GENOCIDE MATTERS

This edited book provides an interdisciplinary overview of recent scholarship in the field of genocide studies. The book examines four main areas:

- The current state of research on genocide
- New thinking on the categories and methods of mass violence
- Developments in teaching about genocide
- Critical analyses of military humanitarian interventions and post-violence justice and reconciliation.

The combination of important scholarship and innovative approaches to familiar subjects makes this essential reading for all students and scholars in the field of genocide studies.

Joyce Apsel is a faculty member in the Liberal Studies Program at New York University and was a recipient of the 2009 NYU Distinguished Teaching Award. She was President of the International Association of Genocide Scholars (2001–03) and is currently President of the Institute for the Study of Genocide. She is Director of RightsWorks International, a human rights and genocide educational initiative.

Ernesto Verdeja is an Assistant Professor of Political Science and Peace Studies in the Department of Political Science and the Kroc Institute for International Peace Studies, University of Notre Dame. Verdeja is on the boards of the Institute for the Study of Genocide and the International Association of Genocide Scholars.

GENOCIDE MATTERS

Ongoing issues and emerging perspectives

Edited by Joyce Apsel and Ernesto Verdeja

Routledge
Taylor & Francis Group

LONDON AND NEW YORK

First published 2013
by Routledge
2 Park Square, Milton Park, Abingdon, Oxon OX14 4RN

Simultaneously published in the USA and Canada
by Routledge
711 Third Avenue, New York, NY 10017

Routledge is an imprint of the Taylor & Francis Group, an informa business

British Library Cataloguing in Publication Data
A catalogue record for this book is available from the British Library

Library of Congress Cataloging in Publication Data
Genocide matters: ongoing issues and emerging perspectives/edited by
Joyce Apsel & Ernesto Verdeja.
  pages cm
Includes bibliographical references and index.
1. Genocide. I. Apsel, Joyce Freedman, 1945- II. Verdeja, Ernesto.
HV6322.7.G4554 2013
364.15'1–dc23   2012039684

ISBN: 978-0-415-81489-8 (hbk)
ISBN: 978-0-415-81496-6 (pbk)
ISBN: 978-0-203-55006-9 (ebk)

Typeset in Adobe Garamond
by Cenveo Publisher Services

Printed and bound in the United States of America by Publishers Graphics,
LLC on sustainably sourced paper.

CONTENTS

CONTRIBUTORS

Joyce Apsel is a faculty member in the Liberal Studies Program at New York University and was a recipient of the 2009 NYU Distinguished Teaching Award. She was President of the International Association of Genocide Scholars (2001–03) and is currently President of the Institute for the Study of Genocide. She is Director of RightsWorks International, a human rights and genocide educational initiative. Research interests include comparative genocide, pedagogy, and peace studies. Her works include: "The Complexity of Genocide in Darfur: Historical Perspective and Ongoing Processes of Destruction" (2009); and *Museums for Peace: Past, Present and Future* (2009) co-edited with Ikuro Anzai and Syed Sikander Mehdi.

Donald Bloxham is Professor of History at Edinburgh University. He is author, inter alia, of *The Final Solution: A Genocide* (Oxford University Press, 2009); *The Great Game of Genocide: Imperialism, Nationalism, and the Destruction of the Ottoman Armenians* (Oxford University Press, 2005); *Genocide on Trial: War Crimes Trials and the Formation of Holocaust History and Memory* (Oxford University Press, 2001); and co-editor of the *Oxford Handbook of Genocide Studies* (Oxford University Press, 2010) and *Political Violence in Twentieth Century Europe* (Cambridge University Press, 2011).

Helen Fein is Board Chairperson of the Institute for the Study of Genocide (ISG), former Executive Director of the ISG and Founding President of the International Association of Genocide Scholars. She is the author and editor of eleven books and monographs on genocide, collective violence, antisemitism and collective altruism, including two prize-winning works, *Accounting for Genocide: National Responses and Jewish Victimization During the Holocaust* (1979) and *Genocide: A Sociological Perspective* (1993). She is an Associate of the Belfer Center for Science and International Affairs at the Kennedy School of Government, Harvard University and a member of the International Genocide Prevention Advisory Network.

Maureen S. Hiebert is Assistant Professor of Political Science and Law and Society and Fellow at the Centre for Military and Strategic Studies, University of Calgary. She has published works on the role of identity construction and genocidal elite decision-making, comparative genocide theory, and genocide prevention. Hiebert is also a faculty member of the Genocide and Human Rights University Program summer school teaching units on comparative genocide theory and the Cambodian genocide.

Alexander L. Hinton is the Founder and Director of the Center for the Study of Genocide, Conflict Resolution, and Human Rights, and Professor of Anthropology and Global Affairs at Rutgers University, Newark. He is the author of the award-winning *Why Did They Kill? Cambodia in the Shadow of Genocide* (University of California Press, 2005) and six edited or co-edited collections. He is currently working on several other book projects, including a book on the Khmer Rouge Tribunal. He is President of the International Association of Genocide Scholars (2011–13) and a Member of the Institute for Advanced Study at Princeton (2011–12). In recognition of his work on genocide, the American Anthropological Association selected Hinton as the recipient of the 2009 Robert B. Textor and Family Prize for Excellence in Anticipatory Anthropology.

Sheri P. Rosenberg is Assistant Clinical Professor of Law, Director of the Program in Holocaust and Human Rights Studies, and Director of the Human Rights and Genocide Clinic, at the Benjamin N. Cardozo School of Law at Yeshiva University, New York City. She was selected as one of two US lawyers to work for the Human Rights Chamber, a quasi-international court established under the Dayton Peace Agreement, in Sarajevo, Bosnia and Herzegovina, and was a recipient of a Human Rights Fellowship at Columbia University where she worked for the United Nations Office for the Coordination of Humanitarian Affairs, Policy Branch. She is Executive Director of the Institute for the Study of Genocide.

Everita Silina is Assistant Professor at the New School Graduate Program in International Affairs, with interests in genocide, theories of justice, representation and democracy in post-national contexts, political economy and theories of integration, the European Union and the politics of Europeanization, human rights and international law.

Roger W. Smith is Professor Emeritus of Government at the College of William and Mary in Virginia. He has written and lectured widely on the nature, history, and prevention of genocide, and on the issue of denial. He is a co-founder and past president of the International Association of Genocide Scholars. From 2002 to 2011 he directed the Zoryan Institute's Genocide and Human Rights University Program, a two-week intensive seminar held annually at the University of Toronto. In 2008 Armenia presented him with its highest civilian award, the Movses Khorenatsi Medal, for his contributions to the international recognition of the 1915 Genocide.

Ernesto Verdeja is an Assistant Professor of Political Science and Peace Studies in the Department of Political Science and the Kroc Institute for International Peace Studies, University of Notre Dame. He is the author of *Unchopping A Tree: Reconciliation in the Aftermath of Political Violence* (2009) and articles on comparative genocide, transitional justice, theories of political reconciliation and critical theory. Verdeja is on the boards of the Institute for the Study of Genocide and the International Association of Genocide Scholars.

Paul D. Williams is Associate Professor in the Elliott School of International Affairs at George Washington University. He writes on the politics of contemporary peace operations, Africa's international relations, and the responsibility to protect. He serves on the editorial boards of the journals *African Affairs* and *Global Responsibility to Protect*.

Foreword

Genocide matters not only to scholars but to citizens, people in neighboring states, and all people concerned with human rights, economic development and refugees. We know that genocide is one of the leading causes of refugee flights, economic regression, and new wars. The flight of *genocidaires* (perpetrators of genocide) from Rwanda triggered the first African inter-state war, whose consequences continue. Genocides in Afghanistan and Iraq led to foreign interventions, which have been costly for the interveners and peoples concerned.[1]

It is important to compare genocides theoretically as in this volume in order to avoid using a single genocide – the Holocaust or another case – as a paradigm. This volume reflects on the state of comparative theorizing. Genocides often also include rape and imposed deaths by deprivation – genocide by attrition – which is actually specified in the United Nations Genocide Convention (Article II, b and c):

> In the present Convention, genocide means any of the following acts committed with intent to destroy, in whole or in part, a national, ethnical, racial or religious group as such:
>
> (a) Killing members of the group;
> (b) Causing serious bodily or mental harm to members of the group;
> (c) Deliberately inflicting on the group conditions of life calculated to bring about its physical destruction in whole or in part;
> (d) Imposing measures intended to prevent births within the group;
> (e) Forcibly transferring children of the group to another group.

Many scholars have also remarked on such acts which do not fit precisely within the scope of groups protected, calling them by a series of terms including genocidal massacres, political killings, or "politicide" (a term coined by Barbara Harff). They agree on the need to react before legal indictment or adjudication. Some have observed how the acts involved in genocides, crimes against humanity, and war crimes overlap and may be called "mass atrocity crimes" as proposed by former US war crimes ambassador, David Scheffer. The present situation in Syria (as of September 12, 2012) illustrates the risks of waiting. The escalating crimes against civilians, whether by government or as an outcome of civil war, threaten all Syrians.

Some call for military intervention but it is not clear which powers would be likely to pay the costs of intervention, for it is not disinterested interveners but interested interveners who are most likely to risk the domestic consequences and cost of intervention. There are other suggestions to limit civilian deaths, such as imposing a "no-fly zone" multilaterally. There has always been and will probably continue to be controversies about what some call "humanitarian intervention" and what some call "humanitarian military intervention," as Paul D. Williams puts it in this volume. Besides the question of legitimacy and unintended consequences, few speak openly about the costs to the intervener, which are not only financial. The domestic consequences of putting "our boys" in "harm's way" in situations where their state is not threatened will continue to plague politicians. Indeed, many commentators believe that the shame associated with the US intervention in Somalia in 1991 explains America's failure to support intervention in Rwanda in 1994. There is an enormous list of books that might be cited here, but it might be worthwhile to go back to the classic on intervention: Michael Walzer's *Just and Unjust Wars*.[2]

Today, there is much domestic and international interest in the prevention of genocide, including groups such as the Institute for the Study of Genocide, the Genocide Intervention Network, and the Genocide Prevention Advisory Network. In order to get public support, teaching about genocide needs to be incorporated in public and higher education in appropriate formats and contexts. The Institute for the Study of Genocide (ISG), a co-sponsor of the conference out of which the essays in this volume emerged, has been engaged in the 35 years I have been associated with it in spreading both consciousness of genocide and deterring hyperbolic uses of the word. A major conference in 1988, *Genocide Watch*, led to an edited volume of that name in 1992. Other volumes stemming from ISG conferences include *The Prevention of Genocide: Rwanda and Yugoslavia Reconsidered* (1994), *Ever Again?: Evaluating the United Nations Genocide Convention on its 50th Anniversary and Proposals to Activate the Convention* (1998), *Teaching about Genocide* (2002), and *Darfur: Genocide Before Our Eyes* (2005). For further details about these works and ISG's biannual newsletters, see the Institute for the Study of Genocide website, www.instituteforthestudyofgenocide.org. The main themes of this volume: the state of genocide studies; different types and methods of violence; pedagogy/education; and intervention/post-conflict issues, are all important ones that have been and continue to be integral to the work of ISG and to genocide scholarship.

Helen Fein
Board Chair, Institute for the Study of Genocide, Associate,
Belfer Center for Science and International Affairs,
Kennedy School of Government, Harvard University

NOTES

1 For a list of genocides from 1915 to 2006 with sources and estimates of victims, see Fein 2007: 128–30.
2 M. Walzer, *Just and Unjust Wars: A Moral Argument with Historical Illustrations*, New York: Basic Books, 2003. Originally published in 1977.

CHAPTER 1

Introduction: Genocide Matters

Ongoing issues and emerging perspectives

Joyce Apsel and Ernesto Verdeja

War and atrocity have been subjects of public and scholarly interest from ancient times to the present. However, the use of genocide as a conceptual lens to focus on the targeting of civilian populations for destruction is a modern phenomenon. The term genocide, from the Greek *genos* (race, tribe), and the Latin *caedere* (to kill), was coined by Raphael Lemkin in 1944 in his book *Axis Rule in Occupied Europe*, which described the laws and policies of occupation that resulted in the domination and annihilation of peoples. Some four decades later, Leo Kuper wrote in one of the first works to use the term in its title: "the term is new but the crime is ancient."[1]

The crime is indeed ancient, even as our understanding of the complexity and dynamics of human destructiveness continues to evolve and as further mass violence takes place before our eyes. This volume aims to deepen how we approach and analyze such destruction. The chapters include re-evaluations of earlier studies, debates and trends, analyses of under-researched subjects such as education, sexual violence, and genocide by attrition, and explorations of the challenges and future directions for studying and thinking about genocide.

■ THE EVOLUTION OF GENOCIDE AS A FIELD OF STUDY

Scholars began focusing on the mass atrocities inflicted on *civilian populations* as a separate subject of research after the traumas of World War I and World War II. The mass killings, rapes and other atrocities, as well as the presence of millions of refugees and survivors across Europe following World War II, drove scholars to conduct new studies on the origins, causes and methods of wide-scale violence and human suffering. In their broadest terms, these studies sought to explain the overwhelming violence of the recent past, while also uncovering disappeared peoples and neglected histories of violence and investigating the complexity of patterns of extermination across numerous cases.

Genocide emerged as a field of scholarly inquiry as historians, political scientists and other social scientists began analyzing the causes and methods of Nazi violence in the years after World War II, an interest that was reinforced by public fascination with Nazism and fascism. Nevertheless, this was a slow and uneven process: most early research on genocide was devoted solely (or primarily) to the Nazi extermination of Europe's Jews, and few studies sought to place the Holocaust in comparison with other cases of mass violence elsewhere in the world. Indeed, in the years after Germany's defeat scholars and others grappled with how to conceptualize the enormity and specificity of Nazism's crimes, and it was not until the 1970s that the term "Holocaust" came into wide use to describe what political scientist Raul Hilberg had earlier termed "The Destruction of the European Jews." Debates about the use and meaning of the term "Holocaust" have continued, with disagreements over whether to include Roma and Sinti, homosexuals and other targeted groups under its umbrella; the term's applicability to slavery, colonialism and other cases of human destructiveness; and whether the Holocaust was "unique" and what implications this may have for studying other genocides and historic atrocities.[2]

This early scholarship on the Holocaust examined the ways in which antisemitism and expansionist policies targeted disfavored and despised minorities, from persecution to physical destruction. These works included investigating the origins, sequencing, and dynamics of mass violence, as well as the roles of dehumanizing cultural views and ideologies that facilitated extermination.[3] On the one hand, scholarship on the nature and significance of the Holocaust provided areas of research and cross-fertilization that were taken up in subsequent studies of different and comparative cases of genocidal events. In some instances, Holocaust studies served as the model or yardstick for comparisons between one or more cases. For example, studies that showed the similarities between the Armenian genocide and the Holocaust provided an interpretive framework that gave attention to a genocide that had largely been ignored. On the other hand, there was considerable tension between scholars from the 1970s and later who debated the analytical and normative consequences of adopting comparative approaches that often times did not privilege any one case as the defining example of genocide. As this volume makes clear, these debates about studying the Holocaust, or what a number of scholars now refer to as Nazi genocides, have given rise to a complex politics of genocide scholarship that continues today, with debates between some Holocaust scholars and comparativists over the value of comparative scholarship.

From the 1990s on, scholarly perspectives on genocide were transformed as the number of studies of both particular cases and comparative analyses multiplied. Public and academic interest in genocide increased in the face of media coverage during and after the mass atrocities in Rwanda and the Balkans. Scholars and policy analysts, influenced by the growing numbers of non-governmental organizations and expanding scholarship on human rights, began to focus on other cases of atrocity, both historical and contemporary. Path-breaking studies on particular cases such as the Armenian genocide, the Cambodian genocide or other singular events of destruction, which tended to provide historically detailed descriptions of the causes and patterns of mass violence in a particular time and place, were synthesized into broader frameworks in the 1990s, generating a sophisticated literature on comparative theorizing and modeling over the past 20 years. For example, Frank Chalk and Kurt Jonassohn's important survey course and text, *The History and Sociology of Genocide* (1990), helped introduce the new comparative approach to the study of genocide. Within two decades, a number of volumes were published that provide world surveys of genocide. Indeed, scholarship has broadened to investigate targeted destruction and violence and their ongoing impact in a range of contexts and times, from colonial policies of elimination to the "national security" doctrines of Latin America.[4] Today, genocide is receiving greater focus from scholars across the social sciences, and the multidisciplinary field of genocide studies itself is growing rapidly. The institutionalization of genocide studies is reflected in the founding of two comparative studies journals[5] and the establishment of two international scholarly associations and other institutes focused on studying genocide.[6] Additionally, the publication of a series of works and analyses on conceptual clarification, necessary conditions, and the various patterns of genocidal violence points to ongoing intellectual and public interest in the subject.

RECENT DIRECTIONS IN THE STUDY OF GENOCIDE

This focus on genocide over the past 20 years has resulted in important research advances. There are now empirically detailed accounts of the best-known cases, including Armenia, the Holocaust, Cambodia, Rwanda, and Bosnia and Herzegovina, as well as on mass killings in China and the Soviet Union.[7] Comparative work also continues to mature, with scholars devoting more attention to the role of contingency in the escalation of violence to genocide and developing sophisticated models of the tipping points that explain how sporadic and targeted killings become a widespread and coordinated plan of destruction.[8] Large databases and quantitative studies on political violence, a mainstay of the civil wars literature, have also deepened our understandings of the general conditions that enable genocide and related forms of violence.[9] Historians provide empirically rich and nuanced analyses of macro-historical processes and detail the complex interactions between agency and structure in genocide,[10] while psychologists adapt classic and contemporary social psychology research on obedience and scapegoating to explain acculturation to violence and popular support for genocidal elites.[11] Political scientists and sociologists employ rational choice and prospect theories of elite strategic action,[12] structuralist analyses of social crises,[13] and theories of state repression, social strati-fication, instability and radical ideology to analyze the onset and development of genocide.[14] Anthropologists in turn provide sophisticated readings of cultural norms and practices to explain popular receptivity and resistance to genocidal propaganda and outgrouping.[15] They also largely lead the way in looking at post-genocidal societies and cultures, a subject of study that is expanding across disciplines.[16] Legal scholars and practitioners draw on the social sciences to inform the prosecution of mass crimes, while simultaneously participating in definitional and methodological debates about the meaning and study of genocide.[17] Genocide studies today is an expanding and rich area of research.

CONTINUING CHALLENGES AND UNSETTLED QUESTIONS

Genocide studies as a subfield or field of study (and where and how to place it in relation to other research fields remains an ongoing debate) has in a number of respects come into its own. However, as the chapters in this volume highlight, there remains both a series of continuing unsettled issues as well as new critiques and analytical directions to pursue. These include disputes over the definition and parameters of the term "genocide," a consequence of ongoing scholarly dissatisfac-tion with what are viewed as the limitations and biases of the United Nations definition.[18] A number of chapters in this volume (Alexander Hinton on "critical genocide studies" and Roger Smith on rape) point to the importance of understand-ing how and why certain cases, patterns, and methods were ignored, and explore ways to rethink genocide and its dynamics. In response, scholars continue to develop various alternative definitions with the aim of giving the concept more coherence and analytical leverage.[19] Some analysts adopt a rather restricted view of what qualifies as genocide, focusing only on instances where extermination was driven by an explicit ideology of national purification and cleansing.[20] Others are less concerned with ideology as a bounding concept, and attempt to explain large-scale atrocity more generally, such as by focusing on the systematic physical destruc-tion of groups, regardless of group identity or perpetrator motivation,[21] while others have generated a complex taxonomy of violence that includes urbicide, politicide, ethnic cleansing, murderous cleansing, and even auto-genocide to explain a variety of phenomena that share family resemblances with one another and with the defini-tion laid out in the UN's 1948 Convention on the Prevention and Punishment of the Crime of Genocide.[22] Further complicating this historiography is the fact that numerous and significant works, such as Michael Mann's *The Dark Side of Democracy: Explaining Ethnic Cleansing*, keep their distance from associating with genocide as a frame of analysis, but analyze the same case studies and processes. These developments reflect new sensitivity to the multiple ways in which mass violence originates and develops, but it also means few scholars use the same opera-tional definitions. Thus they may select different cases for analysis that cohere to their definitions. Variation in case selection in turn makes it difficult to compare alternative causal theories, since these theories focus on a range of different pro-cesses and violent outcomes.

The multiplicity of analytical frames and terms means that there is continued disagreement on the relative strengths and weaknesses of different theoretical frameworks.[23] This raises a series of theoretical and empirical research questions: what are the most fruitful advances and findings in comparative research? What lessons can be drawn from various disciplines and methods? What are the limitations and strengths of pursuing single case and multiple case studies? These questions are important not only for developing sound theory, but also for informing effective strategies for the detection and prevention of genocide – that is, for practical efforts at stopping future genocides.

There is also still very little work that attempts to draw connections between genocide research and research on other forms of political violence.[24] Contemporary comparative literature tends to examine genocidal outcomes across cases, but not how genocide is related to other kinds of violence more generally. This is a fruitful area for further work, and includes investigating connections with the literatures on civil wars,[25] ethnic violence,[26] political repression,[27] "asymmetric" guerrilla warfare,[28] and structural violence.[29] How do these various phenomena connect to one another? For example, under what conditions does civil war become genocidal? How are counterinsurgency warfare and genocide related? Does severe structural violence constitute a form of genocide, and if so how? Are there insights that genocide studies can contribute to the study of other forms of violence, and vice versa?

There is no simple response to the problem of definitional proliferation and its consequences, and it is unlikely that scholars and activists will settle on a single definition. The legal definition of genocide in the UN Genocide Convention undoubtedly will continue to be the standard against which alternative definitions and terminologies are put forth. However, conceptual and theoretical variation may in fact shed light on important similarities and differences across cases that would otherwise be missed by demanding a uniform definition. The key is to be clear about our assumptions in defining and explaining genocide, and encourage reflection on what is "left out" in how we conceptualize genocide for research. Scholars are critically interrogating what Alexander Hinton, in his chapter for this volume, describes as the core "canon" of cases in genocide studies: Armenia, the Holocaust, Cambodia, Rwanda, and Bosnia and Herzegovina. They are asking which groups or cases have been largely ignored in earlier research (such as those of indigenous peoples or Biafra, Burundi, East Pakistan, and Indonesia, to name a few), what explains these omissions, and what the analytical and methodological consequences are of decentering this canon. As the field has become internally more pluralistic and heterogeneous, scholars are including historically ignored victim groups in current studies of already well-known genocides (Assyrians and Greeks in the Ottoman Empire, Hutu in Rwanda, and so forth). This shift in analytical perspectives has occurred in tandem with an expansion of scholarly networks beyond North America and Europe, traditionally the center of research of genocide. The field is rapidly globalizing.

As genocide studies progresses, some researchers are looking from new perspectives at the larger field of Holocaust studies for points of overlap and possible reciprocal enrichment. What are the parameters of Holocaust studies, and which victims of Nazi destruction are included or excluded and why? What different historiographical schools and interpretations predominate? There continue to be areas of contention between the two fields. Donald Bloxham's chapter in this volume discusses some tensions and differences in interpretations between Holocaust studies and genocide studies, pointing to ongoing resistance by some scholars to comparative analyses, particularly in terms of holding on to the status of the Holocaust as unique and paradigmatic. Another example is recent work arguing that there are similarities between the Nazi war of conquest and earlier colonial genocides in the eighteenth and nineteenth centuries, leading to debates over the analytical status of differences between the two phenomena. These examples of debates and differences in emphases will likely continue and expand as different pieces of the mosaics of each field are reconfigured, and new research emerges.

Teaching about genocide has also expanded. Some of this takes as its model the pedagogy used in teaching about the Holocaust and hence is often seen as an important way to sensitize youth to the dangers of hatred, discrimination, and dehumanization, particularly at the pre-university levels. Given the "never again" and memorializing nature characteristic of much pre-university Holocaust education, the curricular focus in the United States was on reading memoirs about the destruction of European Jewry,[30] and the Holocaust often was introduced as the model example of dehumanization.[31] The politicization of debates over Holocaust and Holocaust/genocide educational mandates in the United States in the 1980s resulted in pressure to broaden content to include Native Americans as well as genocides carried out against Armenians, Ukrainians, Cambodians and other groups. Following the genocides in Rwanda, the Balkans, and recently in Darfur, with films, journalistic accounts, and celebrity engagement about the human toll of such gross human rights violations, student interest in contemporary cases provided an impetus for reading memoirs and journalists' accounts as well as viewing films that examine a range of genocidal events. While training instructors about teaching the Holocaust is the predominant pattern and has the greatest amount of resources and institutional backing by far (from organizations like the United States Holocaust Memorial Museum and Israel's Yad Vashem museum, which focuses on Holocaust education and research), new memoirs and histories on Armenia, Bosnia and Herzegovina, Darfur, Cambodia, and Rwanda as well as teacher training courses that educate young people more broadly on issues of civic education (such as those sponsored by Facing History and Ourselves) have expanded the scope of cases and themes taught in the classroom. Most education remains focused on the Holocaust with other cases added on, but scholars are developing new comparative and multi-case textbooks on genocide to educate young people.[32] Nevertheless, there has been little research in genocide studies on examining the challenges in developing and organizing courses and new strategies for classroom teaching,[33] and integrating new research in genocide studies into secondary education and university modules. It is time for researchers to explore the current state of pedagogy on genocide critically. To what extent can studying the causes and methods of dehumanization and genocidal atrocities link with the prospects for promoting tolerance, inclusion, peace, and pro-social behavior? Or is it possible that the moral education rationale of first Holocaust and now genocide studies education, particularly strong at the pre-university level, needs to be re-examined?

As teachers have moved to bring greater awareness about genocide in the classroom, policy makers and activists have devoted increased attention to preventing and intervening to stop genocide and related mass atrocities. There has been an enormous growth in work on prevention and intervention efforts, which constitute a broad spectrum of policies. The 2001 ICISS report, *The Responsibility to Protect* (R2P), identified a host of nonmilitary and military strategies available to third parties, including development assistance in poor and politically destabilized countries, support for good governance and the rule of law, national and local mediation efforts, and other programs to encourage dialogue between oppositional groups. More intrusively, strategies may include economic sanctions (including withholding military aid), political sanctions, and at the most extreme, armed intervention to stop ongoing mass atrocities. The R2P norm gained further support at the 2005 United Nations World Summit, where world leaders affirmed that states have a responsibility to protect the rights of their citizens, and in 2009 when UN Secretary General Ban Ki-moon outlined "three pillars" of international action to promote state responsibility. The R2P norm aims to reframe the traditional tension between sovereignty rights against intervention on the one hand and the obligation to protect universal human rights on the other, so that sovereignty is reinterpreted as requiring the protection of civilian rights. Nevertheless, R2P raises a number of important questions that require further attention: under what conditions are nonmilitary and military interventions justified? What is the role of the United Nations in determining the need for intervention? Under what conditions may regional alliances like NATO or great powers intervene without formal UN support? How can R2P be applied so that "humanitarian intervention" does not become a cover for powerful states pursuing their own interests?

Finally, genocide studies scholars have begun to investigate the various ways to promote justice and reconciliation after large-scale violence, such as through the use of truth commissions, trials, collective memory initiatives, and reparations programs. Nevertheless, genocide studies scholarship has remained curiously detached from advances in the "transitional justice" field, as this area is known. Often, scholars focus on post-genocidal countries, but limit their analysis to a relatively small subset of post-conflict cases and risk missing – or misrepresenting – the complex challenges posed by the use of truth commissions, trials, reparations and similar justice efforts. Greater attention to the full range of these efforts across cases of mass violence can provide more nuanced understandings of the possibilities and limitations of justice and reconciliation.

THIS VOLUME

In sum, there are a number of issues that remain unexplored or unsettled in genocide studies. Indeed, although there is greater awareness of the need to reflect on the field, there are few works that do so. To date the most comprehensive critical re-assessment of the entire field is the *Oxford Handbook of Genocide Studies* edited by Donald Bloxham and Dirk Moses.[34] That important volume includes case studies and thematic essays and is quite broad in scope. Along with essays appearing in genocide and human rights journals, recent works such as René Lemarchand's *Forgotten Genocides*, Donald W. Beachler's *The Genocide Debate: Politicians, Academics, and Victims* and Adam Jones' edited collection *New Directions in Genocide Research* point to re-evaluations of how and what cases are examined, denial and other thematic issues in the field.[35]

This volume complements these works, but also takes a step back and seeks to provide an interdisciplinary, critical examination of where the field is, including its fundamental assumptions and presuppositions. By exploring the epistemological and methodological claims that underpin genocide studies, the book seeks to promote a discussion among scholars of genocide about the current state of research, and advance thinking about the theoretical and practical contributions the field can make to understanding violence and to genocide education and prevention. With this volume, we hope to contribute to identifying research advances, areas for further work, and the challenges the field faces going forward.

The volume focuses on four related, cross-disciplinary themes in genocide studies. These are: the current state of comparative research on genocide; new thinking about the categories and methods of genocidal violence; developments in teaching about genocide; and, critical analyses of military humanitarian interventions and post-violence justice and reconciliation. There are several reasons for focusing on these four themes. For instance, scholars have shown growing interest in questioning the methodological and theoretical assumptions employed in genocide research, but these discussions remain unsettled, and in this volume our contributors explore some of the consequences that follow from the field's most basic presuppositions. There has also been new work exploring forms of violence other than "direct killings" in genocide, but this research is still mostly eclipsed by studies that focus on genocidal killings and massacres. Thus, the deployment of other techniques of violence (such as enslavement, denial of food, and rape) remain relatively underexplored and in need of further analytical elaboration. Pedagogical issues remain mostly ignored in genocide studies, while intervention and post-violence justice and reconstruction are receiving increased attention among genocide scholars, but often in relatively limited, case-specific ways.

None of this is to say that genocide studies is still a small research field. Indeed, the explosion of research on genocide over the past decade means that any assessment of the field must remain partial; there are so many new research questions and publications that no overview can do justice to genocide studies as a whole. Thus, our volume has limited its scope to these four core themes. For instance, the book does not provide new case studies or definitions of genocide, though these issues are discussed in several chapters. Another important area of recent work, on colonialism and genocide, is not engaged in detail but is discussed by Maureen Hiebert in her evaluation of recent advances in causal theorizing, Joyce Apsel in her analysis of historical repositioning and teaching about mass killing, and by Donald Bloxham in his assessment of the methodological and epistemological challenges involved in rethinking the relation between the Holocaust and colonialist extermination. Lastly, we do not systematically investigate the emerging literature on the relation between genocide and environmental degradation and resource scarcity, which is likely to be an important area for future research. Nevertheless, the four themes explored in this volume are central to current genocide studies research, and provide an important lens by which we can assess advances and challenges in the field.

CORE THEMES AND CHAPTERS IN THE VOLUME

The volume begins by examining the state of contemporary genocide research and providing a series of evaluations of the field. Political scientist Maureen Hiebert gives a critical overview of explanatory theories of genocide across disciplines. In an earlier work, Hiebert categorized theories according to whether they focused on agency, structural or ideational factors, or processes of identity construction. Here she deepens this analytical perspective by investigating the ways in which the current literature privileges different levels of analysis – individual, group, systemic – and what consequences this has for our understandings of the onset and diffusion of genocidal violence. Hiebert provides an extensive investigation of the "boundaries" of the genocide studies literature, and critically assesses how epistemological, definitional, geographical, temporal, and supranational boundaries shape what does and does not qualify as genocide. For Hiebert, while there are some current theoretical contributions that are truly novel, much of the recent scholarship is more of a refinement of older insights rather than completely new ideas. She also contends that much of this recent scholarship is in many ways a return to (or at least engagement with) Raphael Lemkin's foundational conceptual-ization of genocide. In evaluating the current research, Hiebert notes continued conceptual confusion and methodological underdevelopment that affect both the parameters and types of research genocide scholars undertake. Her chapter calls for greater clarity of research design and underlying theoretical assumptions in future work.

Alexander Hinton's chapter elaborates the elements of a "critical genocide studies." He uses his anthropological lens to interrogate the presuppositions, biases, and continued blind spots of the field. Beginning with uncovering what he describes as the "origin myth" of genocide studies, Hinton explores a series of assumptions and tensions in genocide research, and provides a reinterpretation of Raphael Lemkin as the foundational figure in the field and the continuation of the scholar–activist model rooted in early scholarship. Hinton provides a conceptual reconstruc-tion of the field's origins and cautions that scholars should be wary of the ways in which their research may be co-opted by the interests of powerful political actors. Such concerns are particularly timely, given the continued public debates over the justifications of humanitarian intervention and its relation to state power.

The roots of genocide studies go back to the Holocaust, the first genocide to be studied extensively. As subsequent generations of scholars began investigating and comparing other cases of mass violence, a division grew between Holocaust research and comparative genocide research, one that is still with us today. Historian Donald Bloxham's chapter explores the continued tensions between Holocaust studies and genocide studies as well as the possibilities for greater synergies between the two fields. Bloxham has been at the center of these debates and highlights several ways in which comparativist scholars (typically found in genocide studies) can learn from historiographical advances in Holocaust research. His chapter begins by problematizing the question of the Holocaust's "uniqueness" (and thus incomparability) and "universality" (as the benchmark of evil). The chapter also looks at crosscutting relationships and similarities between the Holocaust and other genocides, for instance through the ways in which European colonial genocides abroad were reflected in Nazism's colonial project in Europe. Bloxham uses criticisms of his own work to explore a series of tensions he finds between some Holocaust and genocide scholarship. He investigates the differences between the two fields through a theoretical framework that looks at the degree to which each field balances analytical versus commemorative demands, and how scholarship is positioned between calls for historical contemplation versus proscriptive activism. With such a framing, Bloxham provides valuable critical insights into the divisions and similarities between Holocaust and genocide studies.

The following two chapters focus on new theorizing about the categories and methods of destruction. Here, contributors explore how to expand our analyses of mass violence by moving beyond the conceptual frames that have usually been employed in genocide research. Political scientist Roger Smith's contribution investigates the terrible politics of rape and its relationship to genocide. Smith looks at a series of historical cases and traces the fundamental elements of extreme sexual violence, including rituals of degradation employed by perpetrators, and highlights how rape in genocide is part of a policy process rather than merely "excesses" in the normal course of warfare. This interdisciplinary chapter, including psychological and political science theories, examines the functions of rape and range of victimization for the individual and community that continues after the initial acts of physical violence end. Although rape has been explored in studies of single cases of genocide, Smith's work places rape at the center of comparative research on genocides and helps brings sexual violence to the forefront of analysis.

Legal scholar Sheri Rosenberg and political scientist Everita Silina explore another aspect of genocide, namely the destruction of groups through attrition. The range of methods of human destructiveness has been an area of increasing interest in genocide research, and this chapter examines a number of cases by analyzing how groups are destroyed in whole or part through the calculated removal of food and healthcare and other means needed for human survival. Rosenberg and Silina note that genocide's legal definition and the crime's popular representation in Auschwitz as its paradigmatic example often prevent scholars as well as the public from seeing less direct methods of killing, such as starvation and enslavement, as forms of extermination. Through the examination of a number of cases, Rosenberg and Silina reconstruct the legal definition to include slower but no less intentional processes of annihilation. Given that extreme forms of structural and long-term violence have historically been ignored in genocide research, this chapter marks an important contribution to rethinking the contours of the field.

The next chapter turns to an area that has received surprisingly little attention from genocide scholars: the teaching of genocide and links between pedagogy and research. Even though most researchers are housed in academic institutions and thus are also teachers, genocide studies has been slow to reflect on the basic goals and challenges of teaching such a morally complex issue in analytically sophisticated and rigorous ways. Historian Joyce Apsel's chapter investigates the ways in which the literature and research trajectories have changed over the past two decades, and the consequences of these changes for teaching. She considers how to frame genocide studies in relation to other thematic areas of teaching, including human rights, humanitarianism, development studies and postcolonialism, and the ways in which the field rests on the categorization of certain cases of violence as genocide. The fact that genocide studies is interdisciplinary and often solely dependent on the interest of a particular faculty member rather than firmly institutionally anchored has implications for undergraduate and graduate teaching. The chapter also explores how different historians of genocide use various comparative models to analyze genocidal events and related themes. From comparative to transnational analysis, the chapter looks as well at the implication of such frameworks both for teaching and new directions in research.

The final two chapters of the volume are dedicated to issues of intervention to stop genocidal violence and post-conflict efforts at securing justice and reconciliation. Political scientist Paul D. Williams investigates the rise of so-called "humanitarian interventions," where external military force is deployed to stop or minimize severe human rights violations such as genocide, war crimes, crimes against humanity, and ethnic cleansing. Starting with the Responsibility to Protect doctrine endorsed by the United Nations in 2005, Williams identifies five types of obstacles to the theory and practice of intervention, raising serious challenges to the pro-interventionist positions that are at the center of genocide studies prevention activism. His chapter connects the intervention literature to genocide studies by highlighting the complex relations between intervention and the politics of preventing genocide.

Political theorist Ernesto Verdeja follows with a chapter devoted to investigating how insights from the post-conflict literature known as transitional justice can inform genocide studies. Transitional justice is broadly concerned with the strategies, practices, and theories of social repair and transformation for societies dealing with a recent history of authoritarianism, civil war or massive human rights violations, including genocide, and has drawn increased interest from genocide scholars. His chapter critically reconstructs some of the developments and current research advances in the transitional justice field. The chapter is motivated by the concern that much of the best research in transitional justice and genocide studies remains largely unconnected and discrete, with scholarship advances in one area going unnoticed in the other. As genocide scholars continue to focus on post-conflict settings and engage in advocacy for the prevention and punishment of genocide, Verdeja contends that it has become necessary to have a deeper understanding of the transitional justice literature. He maps the transitional justice literature as a way of furthering useful interactions between the two fields.

This volume provides a series of chapters engaged in questions about what the study of genocide entails. It raises important issues for scholars across disciplines and challenges us to rethink how we "see," investigate and explore the complicated issues related to past and present human destructiveness. As scholarly research continues to expand, these essays will be of particular importance for scholars across disciplines working on genocide and political violence. Given the new developments and work being produced in genocide studies, the field is in need of general analyses of its advances, weaknesses, and areas for further research, and it is our hope that this volume will contribute to this critical work.

ORIGINS OF THE PROJECT

The idea for this volume originated from a series of discussions among board members of the Institute for the Study of Genocide (ISG), a nonprofit non-governmental organization that over the last three decades has been dedicated to educating the public about the crime of genocide and promoting scholarly research on genocide. Founded in 1982, the ISG is one of the earliest organizations in North America to use the lens of genocide to critically analyze past and ongoing cases of systematic mass violence, and has produced a series of conferences, roundtables, publications, and newsletters (see www.instituteforthestudyofgenocide.org). The Institute's board members felt that the field required a systematic evaluation of its current state. A number of scholars were invited to contribute to the project, and the main themes were refined through subsequent conversations and exchanges at an authors' workshop held at the University of Notre Dame in 2011. In addition to the contributors to the volume, we would like to thank Scott Appleby, Christian Davenport, Adam Jones, Helen Fein, and Luc Reydams for their valuable contributions to the project. Joyce Apsel expresses her appreciation for the ongoing support from the New York University Liberal Studies Program and Dean Frederic Schwarzbach. We are grateful to the following entities and offices at the University of Notre Dame for providing the resources that allowed us to host the initial workshop and to bring these chapters together in an edited collection: the Kroc Institute for International Peace Studies, the Kellogg Institute for International Studies, the Institute for Scholarship in the Liberal Arts, the Office of Research, and the Nanovic Institute for European Studies. We would also like to thank Kathy Smarrella, Cathy Laake, Maria Surat and the staff at the Kroc Institute for making the workshop so rewarding.

NOTES

1 R. Lemkin, *Axis Rule in Occupied Europe: Laws of Occupation, Analysis of Government, Proposals for Redress*, Washington, DC: Carnegie Endowment for International Peace, 1944; L. Kuper, *Genocide: Its Political Uses in the Twentieth Century*, New Haven, CT: Yale University Press, 1983, p. 1.

2 A. Rosenbaum, *Is the Holocaust Unique? Perspectives on Comparative Genocide*, Boulder, CO: Westview Press, 1988; Y. Bauer, *Rethinking the Holocaust*, New Haven, CT: Yale University Press, 2002; A. D. Moses, "The Holocaust and Genocide," in Dan Stone, ed., *The Historiography of the Holocaust*, New York: Sage, 2004.

3 R. Hilberg, *The Destruction of the European Jews*, London: W. H. Allen, 1961, 3 vols; L. Dawidowicz, *The War Against The Jews, 1933–1945*, New York: Holt, Rinehart and Winston, 1975; L. Poliakov, *Harvest of Hate: The Nazi Program for the Destruction of Jews*

in Europe, New York: History Library, 1956; Y. Bauer, *Holocaust in Historical Perspective*, Seattle: Washington University Press, 1978.

4 D. Feierstein, *El genocidio como práctica social: Entre el nazismo y la experiencia argentina: Hacia un análisis del aniquilamiento como reorganizador de las relaciones sociales*, Buenos Aires, Argentina: Fondo de Cultura Económica, 2008; M. Esparza, H. Huttenbach and D. Feierstein, *State Violence and Genocide in Latin America: The Cold War Years*, New York: Routledge, 2011.

5 The *Journal of Genocide Research* and *Genocide Studies and Prevention*. *Holocaust and Genocide Studies* is devoted mostly to the Holocaust, though it does publish on other cases as well.

6 For example, see the *International Association of Genocide Scholars*, the *Institute for the Study of Genocide*, and the *International Network of Genocide Scholars*.

7 T. Akçam, *The Young Turks' Crime Against Humanity: The Armenian Genocide and Ethnic Cleansing in the Ottoman Empire*, Princeton, NJ: Princeton University Press, 2012; D. Bloxham, *The Great Game of Genocide: Imperialism, Nationalism and the Destruction of the Ottoman Armenians*, Oxford: Oxford University Press, 2005; H. Travis, *Genocide in the Middle East: The Ottoman Empire, Iraq and Sudan*, Durham, NC: Carolina Academic Press, 2010; P. Longerich, *Holocaust: The Nazi Persecution and Murder of the Jews*, Oxford: Oxford University Press, 2010; S. Straus, *The Order of Genocide: Race, Power and War in Rwanda*, Ithaca, NY: Cornell University Press, 2006; B. Kiernan, *Blood and Soil: A World History of Genocide and Extermination from Sparta to Darfur*, New Haven, CT: Yale University Press, 2007; S. Rosefelde, *Red Holocausts*, New York: Routledge, 2009; F. Dikötter, *Mao's Great Famine: The History of China's Most Devastating Catastrophe, 1958–1962*, London: Bloomsbury Publishing, 2010.

8 B. Goldsmith, C. Butcher, D. Semenovich, and A. Sowmya, "Forecasting the Onset of Genocide and Politicide: Annual Out-of-Sample Forecasts on a Global Dataset, 1988–2003." Online. Available HTTP: http://ssrn.com/abstract=2027396 or http://dx.doi.org/10.2139/ssrn.2027396 (accessed March 20, 2012).

9 UCDP/PRIO (2011) *Uppsala Data Conflict Armed Conflict Dataset v.4–2011: 1946–2010*. Online. Available HTTP: www.pcr.uu.se/research/ucdp/datasets/ ucdp_prio_armed_conflict_dataset/; PITF: Political Instability Task Force (2011) *Internal Wars and Failures of Governance: 1955–2008*. Online. Available HTTP: http://globalpolicy.gmu.edu/pitf/pitfdata.htm; ACLED (2012) *Armed Conflict Location and Event Dataset*. Online. Available HTTP: www.acleddata.com/; MAR: *Minorities at Risk Project* (2010). Online. Available HTTP: www.cidcm.umd.edu/mar/. All accessed March 20, 2012. Also see K. Eck, "In Data We Trust? A Comparison of UCDP GED and ACLED Conflict Events Datasets," *Cooperation and Conflict*, forthcoming.

10 C. Gerlach, *Extremely Violent Societies: Mass Violence in the Twentieth Century World*, Cambridge: Cambridge University Press, 2010; B. Kiernan, *Blood and Soil: A World History of Genocide and Extermination from Sparta to Darfur*, New Haven, CT: Yale University Press, 2007; M. Levene, *Genocide in the Age of the Nation State*, London: I. B. Tauris, 2005, 2 vols; M. Marrus, *The Holocaust in History*, New York: Plume Books, 1989.

11 H. Kelman and V. Hamilton, *Crimes of Obedience*, New Haven, CT: Yale University Press, 1990; R. Lifton, *Nazi Doctors: Medical Killing and the Psychology of Genocide*, New York: Basic Books, 2000; C. McCauley and D. Chirot, *Why Not Kill Them All? The Logic and Prevention of Mass Political Murder*, Princeton, NJ: Princeton University Press, 2006.

12 M. Krain, "State Sponsored Mass Murder: The Onset and Severity of Genocides and Politicides," *Journal of Conflict Resolution* 41/3, 1997, 331–60; B. Valentino, *Final Solutions: Mass Killing and Genocide in the Twentieth Century*, Ithaca, NY: Cornell

University Press, 2004; M. Midlarsky, *The Killing Trap: Genocide in the Twentieth Century*, Cambridge: Cambridge University Press, 2005.

13 B. Harff, "No Lessons Learned From the Holocaust? Assessing Risks of Genocide and Political Mass Murder Since 1955," *American Political Science Review* 97, 2003, 57–73.

14 M. Mann, *The Darkside of Democracy: Explaining Ethnic Cleansing*, New York: Cambridge University Press, 2007; H. Fein, *Accounting for Genocide: National Responses and Jewish Victimization During the Holocaust*, Chicago: University of Chicago Press, 1984.

15 A. Hinton, ed., *Annihilating Difference: The Anthropology of Genocide*, Los Angeles, CA: University of California Press, 2002; A. Hinton, *Why Did They Kill? Cambodia in the Shadow of Genocide*, Los Angeles: University of California Press, 2005.

16 A. Hinton and K. O'Neill, eds., *Genocide: Truth, Memory and Representation*, Durham, NC: Duke University Press, 2010.

17 J. Hagan, *Justice in the Balkans: Prosecuting War Crimes at the Hague Tribunal*, Chicago: University of Chicago Press, 2003; S. Ratner and J. Abrams, *Accountability for Human Rights Atrocities in International Law: Beyond the Nuremberg Legacy*, Oxford: Oxford University Press, 2001; W. Schabas, *An Introduction to the International Criminal Court*, Cambridge: Cambridge University Press, 2001.

18 F. Chalk and K. Jonassohn, *The History and Sociology of Genocide*, New Haven, CT: Yale University Press, 1990, pp. 8–12.

19 D. Scheffer, "Genocide and Atrocity Crimes," *Genocide Studies and Prevention* 1/3, 2006, 229–50.

20 J. Sémelin, *Purify and Destroy: The Political Uses of Massacre and Genocide*, New York: Columbia University Press, 2007; E. Weitz, *A Century of Genocide: Utopias of Race and Nation*, Princeton, NJ: Princeton University Press, 2005.

21 V. Dadrian, *Warrant for Genocide: Key Elements of the Turko–Armenian Conflict*, New Brunswick, NJ and London: Transaction Publishers, 1999; H. Fein, *Genocide: A Sociological Perspective*, London: Sage, 1993; Valentino, *Final Solutions*.

22 M. Shaw, *What Is Genocide?* Cambridge: Polity Press, 2007.

23 A. D. Moses, (2008) "Toward a Theory of Critical Genocide Studies," *Online Encyclopedia of Mass Violence*. Online. Available HTTP: www.massviolence.org/Toward-a-Theory-of-Critical-Genocide-Studies (accessed March 20, 2012); S. Straus, "Second Generation Research on Comparative Genocide," *World Politics* 59/3, 2007, 476–501; E. Verdeja, "Genocide: Clarifying Concepts and Causes of Cruelty," *Review of Politics* 72, 2010, 513–26.

24 E. Verdeja, "The Political Science of Genocide: Outlines of an Emerging Research Agenda," *Perspectives on Politics* 10/2, 2012, 307–21.

25 S. Kalyvas, *The Logic of Violence in Civil War*, Cambridge: Cambridge University Press, 2006.

26 A. Varshney, *Ethnic Conflict and Civic Life: Hindus and Muslims in India*, New Haven, CT: Yale University Press, 2003.

27 C. Davenport, "State Repression and Political Order," *Annual Review of Political Science* 10, 2007, 1–23.

28 L. Cederman, A. Wimmer and B. Min, "Why Do Ethnic Groups Rebel? New Data and Analysis," *World Politics* 62/1, 2010, 87–119.

29 K. Weigert, "Structural Violence," in Lester Kurtz, ed., *Encyclopedia of Violence, Peace and Conflict*, Oxford: Elsevier Press, 2008.

30 A. Frank, *Diary of a Young Girl*, New York: Doubleday Books, 1967; E. Wiesel, *Night*, New York: Ballantine Books, 1960; V. Frankl, *Man's Search for Meaning*, New York:

Pocket Books, 1997; P. Levi, *Survival in Auschwitz*, New York: Classic House Books, 2009.

31 S. Totten, P. Bartrop and S. Jacobs, eds., *Teaching About the Holocaust: Essays by College and University Teachers*, New York: Praeger Books, 2004.

32 M. Derdarian, *Vergeen: A Survivor of the Armenian Genocide*, Los Angeles, CA: Atmus Press, 1996; R. Hukanovic, *The Tenth Circle of Hell: A Memoir of Life in the Death Camps of Bosnia*, London: Little, Brown, 1997; J. Apsel, ed., *Darfur: Genocide Before Our Eyes*, 3rd edition, New York: Institute for Study of Genocide, 2007; C. Him, *When Broken Glass Floats: Growing Up Under the Khmer Rouge*, New York: W. W. Norton, 2001; L. Ung, *First They Killed My Father: A Daughter of Cambodia Remembers*, New York: Harper Perennial, 2001; P. Gourevitch, *We wish to inform you that tomorrow we will be killed with our families*, New York: Picador Books, 1999; A. Jones, *Genocide: A Comprehensive Introduction*, 2nd edition, New York: Routledge, 2010.

33 For exceptions, J. Apsel, ed., *Teaching About Human Rights*, Washington, DC: American Sociological Association, 2005; J. Apsel and H. Fein, *Teaching about Genocide: A Guidebook for College and University Teachers: Critical Essays, Syllabi and Assignments*, 3rd edition, Washington, DC: American Sociological Association, 2002.

34 D. Bloxham and A. D. Moses, eds., *The Oxford Handbook of Genocide Studies*, Oxford: Oxford University Press, 2010.

35 R. Lemarchand, ed., *Forgotten Genocides: Oblivion Denial and Memory*, Philadelphia: University of Pennsylvania Press, 2010; A. Jones, *New Directions in Genocide Research*, London: Routledge, 2012. Also see D. Stone, *The Historiography of Genocide*, London: Palgrave Macmillan, 2010; and the special issues of *Genocide Studies and Prevention* 6/3, 2011, and 7/1, 2012, which were devoted to examining the field.

CHAPTER 2

Questioning Boundaries
What's old and what's new in comparative genocide theory

Maureen S. Hiebert

INTRODUCTION

Genocide studies has always been a goal-oriented area of scholarship that has sought to make the post-Holocaust injunction, "never again" a reality. Whether through comparative or single case studies, much of genocide research has focused on unlocking the secret of why whole groups of people are targeted for destruction so that we might find the key to prevent future genocides. This project has attracted scholars from varied academic disciplines as well as the interest of artists, journalists, human rights activists and others.

First developed as a distinct academic field in the 1980s by a small group of mostly historians, sociologists, and political scientists, the early years focused on forging a comparative project of inquiry in which scholars searched for common patterns of causation and processes of destruction across a relatively small set of twentieth-century genocides.[1] In consciously adopting a comparative approach to explaining genocidal destruction, theory generation and testing, it involved overcoming opposition by some academics and genocide survivors to the idea that what were understood to be unique instances of victimization and suffering could be compared to other instances of mass killing. Opposition to comparative analysis was particularly acute in the Holocaust "uniqueness" debates. Many (but not all) genocide scholars challenged the idea that because the Holocaust was a particularly intense, continent-wide, technologically advanced example of genocide not repli-cated in form or scope elsewhere, it was in a category of its own. Instead they argued that the Holocaust was one instance of genocide among other cases of the same phenomenon. Interestingly, the recognition of the Holocaust as one of several cases of genocide did not dispense with Holocaust uniqueness in genocide studies. Once it became "normalized" as the ultimate case of root-and-branch genocidal destruction, the Holocaust emerged as the standard from which much comparative genocide theory was generated and then tested in other mostly twentieth-century cases. Early comparisons involved the identification of broad structural variables such as ethnic and social divisions in society, authoritarian and totalitarian regime types, the amoral bureaucratized structures of modern nation-states possessing a monopoly over the means of violence, and ideational structures such as radical eliminationist ideologies as the key precursors to genocidal violence. Other scholars concentrated on the role of individual and social psychological processes of dehumanization of the victim group.[2]

Over time genocide studies has expanded in almost every dimension. Cases now include pre-modern, colonial, and twentieth/twenty-first century genocides across the globe. The Holocaust is no longer seen as necessarily *the* case against which all others must be measured and compared or as the main source of explana-tory models of genocidal violence, although it continues to be a central case in genocide studies in its own right and in comparative perspective. Further, it is now acknowledged that genocide, while constituted of a minimum set of shared features (about which genocide scholars continue to disagree), has and continues to manifest itself in a variety of forms, and as such, is sparked by different sets of micro-, meso-, and macro-level factors and processes. Comparative theorizing has expanded both the levels and units of analysis to include individual and social psychological dynamics in hierarchical organizations, the social construction of collective identity, the association under some circumstances of democracy and democratic regimes with genocidal projects, the role of global system-level processes of colonization, nation-state formation, and the decline and rise of old and new empires in shaping both the global and local contexts in which genocidal violence has occurred across time and space. The expansion of genocide scholarship has been driven by an influx of scholars into the field from a number of disciplines in the social sciences and humanities. Genocide scholarship is also no longer confined to positivist social sciences and now includes critical theory and post-colonial approaches, and is pur-sued by scholars not just from North America, but around the world.

The diversification of theorizing in genocide studies has occasioned the "ques-tioning" or "problematizing" of several boundaries within the field. The embrace of critical theory approaches, for instance, signals a questioning of *epistemological* boundaries. Meanwhile genocide scholars continuously, some might argue obses-sively, question *definitional* boundaries. Definitional challenging revolves around not only the perennial question of how to distinguish genocide from other forms of mass violence and destruction, but also the formulation of cognate concepts designed to widen the scope of inquiry beyond a limited number of cases. Labels include, for example, "mass killing," "ethnic cleansing," "extraordinary human evil,"[3] and a plethora of "cides" from the familiar politicide[4] and democide[5] to newer incarnations like ethnocide, gendercide,[6] or indigenocide[7] that denote in specific terms the kind of destruction or the group destroyed. Definitional questioning has also involved, at least for some scholars, a transition away from defining genocide as strictly physical and/or biological destruction of the kind defined under international law in the UN Convention on the Prevention and Punishment of the Crime of Genocide (UNCG 1948), to other forms of group destruction such as cultural genocide, forced assimilation, or the biological subsuming of one population into another. The latter trend is in many ways a return to genocide studies' pre-UNCG roots and the work of Raphael Lemkin, who coined the term "genocide" in the 1940s.[8] By challenging and expanding definitional boundaries, genocide studies, for better or worse, now finds itself with not only the boundaries and content of the concept genocide to contemplate, but a host of related and overlapping forms of direct and indirect group destruction.

Definitional challenging has gone hand in hand with another exercise in questioning: the questioning of *geographical* boundaries as well as of case selection. More expansive definitions of genocide focused mostly on outcomes as opposed to restrictive definitions based on genocidal intent and perpetrated through a wider variety of direct and indirect, violent and non-violent, physical, biological, and cultural methods. This has opened the door for a correspondingly wider variety of case selection and comparison across the globe. This trend has moved the field away from genocides committed in Europe in the twentieth century to genocides perpetrated in the Global South and genocides carried out in an earlier era by Europeans and settler colonies in the Americas and Australia.[9] Definitional and geographical/case boundary questioning has similarly given rise to the questioning of *temporal* boundaries. Here the movement is away from seeing genocide as a strictly "modern" twentieth-century (and beyond) phenomenon, to a form of violence and group destruction still most often found in modernity but in a greatly expanded conceptual and temporal understanding of what modernity is and when it begins.[10]

Boundary questioning has also meant moving beyond identifying authoritarian and/or totalitarian regimes as the only perpetrators of state-sponsored genocidal violence. While not dismissing the connection between the structure, ideology, and the destructive capacity of non-democratic regimes and genocide, *regime* questioning introduces the thesis that some of the foundational concepts of democracy – the people, the nation, and majority rule – understood and manipulated in particular ways has underpinned genocidal violence. Regime questioning also extends the role of established democracies in the perpetration of genocide against indigenous populations constructed as outside of the democratic political community and "in the way" of settlement and resource exploitation.

Questioning the boundaries of *violence* further problematizes what forms of violence against civilian populations constitute genocide versus the targeting of civilians in other forms of struggle and conflict. The identification of a nexus between warfare and genocide suggests, for instance, that while these two forms of violence are distinct from each other they often coexist in complex ways, with warfare variously providing the context, cover, organizational structures, personnel, materiel and sometimes even the rationale for genocidal violence.[11] Indeed, certain forms of warfare are said to be more likely to occasion genocide.[12]

Finally, genocide studies has begun to question the established practice of relying almost solely on *nation-state* level explanatory factors and dynamics. Somewhat late compared to other areas in the social sciences, genocide studies has recently discovered the importance of global system-level explanations, mostly in the form of large historical processes of change across and between political entities in the international system. This examination involves confronting the complex process of nation-state formation first begun internally in Western Europe and then exported to other parts of the world through colonialism and the expansion of vast overseas empires just as old empires (Ottoman, Russian, Habsburg) began to collapse into multiethnic, religiously and linguistically plural neo-natal states in a world increasingly dominated by homogeneous nation-states.

As noted with respect to definitions, much of the questioning and boundary testing in genocide studies has taken its inspiration from the founding father of genocide studies, Raphael Lemkin. In an "old–new" approach to theoretical innovation, a new generation of genocide scholars seems to be (re)turning to the roots of the field to broaden and deepen understanding of how we conceptualize genocide, why genocide occurs in different forms, in different contexts, aimed at different kinds of groups, across geographical location and historical time period. That Lemkin is the source of new ideas and new research agendas is entirely appropriate given the richness and complexity of his scholarship on what he considered to be an old crime that manifests itself in multiple forms historically and currently around the world. Lemkin has left us much to work with and the return to his work suggests a cautionary tale about failing to recognize what is truly new and what is not in genocide studies.

Described as "generations" of genocide scholarship,[13] it is important to think critically about how novel these new theoretical approaches really are. As the analyses of different theoretical explanations of genocide discussed in this chapter will show, some recent genocide scholarship, although innovative in many respects, clearly builds on rather than overturns the work of earlier scholars. Theoretical insights that are sometimes claimed by their authors to be significant departures from, or even repudiations of, existing explanations are usually more of a questioning or problematizing of existing assumptions or proposed explanatory relationships between variables that refine an explanation, rather than a new account of genocidal violence.

That new scholarship in the field has not yielded perhaps as much innovation as has sometimes been claimed does not discount the variety of key concepts, theoretical explanations, and possible cases for study and comparison. The lack of agreement on concepts, explanations, cases, and methodology is unsurprising given the complexity of the subject and the inter/multidisciplinary nature of the field. But is the lack of definitional and theoretical agreement in genocide studies a problem? Some scholars argue that it is, suggesting that genocide studies is now so incoherent as to be mired in a state of "crisis."[14] But given the intricacies of genocidal destruction and its variability across time, space, regime type, actors, processes and structures, and the difficulty of fashioning and validating comparative theory to explain genocide under such varied circumstances, can we really expect genocide studies to be a tidy field of research?

Instead of "crisis" we can more charitably describe comparative genocide theorizing as "diverse." Genocide studies cannot contribute to our knowledge of this particular form of human destruction without continuously questioning what we think we know, without challenging our assumptions and conclusions, without exploring new theoretical approaches and empirical evidence. This does not mean different definitions, theories, and research should not be subject to rigorous testing and critical evaluation. It does mean that there are multiple ways to account for genocidal violence, be it epistemologically, theoretically, or methodologically. We need to be conscious of the limitations of our theories and research in terms of both generalizability and comparability. A given definition and theoretical model will likely only explain a subset of cases rather than the entire universe of possible cases of genocide. The diversity of genocide scholarship would thus seem to indicate that mid-range rather than grand theorizing is a more realistic goal for the definition of key concepts, comparative theory, and theory testing across cases.

The following discussion is primarily a retrospective (rather than prescriptive) analysis of the field to date. I will trace the evolution of theorizing in genocide studies on the causes and processes of genocidal violence and the ways in which theorizing has been established, and then question the "boundaries" identified above. Since comparative genocide studies has developed across disciplinary lines the chapter will eschew a disciplinary division of the literature and instead concentrate on the relative importance of different causal mechanisms and processes of destruction across three broad levels of analysis: individual, national, and system.[15] Theories that adopt an individual level of analysis focus on the role of individual actors, be they elite perpetrators, front-line killers, military personnel, civilians, or ordinary bystanders as the unit of analysis, often acting within institutional or organizational structures. The national level of analysis includes the state as a whole, institutions within the state, ethno-racial and socio-economic social structures and society-wide ideational structures based on cultural beliefs and practices. System-level theories look beyond the boundaries of the nation-state to global processes, including the decline of old and the rise of new empires, modernity, the rise of the modern state, and colonialism.

INDIVIDUAL-LEVEL APPROACHES

Individual and social psychology

Genocide is so malevolent that it can appear at first blush to be an act of supreme insanity conceived of and executed by psychologically abnormal people. Some Holocaust scholars tried to account for genocidal violence and other extremist policies by interrogating the role of individual psychology, personal and professional life experience, leadership styles, world views, ideological beliefs, and other personality traits on the assumption that the central driver behind some of the greatest crimes in history are the particularities of specific leaders.[16]

Social scientific explanations of genocide now reject the notion that one person, even at the very top of the political hierarchy, can be *the* single cause of genocidal destruction given the complexity and multiple actors and institutions involved in the perpetration of genocidal violence. Indeed, more recent research notes that the long-term indirect destruction of indigenous populations in the Americas and Australia did not occur under the guiding hand of one or a few leaders in distant colonial capitals but rather occurred as a result of a confluence of policies set in motion by officialdom near and far, and in some cases, at the hands of settlers themselves, culminating in what Patrick Wolfe calls the "logic of elimination."[17] Even in the Holocaust, with the central role played by Hitler and his lieutenants, it is now evident that this vast program of destruction varied significantly over time and location in part as a result of differences in the roles played by local leadership within various Nazi organizations, local collaborators, and local populations.[18]

Early attempts by psychologists and social psychologists to explain why members of society participate in or tacitly accept genocidal policies similarly assumed that the low-level perpetrators of genocide were outside the psychological norm. One approach emphasized that this was the result of a culturally conditioned society-wide "authoritarian personality."[19] Later research determined that genocidal killing is perpetrated by ordinary people who are not psychologically disturbed, highly ideological, or socialized into a common destructive or exclusionary social pathology.[20]

Current social psychological approaches offer several explanations of elite and mass behavior in genocide. The first of these arguments suggests that there are natural human tendencies that make genocidal behavior possible across time, space, and circumstance. One tendency is the cognitive practice of "double essentializing" in which fidelity to one's own group necessarily results in hate for a threatening out-group[21] while a second tendency is the presence of a human "ancestral shadow" that produces ethnocentrism, xenophobia and the desire for social dominance in response to authority. Another set of psychological arguments focuses on human motivations and emotions. Daniel Chirot and Clark McCauley, for example, argue that political killing is motivated by four often mutually reinforcing motivations: convenience (getting rid of groups that are in the way); revenge; "simple" fear (fear of retribution by the victim group and of extermination); and fear of pollution. These motivations are shared by elites but elite actors also manipulate these motivations to induce society to support and execute genocidal policies.[22]

Broader social psychological approaches suggest further that psychologically distressing political, economic, security or other crises produce what Ervin Staub calls "difficult life conditions" that in turn can act as a trigger for genocidal violence. Once crises take hold, members of society blame their frustrations and hardships on historically marginal groups. As crises deepen, and as the state begins to use repression and violence against the victim group, the wider society gradually becomes psychologically disposed to accept the victimization of the group, and some individuals become ripe for recruitment into the genocidal process as low-level killers.[23] In accounting for how ordinary people can become front-line perpetrators of genocide, social psychological explanations also track how individuals' beliefs and behaviors are transformed by social organizational structures. For James Waller, professional socialization into military and security organizations reinforces members' "commitment to the group and its activities" such that "evil-doing organizations change the people within them."[24] Social interaction between different kinds of perpetrators and group dynamics are also identified as explanations for how ordinary law-abiding citizens can be co-opted into the genocidal process.[25]

The idea that human psychology and group dynamics predispose humanity to genocidal violence has been questioned by scholars such as Alex Alvarez, who disputes the idea that humans are naturally prone to violence against out-groups. Alvarez contends that the real question is not "Why do they kill?" but how do ordinary people overcome internalized norms against violence and become the executioners of genocidal regimes? Low-level perpetrators repress personal beliefs and feelings so that their actions are reframed as acceptable to themselves and others through "neutralization" techniques.[26] These include denial of responsibility, of injury, and of victims.[27]

Strategic choice

Strategic actor models keep the focus on individuals but instead treat them as rational actors. Whether elites, front-line perpetrators, or bystanders, strategic actor models assume that actors engage in cost–benefit calculations and consciously order their preferences and goals through a process of calculating subjective "expected utility."[28] The idea that genocide is a goal-oriented policy that is "rationally instrumental" to the realization of elite perpetrators' goals has been a part of the genocide studies literature from the beginning,[29] but has only more recently been explored in explicit strategic actor models. Benjamin Valentino[30] sees mass killing as a seemingly illogical act but one that is the product of a rational choice made by elites to achieve other policy goals. Perpetrator elites commit genocide against a target group to force its members to do something they would otherwise not do but which is required, from the perpetrators' perspective, to realize preferred policy outcomes. Elites commit genocide when they conclude that less violent forms of repression or concessions to the target group have failed or are impractical.[31] Using prospect theory, Manus Midlarsky also links the strategic choice to commit genocide to policy failure but suggests that genocide is a response to external, particularly territorial, losses.[32]

Strategic actor models of front-line perpetrator and bystander behavior challenge the notion that non-elite actors only participate in genocidal violence or allow it to occur unopposed because of innate human propensities for exclusion and violence, powerful emotions triggered by crises, or obedience to authority. While individual psychological and group dynamics are certainly not irrelevant, there is a growing body of evidence that suggests at least some ordinary perpetrators and bystanders engage in cost–benefit calculations over increased access to resources held by members of the victim group (e.g. land, housing, employment, education), career advancement, or prestige.[33]

The strategic actor approach is useful in that it rejects even more strongly than individual and social psychological approaches the belief that the perpetrators of genocide must be crazies, zealots, ideologues, or blind followers, or that extreme circumstances leave members of society vulnerable to powerful exclusionary human proclivities and emotions and the influence of authority figures and hierarchical organizational structures. The strategic actor models of genocide are problematic, however, since they suffer from some of the same shortcomings as rational actor models in general. First, strategic actor models either do not inquire at all or deeply enough into how actors arrive at and order their preferences and goals. Doing so is said to be an "unnecessary convolution,"[34] but without this knowledge we cannot know why genocide becomes a preference or goal in the first place. Tracing the influence of psychological and social psychological factors, cultural beliefs, values, and practices, historical social relationships between groups, and perceptions of group identity, for example, are key to understanding how genocide can be entertained by elites as a policy option to achieve certain ends or become a behavior ordinary people are willing to participate in or tolerate. Further, strategic/rational actor explanations fail to realize that actors do not always rationally order preferences according to subjective expected utility calculations, particularly under conditions of risk.[35] The Nazi, Khmer Rouge, and Hutu Power regimes saw essentially defenseless civilians as the most threatening of enemies, despite objective evidence to the contrary. Thus, they were willing to divert crucial resources away from military operations against real enemies to carry out their exterminationist policies. Finally, the strategic actor thesis only works to explain elite behavior if we agree that genocide is in fact a means to some other policy end. For scholars who believe that genocide is a deliberate and systematic policy designed specifically to bring about the complete or partial destruction of a group, the means–ends logic of the strategic actor model would seem not to apply, since genocide is ultimately an end in itself. Whether genocide is a strictly intentional act or not continues to be a matter of dispute among genocide scholars.

Identity construction

Finally, individual-level approaches look at how actors construct the identities and interest of other actors, or more precisely, how perpetrators construct the collective identity of their victims. The literature tends to group a number of different constructions under one generic label such as dehumanization or demonization. But, if we look carefully, there are three distinct yet interrelated conceptions held by perpetrators of their victims: the victim as an "alien" other; as sub- or non-human; and as a threatening "enemy within."

From a social psychological perspective human beings are said to have the capacity to target for genocidal destruction any kind of "self-reproducing social category"[36] because we naturally divide the world into in-groups and out-groups and imbue groups with "an unchanging quality that makes a group what it is."[37] Under the right contextual and institutional conditions this capacity leads to what Waller calls the "social death" of the victim whereby the victim group is psychologically removed from the wider society.[38] This severs any emotional connection with the victims which in turn neutralizes popular aversion to authoritarian politics in general and the genocidal destruction of other groups in particular.[39]

For Helen Fein, the process of cognitively separating out the victims constitutes a key precondition for genocide through the removal of the victim group from the "sanctified universe of obligation."[40] The exclusion of victims from society and their definition as aliens is not ahistorical or innately psychological but rather follows from already existing exclusionary practices and beliefs in society, although the exact content of these practices and beliefs may change over time. Those who are deemed to no longer belong to the community are stripped of any protection, formal and informal, that membership in the community provides against a predatory state.[41] Lacking the legal and social protection of citizenship, vulnerable groups are ripe for victimization in the era of the nation-state since such peoples are rendered, as Hannah Arendt notes, "stateless" and thus "superfluous."[42] Defining the victims of genocide as out-groups through a variety of techniques not only marks one group off as different from other groups and apart from the wider society, but also involves the dehumanization of the members of the group and culminates in calls for concrete action to bring about the "moral disengagement" of bystanders and perpetrators from the victims,[43] and ultimately the latter's extermination.[44]

For genocide to occur the victim group must be seen as more than the "other" or "foreign"; after all, this kind of thinking is the hallmark of other forms of violence such as warfare and terrorism. To explain why elites and society commit genocide against out-groups, some scholars have argued that the dehumanization of the victim group is an essential social construction in the genocidal process. The group is conceived as something other than a member of the human species[45] since the victims are seen to stand not only outside of a particular political, national, ethnic, or racial community, but outside of humanity itself.

The denial of humanity also performs the crucial functions of overcoming the normal human revulsion against murder[46] and moral inhibitions against violence,[47] creating a context in which it becomes morally and psychologically possible for the perpetrators, high and low, to engage in efficient and guilt-free programs of group destruction. The dehumanization of victim groups is most easily projected onto people belonging to different racial, ethnic, religious, or political groups who are "regarded as inferior or threatening."[48]

Finally, the identity construction literature focuses on perpetrator conceptions of the victim group as a source of danger or threat that the perpetrators believe must be countered through physical destruction. Psychological approaches to identity construction contend that since humans tend to project onto others what they fear most, perpetrators' fear of death itself is projected onto the victims. Perpetrators thus believe they are justified in sparing their own lives by causing the deaths of others.[49] Beyond this rather generalized fear of death, fear of "pollution," which stems historically from concerns with religious purity, and in the twentieth century with racial and class purity, is said to be the "most extreme reason" for genocidal and mass killing and other policies such as deportation.[50] Perceptions of threat can also produce other powerful emotions such as hatred of the victim group grounded in a conception of them as so "fundamentally flawed" that they "cannot be fixed."[51]

Further, the "victims as threat" conception is amplified by the perception of the victims as a powerful force bent on the extermination of the perpetrators, whether the state, society, nation, race, or new revolutionary order. Faced with what is perceived to be the very real possibility of one's own extermination at the hands of the victim group, the latter must be exterminated first.[52] Once the genocide is underway, perpetrators also become motivated by the short-term fear that failure to "finish the job," so to speak, will allow the victims to regain strength and retaliate.[53]

The existing literature on identity construction, while promising, needs to consider more systematically how the identities of the victim group are constructed in the first place and how this construction can change over time. Key to this inquiry is, as Martin Shaw suggests, a conception of genocide as an evolving social relationship, or as Daniel Feierstein puts it, social practices, between victims and perpetrators.[54] A careful exercise in process tracing built on this conceptual foundation can unpack the evolution of the relationship and local perceptions of the relationship between societal groups as they transform from relatively benign conceptions of the victims as marginal insiders to malevolent constructions of the victims as foreigners, enemies, threats, and sub-human vermin. Part of the effort in process tracing is the identification of critical junctures such as sharp political, economic, and/or security crises, and an examination of the way in which these experiences can turn longstanding anti-group attitudes and practices into threatening conceptions of the target group as "enemies within" requiring extermination.

The identity construction literature also needs to develop further the exact relationship between collective identity construction, on the one hand, and the initiation and acceptance of genocidal policies on the other. As it is, the causal mechanisms that connect perceptions of the victim group to genocidal policies specifically, and not some other form of repression and violence, remain undefined. To uncover causal mechanisms linking identity construction to genocide we need to avoid conflating, as is sometimes the case in the literature,[55] different but interrelated conceptions of the victim group. This conflation obscures our understanding of the specific content of and functions that each of these conceptions plays in the genocidal process. Groups conceived of as outsiders or foreigners are conceptualized as non-members of the community and, therefore, are owed neither rights nor obligations. But this conception on its own does not threaten the community and as such does not lead to a genocidal response. Similarly, while dehumanization is crucial to loosening moral and psychological inhibitions against the destruction of other human beings, dehumanization alone is not the rationale for genocide. As I have argued elsewhere, only the mortal threat conception of the victim group leads elites to initiate, and society to accept, root-and-branch genocidal policies because only this conception sees the victim group as so threatening as to imperil the very existence of the state and society despite the objective powerlessness of the victims.[56]

NATIONAL-LEVEL APPROACHES

Culture

Conceived as a national-level variable, culture would seem to be a logical place to begin to explain why genocide has occurred in certain societies but not others.

But the search for a set of society-wide cultural beliefs and practices that cause genocidal destruction has been highly problematic. Cultural explanations can easily slide into stereotypical "national character" arguments in which all the members of a society are said to possess the same exclusionary beliefs and practices that inexorably lead to genocide. Aside from the obvious methodological problem of proving such a thesis, the notion of a collectively shared genocidal culture specific to a given society, as articulated by Daniel Goldhagen in his "eliminationist antisemitism" explanation of the Holocaust,[57] or across all cases of genocide has been roundly dismissed in the literature.

Such problems do not mean that culture is irrelevant to an account of why genocide happens or the way in which genocidal destruction manifests itself in specific cases. Shifting the geographical boundaries of cultural research, anthropologists and other genocide scholars have largely avoided the pitfalls of large macro-level studies in more recent research by concentrating on close ethnographic studies of subnational communities and local cultural knowledge as a determinant of the exact form that genocidal destruction takes on in local circumstances. Anthropologist Alexander Hinton suggests that the "cultural knowledge" of disproportionate revenge as a response to a long-standing grudge in Cambodia, for example, "constitutes a crucial site upon which genocidal regimes can work," with perpetrator elites "us[ing] these highly salient cultural models to motivate individuals to commit violent atrocities."[58] Historian Omer Bartov in a similar micro-level examination suggests that the nature of interaction between friends and neighbors and the reception of local communities to external forces tasked with carrying out genocidal policies is key to the success or failure of genocide at the local level.[59] Ethnographic studies have turned to a different methodological approach than macro-level cultural research, employing an "experience-near" methodology grounded in extensive "face-to-face engagements with communities" that have endured genocidal violence and other gross human rights abuses. This approach yields "thick descriptions" to reveal the actual lived experiences[60] of both survivors and perpetrators. While the near-experience method avoids imputing sweeping generalizations about the content and effects of cultural beliefs and practices onto whole societies, these are self-consciously idiographic, even idiosyncratic, single-case studies that do not provide the foundation for the creation of comparative cultural theories of genocide. Thus the cultural variable finds its utility in sub-national studies but remains problematic at the national level or for cross-national comparison.

Divided societies

A more common national-level approach is the divided society thesis. Indeed, ethnocultural stratification was identified by early genocide scholars as the "structural base for genocide"[61] and a key causal factor in ethnic, racial, or religiously-based genocides.[62] Socio-economic or ethno-religious cleavages, however, do not on their own directly cause genocide. Rather it is only societies riven by severe ethnic, religious, socio-economic, or other cleavages reinforced by segregationist policies, and other "differential legal, sociocultural, political, educational, and economic opportunities afforded to social groups"[63] that are particularly vulnerable to genocide. Plural societies in which cleavages are "persistent and pervasive" and where economic inequality is "superimposed" on ethnic, religious, racial or socio-economic "differentiation" allow for the aggregation of the population into "distinctive sections," thereby facilitating, as Leo Kuper noted in an early work, "crimes against collectivities."[64] In their quantitative analysis, William Easterly and his colleagues find that societies in which the population is distributed more or less evenly across two main communal groups are more likely to experience mass killing than societies "fracturalized" into a large number of smaller communal groups.[65]

Although critics of the divided society thesis argue that not all societies that have experienced genocide have been characterized by deep societal divisions and that large-N extensive quantitative analyses suggest that societal divisions are not a principal cause of genocide,[66] it is important to remember that quantitative studies simply establish correlative relationships but they do not account for the complex causal mechanisms and processes at play in any given case. Determining whether and under what circumstances deep societal divisions make genocide more likely should involve tracing the complex interplay of additional national-level variables with the divided society variable, to establish how intense societal divisions are transformed into malevolent forms of social stratification and social interaction that culminate in the targeting of certain groups for destruction. The impact of serious political, economic, security or other crises and a history of exclusionary intergroup attitudes and practices in society are two possible factors that may allow us to account for this transformation. Crises of various kinds create extremist conditions under which elites and ordinary people alike begin to search for the source of and solution to their deepening woes. Already existing societal divisions reinforced by legal and other restrictions, and a concomitant history of exclusionary conceptions of marginal groups in society and/or restrictive understandings of genuine membership in the political community, establish a ready set of possible candidates for blame, punishment, and possibly extermination as a means of realizing a "final solution" to "problems" or "questions" posed by the continued existence of certain groups.

Crises, revolution, and war

The next set of national-level explanations leaves aside the ideational and social structure of society and instead looks at the impact of a variety of severe, often violent, society-wide upheavals. The literature has identified crises, revolution, and war as extreme events that either precede or occur concurrently with genocide, with each phenomenon playing similar but distinct functions in the genocidal process.

From the advent of genocide studies onward, qualitative and quantitative studies have consistently highlighted crises as a prelude to and predictor[67] of genocide, but mostly as a triggering mechanism rather than as a condition that on its own causes genocide. External and internal security crises, including loss in war and loss of territory, have been linked to the onset of "crises of national identity"[68] and the quest for "loss compensation" at the expense of the victim group.[69] More generally crises are said to trigger society-wide "frustration" and "normative upheavals"[70] that heighten social cleavages, produce distress,[71] or lead to the "break-down of existing social mechanisms" and power struggles in society.[72] Other arguments treat crises as opportunities that can be seized on and manipulated by elite actors to further their own policy goals, or as "political opportunity structures"[73] for radical elites to capture the reins of power in order to execute already formulated genocidal policies.[74] Matthew Krain finds in his quantitative analysis that genocides and politicides (the destruction of political groups) are more likely to occur in the presence of "big opportunity" structures, particularly civil wars, and to a lesser extent wars in general and decolonization. Krain concludes that these opportunity structures also best account for the severity of genocides and politicides while other variables such as ethnic "fractionalization" and power concentration are of only marginal impact.[75]

Whether as a trigger or opportunity, what is important about crises is not so much the specific nature of crises themselves but how they are perceived by ordinary people and elites in terms of cause, blame, and solution. To borrow Alexander Wendt's phrase about anarchy in the international system, crisis is what elites and society "make of it."[76] What elites and society "make" of crises rests, at least to some degree, on prevailing cleavages, attitudes, beliefs, and practices. In genocidal situations crises are interpreted to be illustrative of an ongoing struggle between the political community on the one hand and a specific group on the other.

Revolutions also create circumstances through which radical elites assume political power and implement highly ideological, exclusionary, and sometimes genocidal policies designed to radically reshape society.[77] But as with divided societies, not all revolutions give way to genocide. For Edward Kissi, genocidal revolutions only occur when the targets of mass political killing are atomized to such an extent that they cannot defend themselves against the state, when the state is able to dominate society, and when the state targets for liquidation ethnic, religious, socio-economic, and inactive or already defeated political groups.[78]

A detailed body of literature has similarly investigated the complex relationship between two hugely violent national-level forms of collective human action: war and genocide. Despite the fact that genocidal violence often occurs during war,[79] genocide and war are not synonymous. Nonetheless warfare and genocide are said to share several ideational, social–psychological, and organizational foundations. Ideationally, war and genocide are underpinned by ideologies that dehumanize the targets of violence and feature the use of dehumanizing propaganda to vilify "enemies" designed to diminish "popular awareness of, and resistance to, ruthless governmental actions."[80]

Wars expose societies to threats to national survival that Eric Markusen and David Kopf argued in an early work can inflame already existing inter-group tensions with a fearful majority punishing marginalized minorities for an existential security crisis.[81] Further, killing in war psychologically desensitizes soldiers and civilians to the widespread use of violence not only against other soldiers but civilian victims of genocide.[82] Meanwhile soldiers become, according to Scott Straus, "specialists in violence" allowing for their mobilization for genocidal killing.[83] Wars and genocides are also identified as the product of bureaucratized modern states capable of planning and using force on a massive scale, with an array of destructive modern weaponry that inflicts mass casualties in a manner that insulates the killers from the suffering of their victims.[84] Finally, warfare can be used to hide the execution of genocidal policies from domestic and international audiences, which can then be denied afterward as a result of the "fog of war" or the alleged perpetration of atrocities by all sides.

Not all kinds of warfare have been linked to genocide, however. Markusen and Kopf suggest that genocide shares many parallels with "total war"[85] in which entire societies are mobilized for the prosecution of armed conflict against similarly mobilized societies. More recently, Martin Shaw has pressed the boundaries of the kind of war most closely associated with genocide, arguing that "degenerate wars" are most likely to slide into the genocidal destruction of deliberately targeted civilian groups. Degenerate war involves "the deliberate and systematic extension of war against an organized armed enemy," or what Shaw calls legitimate or "real war," to war against a largely unarmed civilian population.[86] While degenerate war and genocide share a similarly destructive "character of the action," "violent modality," and "typical actor" (i.e. the armed organized power of the state), and are both forms of conflict, degenerate war and genocide remain different phenomena for Shaw since only genocide involves the "construction of civilian groups as enemies, not only in a social or political but also in a military sense, to be destroyed."[87] Using more conventional categorizations of warfare, Benjamin Valentino, Paul Huth, and Dylan Balch-Lindsay find in their quantitative analysis of 147 post-World War II instances of armed conflict, that mass killing of noncombatants by states is most likely to occur when states feel their security is significantly threatened and when the state's adversaries engage in guerrilla warfare in which insurgents maintain high levels of support from surrounding populations.[88]

Regime type and the state

A final national-level of analysis links the modern state to the initiation, planning, and perpetration of genocidal violence. Early theorizing focused on regime type specifically, suggesting that non-democratic political systems are the exclusive perpetrators of genocide in the modern era. The totalitarianism version of this thesis suggests that the underlying logic of totalitarian regimes fuels genocide because of the state's single-minded attempt to exert what Arendt called "total domination"[89] over all aspects of society in an effort to overcome societal differentiation (ethnic, religious, racial, class), or eliminate dissent to the radically transformative policies of the state.[90] Totalitarian regimes are the most capable of executing genocidal policies given the state's coercive capacity and high degree of autonomy from society.

The authoritarianism version of the argument holds that non-democratic regimes are generally more likely to perpetrate genocide and other forms of political violence against their own people because of what Rudolph Rummel calls the "power principle": "the more power a government has, the more it can act arbitrarily ... and murder its foreign and domestic subjects," while "the more constrained the power of governments, the less it will aggress on others."[91] Rummel thus concludes that the best prophylactic against genocide is the promotion of democratic governance. Barbara Harff's quantitative study shows that failed authoritarian states are three and a half times more likely to perpetrate genocide or politicide than failed democratic states.[92] Easterly and his colleagues have found that Rummel's democracy thesis is confirmed but only with regard to countries with high levels of development and democracy and then only in the twentieth century. Wealthy colonial powers and settler societies were the most likely to perpetrate massacres against indigenous populations in the nineteenth century, which suggests that there is non-linear relationship between mass killing and democracy or mass killing and development. Indeed, in the twentieth century mass killing is most frequent in middle-income countries and in countries considered to be "intermediate" level democracies.[93] Krain, while not dismissing Rummel's power principle altogether, finds in his quantitative analysis that power concentration does not determine the outbreak of genocides and politicides and is only important as one among other factors that in concert create an environment in which openings in the opportunity structure trigger genocidal policies.[94]

Other scholars have examined how the modern state is particularly well equipped to conceive and implement genocidal policies. The modern state possesses power resources and institutions, including coercive institutions, that can be harnessed by genocidal elites to pursue policies of group destruction.[95] Aside from military and security organizations, civil services are instrumental in perpetrating genocide since bureaucracies prize fidelity to rules, procedures, and the law, regardless of their content and the moral and physical consequences of policy outcomes.[96] In genocide, military and civilian institutions engage in a form of "state criminality" perpetrated by what have become criminal organizations.[97] Pierre van den Berghe goes further, claiming that the modern state is at its core a fundamentally violent form of political organization.[98]

Powerful centralized bureaucratic states are also said to conceive of and implement grand projects of social engineering, turning the state into genocidal "gardener states." For Zygmunt Bauman the state engages not in destruction through genocide, but in *construction* of new social, economic, demographic, or political orders in a way similar to a landscaper who plants and tends a garden. Just as weeds inevitably grow that do not belong in a meticulously designed garden, so too new racial, national, or revolutionary systems that contain human beings who do not belong in the new order must be "weeded out" by the gardener state.[99]

SYSTEM-LEVEL APPROACHES

Ideas of modernity

Some of the most innovative contemporary research in genocide studies has refocused theorizing around the system-level of analysis while at the same time engaging, in one way or another, with the advent of modernity and its consequences. The *ideas of modernity* approach adopts an ideational perspective by examining the rise and effect of exclusionary conceptions of nations and nationalism, class, and scientific thinking as well as race thinking and racism resulting from contact between Europeans and indigenous populations through the spread of colonialism.[100] A particularly pernicious idea, race came to be conceived as physiological differences between human groups mapped onto a hierarchical ordering of intellectual, cultural, and moral capacities, thus encouraging the notion that "superior" races could be polluted biologically or culturally by "inferior" races, that all races are locked in a struggle of the survival of the fittest,[101] and that victory in this struggle may necessitate the physical elimination through eugenics or even genocide of "inferior" yet biologically threatening individuals and groups.

Some scholars have expanded the modern ideas linked to genocide to include a concept that is usually seen as progressive: democracy. For Mark Levene, Rousseau's general will is simultaneously the philosophical basis for an exclusionary conception of the nation and the democratic conception of rights articulated in the *Declaration of the Rights of Man and Citizen* – rights that are derived from membership in a naturally pre-existing national community. Michael Mann argues that ethnic cleansing is the "dark side of democracy"[102] and occurs when the democratic idea of "rule of the people" fuses the *demos* (the people) with the dominant *ethnos* (people of the same ethnicity or nationality), or when socialist conceptions of democracy entwine *demos* with the proletariat. In both circumstances, a perversion of the democratic ideal can be used to sanction the cleansing of ethnic minorities or socio-economic classes.[103] Along with Mann, scholars such as A. Dirk Moses, Dan Stone, Tony Barta and their collaborators directly challenge the notion that Western democracies do not commit genocide, laying bare the direct role European colonial powers and Western settler societies in North America and Australia have played in the physical, biological, and cultural extermination of indigenous populations.[104] Further, the prescription that democratization is the most effective long-term genocide prevention strategy has been called into question. For Mann the dangerous intertwining of the *demos* and *ethnos* is most likely to occur when multi-ethnic authoritarian regimes begin to liberalize.[105] Easterly and his co-authors found that intermediate democracies, rather than highly authoritarian or highly democratic regimes, are most likely to experience mass killing. As Western democracies press for democratic regime change they may risk creating the conditions for genocide, not genocide prevention,[106] while simultaneously sanctioning neo-colonial foreign adventurism by accident or design.

The modern ideas (and institutions) approach is a useful corrective to the early argument that the Holocaust and other genocides were occasioned by an abandonment of the civilizing restraint of modernity and a descent into murderous barbarism. But while the modernity thesis tells us what modern ideas and institutions have been central to the conceptualization and implementation of genocidal policies, these "products" of modernity are still one step removed from what is foundational about modernity and its connection to genocidal violence. What genocide scholarship is missing is an inquiry into the *necessary* rather than *instrumental* ways in which modernity is bound up with genocide. We need to go further to conceptualize modernity not just as a chronological category characterized by certain features of violence at a particular time in history, but also as an ontological category whose very structure contains an internal logic tending towards total violence, a particular shape of self-consciousness which provides a way to distinguish between ontologically and chronologically modern genocides.[107]

The negative connection in the literature between democracy and genocide has gone as far as it can go. While a credible argument can be made that the democracies of the colonial era committed physical/biological and cultural genocide, it is important to emphasize, as Mann and Easterly and his co-authors do, that these were limited democracies and as such did not extend truly universal citizenship and respect for minority and individual rights. In short, the democracies of old are certainly implicated in genocide but contemporary thoroughly democratic liberal democracies are not.

The declining empires, new nation-states, and colonialism

A second system-level approach turns to the international system itself to find what Shaw calls the "international production" of genocide.[108] It traces the influence of the multiple overlapping historical processes by which multinational European and Near East land empires dissolved and transformed into nation-states at the same time that the early modernizing states of Western Europe embarked on a new program of colonialism and empire building around the world, and more recently, how powerful international actors foster genocidal policies in regional client regimes.[109] The first two processes of imperial decline and the rise of the nation-state occasioned the forcible pulling apart of populations living inside multicultural empires and the reordering of these populations into more or less homogeneous nation-states. The geographical, political, economic, and social points at which these dramatic geo-political and societal changes took place in the nineteenth and twentieth centuries have been identified by Mark Levene as "tectonic plates"[110] and Timothy Snyder as "the bloodlands."[111] Dominik J. Schaller and Jürgen Zimmerer, to name but one example, have traced these developments in the late Ottoman genocides.[112] This argument draws on much of the modern ideas thesis, particularly the notion that human beings and institutions (re)make whole societies, nations, regions, and the geo-political foundations of the international system at will regardless of the cost to human life. A relatively new body of literature, this approach succeeds at moving beyond the societal level and problematizing the domestic/international distinction to see genocide as constitutive of global systemic changes. But contrary to Shaw's insistence on a strictly system-level historical sociology,[113] global changes and social relationships between actors at the system level are not themselves the direct drivers of genocide. Rather they are the highly disruptive and sometimes destructive contexts within which genocidal policies, either in intent, effect, or both, are crafted to restructure whole regions of the world and the societies within them. As the works of Levene and Donald Bloxham show, for example, other more proximate variables and/or processes must be included to connect the tectonic shifts of nation-building to the initiation and implementation of genocide by specific perpetrators against specific victim groups.[114] No one level of analysis can fully unpack the genocidal process, and as such we should, as Ugur Ümit Üngör suggests, incorporate macro (inter-state), meso (intra-societal), and micro ("ordinary people") level contexts into our analyses.[115]

Another variant of this approach that looks specifically at colonialism, colonization, and genocidal destruction in what we now call the Global South has proved to be a fertile avenue of research on a number of different fronts. In his exploration of the interplay of the advent of modern ideas and historical processes, Eric Weitz suggests that contact between white Europeans and non-white indigenous populations in the South and the infection of non-white peoples with tropical diseases for which they had little to no immunity reinforced the idea that non-whites, and by extension ethnic or racial out-groups in general, were dangerous racial "parasites" or sources of deadly contagion.

While Weitz used this explanation to account for the Holocaust and other non-colonial genocides, scholars who study genocidal destruction under colonialism from a post-colonial perspective have begun to press the boundaries of what we consider genocide and the methods of genocidal destruction. Colonial genocides have been marked by direct (e.g. killing) and indirect methods of destruction (e.g. spread of diseases, removal to marginal lands, the banning of important cultural practices crucial to group identity and function); the latter suggests less explicit intent than policies that either alone or in concert produced genocidal outcomes for indigenous populations.[116] This line of inquiry employs an outcomes-based definition of genocide that is not new in the literature and in fact dates back to Lemkin, but it is developed in greater detail with reference to a larger number of cases. By pushing the boundaries of how we define genocide and what cases to include, the literature on colonial genocides insists that there are multiple kinds of genocides: those that are perpetrated with a specific intent to destroy a group or groups; those that have this effect but which are the result of an accretion of at times uncoordinated policies not specifically designed to bring about the destruction of a group or groups; those that involve the direct application of violence; and those that involve indirect (intentional or not) physical, biological, and cultural methods and processes of destruction.

Much of the post-colonial critical theory literature also questions who the perpetrators are. Genocide studies has long assumed that states or other comparable authorities are the only actors who plan the dirty deed. Research into colonial settler violence, the nature of colonial administrations and home country policy suggest that determining who the perpetrators of genocide are, who formulates genocidal policies, and whether colonial policies concerning indigenous populations are intentionally genocidal is not entirely clear. Settler violence in Australia, for example, appears to have been mostly spontaneous and self-generated but occurred in a context within which colonial administrators either did not try, or did not consistently try, to curb violence against indigenous populations. Critics will argue that the lack of clarity in identifying the perpetrators of colonial genocide and perpetrator intentions proves that colonialism, destructive though it may have been, was not genocidal. Whether one accepts the conclusions of the post-colonial research agenda in part depends on whether one accepts its underlying logic and a pluralist understanding of how to define and account for genocide across significantly different contexts.

Finally, the post-colonial approach problematizes the role of the mostly indigenous victims of genocide. Typically the victims of genocide in both colonial and non-colonial cases are seen to be passive objects of deadly forces beyond their control or capacity to resist. Post-colonial critical theory studies instead search for sites of resistance to colonial control and processes of group eradication.[117] Rather than conceptualizing a one-way destructive relationship in which perpetrators visit unrelenting violence, deprivation, and degradation on hapless victims, post-colonialism tries to unpack the often complex inter-relationship *between* perpetrators and victims to uncover the ways that both groups are active participants whose actions shape and reshape their mutual, albeit unequal and obviously destructive, relationship.

CONCLUDING OBSERVATIONS

A somewhat unusual three-way split seems to be unfolding in genocide studies. First there is a status quo strand of genocide scholarship that continues to engage in state-level single or comparative qualitative case studies. Meanwhile an increasing number of large-N quantitative studies, mostly by American scholars influenced by the continuing dominance of quantitative methods in American social sciences, are pushing some genocide scholarship even more squarely into the positivist social scientific camp. Finally, a simultaneous embrace of critical theory based research, mostly but not entirely by non-US based scholars, shifts another segment of the field closer to, but not yet entirely within, a post-modern framework. What do each of these trends suggest for the future of genocide studies?

More traditional qualitative single and comparative case studies afford the opportunity to explore the influence of a small number of variables under limited circumstances with plenty of "thick description" of the relevant causes and processes. The drawback with this method is the inability to confidently make generalizable claims. Large-N quantitative research seeks to discover, using many cases across time and space, to establish, or discard, causal and/or correlative relationships between variables and genocidal outcomes. Valentino, Easterly and their respective co-authors, Rummel, Harff, and Krain, for example, have all attempted to test many of the causal claims generated by the comparative qualitative literature on genocide and political violence, and have, interestingly, reached somewhat mixed conclusions, finding confirmation (Easterly and Rummel) and not (Krain) for the inhibitive effect of democracy on genocidal violence; and confirmation (Easterly) and not (Krain) for the effect of "ethnic fractionalization" on outbreaks of genocides and politicides, to take just two examples. The apparent lack of confirmation in some quantitative studies of certain causal variables identified in the qualitative literature seems, however, to be the result of either a failure to understand or test the nuances of these variables as theorized by qualitative theorists. In testing the divided society thesis, for example, quantitative researchers rely on the relatively easily measurable variable "ethnic fractionalization," which only taps how populations are divided among the number of communal groups found in a society. This measure leaves out the qualification in the qualitative "divided society" literature that communal divisions in and of themselves are not predictive of genocide and that genocide is only associated with severe divisions that are created and reinforced by segregationist legal, economic, and social institutions and cultural beliefs and practices.

What is perhaps more important is that quantitative analysis, no matter how sophisticated, cannot get us beyond broad correlative relationships or probabilities. That Krain, for example, finds certain opportunity structures such as civil war and war in general to be predictive of genocidal or politicidal outbreaks is instructive but it cannot tell us exactly how and why elite actors take the opportunities created by a civil war, for instance, to try to exterminate whole groups of people as opposed to other less "final solutions," or *why* (not just *that*) warfare is closely tied to genocide. We can only fully answer these questions about warfare and genocide by turning to the qualitative works of sociology, social psychology, collective identity, and institutional behavior scholars. By way of prescription, once statistical relationships have been established, it would be wise to return to close detailed qualitative analyses that uncover exact causal mechanisms and processes in specific cases. To get the full picture we should follow Sidney Tarrow's advice to adopt, when appropriate, a mixed-methods quantitative and qualitative approach.[118]

It is also advisable to ask research questions first and then determine what methodology and research design best helps us answer these queries. Question-driven, rather than method-driven, research seems most appropriate to the goal-oriented foundation of genocide scholarship: the quest to understand and explain the causes and processes of genocide in the service of effective genocide prevention. An unreflective approach to the adoption of alternative methodologies or epistemologies also risks ignoring the contribution of earlier works in the field. Although the quest by critical theorists, for example, to problematize the discipline of genocide studies, uncover power relationships within genocidal contexts, and more fully understand the dynamics of genocide is extremely valuable, this approach does not always produce insights as new as the authors claim. That democracy, for example, as an idea and in practice has been implicated in genocidal violence by some critical theorists at first blush seems to radically overturn our understanding of democracy as a preventive factor against genocidal violence. But upon closer examination it is clear that long-standing, fully consolidated constitutional democracies with robust human and minority rights instruments still are the least likely regimes to execute genocidal policies. Further, problematization and deconstruction should be a new and fruitful means toward advancing knowledge about the genocidal process and genocide prevention, not simply intellectual exercises in themselves.

So what is new and what is old in genocide studies? New is the diversity of the field in terms of the definition and addition of key concepts, temporal and spatial comparisons, the problematization of the identity and role of victims and perpetrators in the genocidal process, the addition of system-level historical processes of imperial collapse and colonialism, and the adoption of a wider set of methodological and epistemological approaches. Old is the continued importance of a set of key precursors and occurrences of certain kinds of phenomena, some proximate and some more indirect, that are associated with outbreaks of genocide: warfare and other destabilizing tectonic events such as revolutions and nation-state formation;

the social–psychological propensity to exclude out-groups and the victimization of out-groups based on specific negative conceptions of the victims as both sub-humans and overwhelming threats; and, the influence of hierarchical authority-based organizations capable of turning quite ordinary people into the executioners of genocidal policies. The way forward is to profitably marry both the old (and still useful) and the new in interesting and creative ways. Genocide studies' diversity is not a crisis or a liability but a rich vein of intellectual inspiration and, yes, debate.

NOTES

1 Some scholars, including Chalk and Jonassohn, examined both modern and pre-modern genocides. See F. Chalk and K. Jonassohn, *The History and Sociology of Genocide: Analyses and Case Studies*, New Haven, CT: Yale University Press, 1990.
2 E. Staub, *The Roots of Evil: The Psychological and Cultural Origins of Genocide and Other Forms of Group Violence*, Cambridge: Cambridge University Press, 1989; I. Charny, *How Can We Commit the Unthinkable? Genocide: The Human Cancer*, Boulder, CO: Westview Press, 1982.
3 J. Waller, *Becoming Evil: How Ordinary People Commit Genocide and Mass Killing*, Oxford: Oxford University Press, 2007.
4 B. Harff, "No Lessons Learned from the Holocaust? Assessing Risks of Genocide and Mass Murder Since 1955," *American Political Science Review* 97, 2003, 57–73.
5 R. Rummel, *Death by Government*, New Brunswick, NJ: Transaction Publications, 1994.
6 A. Jones, *Gendercide and Genocide*, Nashville, TN: Vanderbilt University Press, 2004; O. Holter, "A Theory of Gendercide," *Journal of Genocide Research* 4/1, 2010, 11–38.
7 R. Evans, "'Crime Without a Name': Colonialism and the Case for 'Indigenocide,'" in A. Dirk Moses, ed., *Empire, Colony, Genocide: Conquest, Occupation, and Subaltern Resistance in World History*, New York: Berghahn Books, 2008, pp. 133–47.
8 R. Lemkin, *Axis Rule in Occupied Europe: Laws of Occupation, Analysis of Government, Proposals for Redress*, New York: Carnegie Endowment for International Peace, 1944.
9 A. Dirk Moses, ed., *Empire, Colony, Genocide: Conquest, Occupation, and Subaltern Resistance in World History*, New York: Berghahn Books, 2008; A. D. Moses and D. Stone, eds., *Colonialism and Genocide*, Abingdon: Routledge, 2007.
10 M. Levene, *Genocide in the Age of the Nation State Vol. II: The Rise of the West and the Coming of Genocide*, London: I. B. Tauris, 2005.
11 E. Markusen, "Genocide and Total War: A Preliminary Comparison," in Isidor Wallimann and Michael N. Dobkowski, eds., *Genocide and the Modern Age: Etiology and Case Studies of Mass Death*, Syracuse, NY: Syracuse University Press, 1987, pp. 97–123; E. Markusen and D. Kopf, *The Holocaust and Strategic Bombing: Genocide and Total War in the Twentieth Century*, Boulder, CO: Westview Press, 1995.
12 M. Shaw, *War and Genocide: Organized Killing in Modern Society*, Cambridge: Polity Press, 2003; M. Shaw, *What Is Genocide?* Cambridge: Polity Press, 2007, pp. 109–12.
13 S. Straus, "Second Generation Comparative Research on Genocide," *World Politics* 29, 2007, 476–501.
14 A. Weiss-Wendt, "Problems in Comparative Genocide Scholarship," in Dan Stone, ed., *The Historiography of Genocide*, New York: Palgrave Macmillan, 2010, pp. 42–70.
15 J. Singer, *A General System Taxonomy for Political Science*, New York: General Learning Press, 1971, p. 16.

16 G. Fleming, *Hitler and the Final Solution*, Berkeley: University of California Press, 1982; D. Chandler, *Brother Number One: A Political Biography of Pol Pot*, revised edition, Boulder, CO: Westview Press, 1999; I. Kershaw, *Hitler 1936–1945: Nemesis*, London: Allen Lane, Penguin Press, 2000; A. Bullock, *Hitler: A Study in Tyranny*, New York: Harper Perennial, 1991; R. Conquest, *Stalin: Breaker of Nations*, New York: Penguin Books, 1991.

17 P. Wolfe, "Structure and Event: Settler Colonialism: Time and the Question of Genocide," in A. Dirk Moses, ed., *Empire, Colony, Genocide: Conquest, Occupation, and Subaltern Resistance in World History*, New York: Berghahn Books, 2008.

18 As one of several possible examples see C. Browning, *The Origins of the Final Solution: The Evolution of Nazi Jewish Policy, September 1939–March 1942*, Lincoln: University of Nebraska Press and Jerusalem: Yad Vashem, 2004.

19 T. Adorno, E. Frenkel and D. Levinson, *The Authoritarian Personality: Studies in Prejudice*, New York: W. W. Norton, 1993.

20 C. Browning, *Ordinary Men: Reserve Police Battalion 101 and the Final Solution in Poland*, New York: Harper Perennial, 1992; D. Chirot and C. McCauley, *Why Not Kill Them All?: The Logic and Prevention of Mass Murder*, Princeton, NJ: Princeton University Press, 2006; J. Waller, *Becoming Evil: How Ordinary People Commit Genocide and Mass Murder*, Oxford: Oxford University Press, 2002; A. Alvarez, *Governments, Citizens, and Genocide: A Comparative and Interdisciplinary Approach*, Bloomington: Indiana University Press, 2001.

21 Chirot and McCauley, *Why Not Kill Them All?* p. 86.

22 Ibid., pp. 20–44.

23 See for example E. Staub, *The Roots of Evil: The Psychological and Cultural Origins of Genocide and Other Forms of Group Violence*, Cambridge: Cambridge University Press, 1989.

24 Waller, *Becoming Evil*, pp. 19–20; see also Chirot and McCauley, *Why Not Kill Them All?* pp. 52, 90.

25 A. Smeulers and L. Hoex, "Studying the Microdynamics of the Rwandan Genocide," *British Journal of Criminology* 50, 2010, 435–54.

26 Alvarez, *Governments, Citizens, and Genocide*, p. 110.

27 Ibid., pp. 114–28.

28 W. Riker, "The Political Psychology of Rational Choice Theory," *Political Psychology* 16/1, 1995, 24–6.

29 H. Fein, *Accounting for Genocide: National Responses and Jewish Victimization During the Holocaust*, New York: The Free Press, 1979, pp. 4–5, 7–8. Also see P. du Preez, *Genocide: The Psychology of Mass Murder*, London: Boyars/Bowerdean, 1994, p. 3; R. Smith, "State, Power, and Genocidal Intent: On the Uses of Genocide in the Twentieth Century," in Levon Chorbajian and George Shirinian, eds., *Studies in Comparative Genocide*, New York: St. Martin's Press, 1999, pp. 3–14.

30 B. Valentino, *Final Solutions: Mass Killing and Genocide in the 20th Century*, Ithaca, NY: Cornell University Press, 2004.

31 Ibid., pp. 4, 72–3.

32 M. Midlarsky, *The Killing Trap: Genocide in the Twentieth Century*, Cambridge: Cambridge University Press, 2005.

33 Smeulers and Hoex, "Studying the Microdynamics of the Rwandan Genocide," pp. 435–54.

34 W. Riker, "The Political Psychology of Rational Choice Theory," *Political Psychology* 16/1, 1995, 26.

35 D. Kahneman and A. Tversky, "Prospect Theory: An Analysis of Decision Under Risk," *Econometrica* 47/2, 1979, 263–92.

36 Chirot and McCauley, *Why Not Kill Them All?* p. 82.

37 Ibid., p. 82.

38 Waller, *Becoming Evil*, pp. 19–20.

39 Ibid., p. 43.

40 Fein, *Accounting for Genocide*, pp. 4–5.

41 H. Hirsch and R. Smith, "The Language of Extermination in Genocide," in Israel W. Charny, ed., *Genocide: A Critical Bibliographic Review, Volume Two*, London: Mansell Publishing Limited, 1991, p. 387. A publication of the Institute on the Holocaust and Genocide.

42 H. Arendt, *The Origins of Totalitarianism*, New York: Harcourt Brace, 1973, pp. 275–90.

43 Waller, *Becoming Evil*, p. 20; I. Charny, *How Can We Commit the Unthinkable? Genocide: The Human Cancer*, Boulder, CO: Westview Press, 1982, pp. 206–7.

44 H. Hirsch and R. Smith, "The Language of Extermination in Genocide," pp. 388–91.

45 Charny, *How Can We Commit the Unthinkable?* p. 207; Chirot and McCauley, *Why Not Kill Them All?* pp. 84–5.

46 G. Stanton, "The 8 Stages of Genocide." Online. Available at: www.genocidewatch.org/aboutgenocide/8stages.htm. Accessed February 20, 2012.

47 H. Kelman, "Violence Without Moral Restraint: Reflection on the Dehumanization of Victims by Victimizers," *Journal of Social Issues* 29/4, 1973, 48–9.

48 Waller, *Becoming Evil*, pp. 20, 245; Chalk and Jonassohn, *The History and Sociology of Genocide*, p. 28.

49 Charny, *How Can We Commit the Unthinkable?* pp. 186, 192.

50 Chirot and McCauley, *Why Not Kill Them All?* pp. 36–42.

51 Ibid., pp. 72–3.

52 R. Lifton, *The Nazi Doctors: Medical Killing and the Psychology of Genocide*, New York: Basic Books, 1986, p. 477.

53 Chirot and McCauley, *Why Not Kill Them All?* pp. 31–2.

54 M. Shaw, *What Is Genocide?* Cambridge: Polity Press, 2007, pp. 81–96; D. Feierstein, "The Concept of Genocidal Social Practices," in Adam Jones, ed., *New Directions in Genocide Research*, London: Routledge, 2012, pp. 18–22.

55 Chalk and Jonassohn, for instance, argue that one of the key precursors to genocide is the perception that the victim group is not equal to, and fundamentally different from, the wider community. Yet subsequent references in their analysis are to the victims as "less than fully human" ("pagans, savages, and even animals"), "worthless, outside the web of mutual obligations, a threat to the people, immoral sinners, and/or sub/human." Here the authors conflate conceptions of the victim group as foreigners and as sub-humans. Chalk and Jonassohn, *The History and Sociology of Genocide*, p. 28.

56 M. Hiebert, "The Three 'Switches' of Identity Construction in Genocide: The Nazi Final Solution and the Cambodian Killing Fields," *Genocide Studies and Prevention* 3/1, 2008, 5–29.

57 D. Goldhagen, *Hitler's Willing Executioners: Ordinary Germans and the Holocaust*, New York: Vintage Books, 1997.

58 A. Hinton, "A Head for an Eye," p. 353.

59 O. Bartov, "Seeking the Roots of Modern Genocide: On the Macro and Microhistory of Mass Murder," in Robert Gellately and Ben Kiernan, eds., *The Specter of Genocide: Mass Murder in Historical Perspective*, Cambridge: Cambridge University Press, 2003, p. 85. See also J. Gross, *Neighbors: The Destruction of the Jewish Community in Jedwabne Poland*, Princeton, NJ: Princeton University Press, 2001.

60 K. O'Neill and A. Hinton, "Genocide, Truth, Memory, and Representation: An Introduction," in Alexander Laban Hinton and Kevin Lewis O'Neill, eds., *Genocide: Truth, Memory, and Representation*, Durham, NC: Duke University Press, 2009, p. 4.

61 L. Kuper, *Genocide*, New Haven, CT: Yale University Press, 1981, p. 57.

62 H. Fein, "Accounting for Genocide After 1945: Theories and Some Findings," *International Journal on Group Rights* I, 1993, 88–92.; R. Hovannisian, "Etiology and Sequelae of the Armenian Genocide," in George J. Andreopoulos, ed., *Genocide: Conceptual and Historical Dimensions*, Philadelphia: University of Pennsylvania Press, 1994, p. 112.

63 A. Hinton, "Toward and Anthropology of Genocide," in Alexander Laban Hinton, ed., *Annihilating Difference: The Anthropology of Genocide*, Berkeley: University of California Press, 2002, p. 29.

64 Kuper, *Genocide*, p. 58.

65 W. Easterly, R. Gatti and S. Kurbat, "Development, Democracy, and Mass Killing," *Journal of Economic Growth* 11, 2006, p. 142.

66 See, for example, Valentino, *Final Solutions*, pp. 16–22. Valentino cites large-N quantitative studies by J. Fearson and D. Laitin, "Ethnicity, Insurgency and Civil War," *American Political Science Review* 97/1, 2003, 75–90; and M. Krain, "State Sponsored Mass Murder: The Onset and Severity of Genocides and Politicides," *Journal of Conflict Resolution* 39/1, 1995, 21; B. Harff, "No Lessons Learned from the Holocaust? Assessing Risks of Genocide and Political Mass Murder Since 1955," *American Political Science Review* 97/1, 67–8. While these kinds of studies are useful they attempt to control for, and therefore factor out as much as possible, the effect of contextual factors. They are also much more vulnerable to coding errors because of the sheer number of cases and the lack of specific expertise by the researcher(s) in most of the cases in the comparison.

67 Harff, "No Lessons Learned from the Holocaust?," p. 66.

68 H. Fein, *Accounting for Genocide: National Responses and Jewish Victimization During the Holocaust*, Chicago: University of Chicago Press, 1979, p. 9.

69 Midlarsky, *The Killing Trap*, pp. 103–7.

70 F. Mazian, *Why Genocide: The Armenian and Jewish Experiences in Perspective*, Ames: Iowa University Press, 1990, pp. 21–42, 145–56.

71 Staub, *The Roots of Evil*, pp. 107–10.

72 Hinton, "Toward an Anthropology of Genocide," p. 29.

73 S. Tarrow, *Power in Movement: Social Movement, Collective Action, and Politics*, Cambridge: Cambridge University Press, 1994.

74 L. Dawidowicz, *The War Against the Jews: 1933–1945*, New York: Bantam Books, 1975.

75 M. Krain, "State Sponsored Mass Murder: The Onset and Severity of Genocides and Politicides," *Journal of Conflict Resolution* 41/3, 1997, 331–60.

76 A. Wendt, "Anarchy is What States Make of It: The Social Construction of Power Politics," *International Organization* 46/2, 1992, 391–425.

77 R. Melson, *Revolution and Genocide: On the Origins of the Armenian Genocide and the Holocaust*, Chicago: University of Chicago Press, 1992, pp. 260, 267.

78 E. Kissi, *Revolution and Genocide in Ethiopia and Cambodia*, Lanham, MD: Lexington Books, 2006, pp. 79–120.

79 W. Easterly, R. Gatti and S. Kurlat, "Development, Democracy, and Mass Killing," p. 142. The authors find through quantitative analysis among other things a positive correlation between mass killing and civil war, colonial, imperial, and international wars.

80 E. Markusen, "Genocide and Total War: A Preliminary Comparison," in Isidor Wallimann and Michael N. Dobkowski, eds., *Genocide and the Modern Age: Etiology and Case Studies of Mass Death*, Syracuse, NY: Syracuse University Press, 1987, pp. 97–123; E. Markusen and D. Kopf, *The Holocaust and Strategic Bombing: Genocide and Total War in the Twentieth Century*, Boulder, CO: Westview Press,1995, p. 64.

81 Markusen and Kopf, *The Holocaust and Strategic Bombing*, p. 64.

82 Ibid., p. 65.

83 S. Straus, *The Order of Genocide: Race, Power, and War in Rwanda*, Ithaca, NY: Cornell University Press, 2006, p. 7.

84 Markusen, "Genocide and Total War: A Preliminary Comparison," in *Genocide and the Modern Age: Etiology and Case Studies of Mass Death*, pp. 97–123; Markusen and Kopf, *The Holocaust and Strategic Bombing: Genocide and Total War in the Twentieth Century*, pp. 55–92; M. Shaw, *War and Genocide: Organized Killing in Modern Society*, Cambridge: Polity Press, 2003, pp. 44–5.

85 Markusen, "Genocide and Total War: A Preliminary Comparison," pp. 97–123; Markusen and Kopf, *The Holocaust and Strategic Bombing*, pp. 55–92.

86 Martin Shaw, *War and Genocide*, p. 5.

87 M. Shaw, *What Is Genocide?* Cambridge, Polity Press, 2007, p. 111.

88 B. Valentino, P. Huth and D. Balch-Lindsay, "'Draining the Sea': Mass Killing and Guerrilla Warfare," *International Organization* 58, 2004, 375–407.

89 H. Arendt, *Origins of Totalitarianism*, New York: Harcourt Brace, 1979, pp. 437–59.

90 I. Horowitz, *Taking Lives: Genocide and State Power*, 4th edition, New Brunswick, NJ: Transaction Publishers, 1997.

91 R. Rummel, *Death by Government*, New Brunswick, NJ: Transaction Publishers, 1994, pp. 1–2.

92 Harff, "No Lessons Learned from the Holocaust?" p. 66.

93 Easterly, Gatti and Kurlat, "Development, Democracy, and Mass Killing," p. 135.

94 M. Krain, "State-Sponsored Mass Murder: The Onset and Severity of Genocides and Politicides," *Journal of Conflict Resolution* 41, 1997, 355.

95 R. Rubenstein, *The Cunning of History: The Holocaust and the American Future*, New York: Harper Torchbooks, 1975, p. 2.

96 Z. Bauman, *Modernity and the Holocaust*, Ithaca, NY: Cornell University Press, 1989, pp. 98–111; Alvarez, *Governments, Citizens, and Genocide*, pp. 97–100.

97 Alvarez, *Governments, Citizens, and Genocide*, pp. 57, 59.

98 P. van den Berghe, *State Violence, and Ethnicity*, Niwot: University of Colorado Press, 1990, p. 1.

99 Bauman, *Modernity and the Holocaust*, pp. 66–76.

100 E. Weitz, *A Century of Genocide: Utopias of Race and Nation*, Princeton, NJ: Princeton University Press, 2003, pp. 39, 45–6.

101 For an analysis of how Darwin's encounters with colonized peoples influenced his thinking about the relationship between human communities, and how his ideas provided the foundation for Social Darwinism, see T. Barta, "Mr. Darwin's Shooters: On Natural Selection and the Naturalization of Genocide," in A. Dirk Moses and Dan Stone, eds., *Colonialism and Genocide*, New York: 2007, pp. 20–41.

102 M. Mann, *The Dark Side of Democracy: Explaining Ethnic Cleansing*, Cambridge: Cambridge University Press, 2005, pp. 2–4.

103 Ibid., pp. 3–4.

104 Ibid., pp. 70–110; A. Dirk Moses, ed., *Empire, Colony, Genocide: Conquest, Occupation, and Subaltern Resistance in World History*, New York: Berghahn Books, 2008; A. D. Moses and D. Stone, eds., *Colonialism and Genocide*, London: Routledge, 2007.

105 Mann, *The Dark Side of Democracy*, p. 4.

106 A. Chua, *World on Fire: How Exporting Free Market Democracy Breeds Ethnic Hatred and Global Instability*, New York: Anchor Books, 2004.

107 Many thanks to my colleague Joshua D. Goldstein for this insight. See G. Cameron and J. Goldstein, "Cosmos and History: The Ontology of Modern Terrorism: Hegel, Terrorism Studies, and Dynamics of Violence," *The Journal of Natural and Social Philosophy* 6/1, 2010, 60–90.

108 M. Shaw, "From Comparative to International Genocide Studies: The International Production of Genocide in 20th-century Europe," *European Journal of International Relations* 7, 2001, 1–24.

109 M. Esparza, H. Huttenbach and D. Feierstein, eds., *State Violence and Genocide in Latin America: The Cold War Years*, New York and London: Routledge, 2010.

110 M. Levene, *Genocide in the Age of the Nation State II: The Rise of the West and the Coming of Genocide*, London: I. B. Tauris, 2005.

111 T. Snyder, *Bloodlands: Europe Between Hitler and Stalin*, New York: Basic Books, 2010.

112 D. Schaller and J. Zimmerer, "Late Ottoman: The Dissolution of the Ottoman Empire and Young Turk Population and Extermination Policies – Introduction," *Journal of Genocide Research* 10/1, 2008, 7–14.

113 M. Shaw, "From Comparative to International Genocide Studies," pp. 15–20.

114 D. Bloxham, *The Final Solution: A Genocide*, Oxford: Oxford University Press, 2009.

115 U. Üngör, "Fresh Understandings of the Armenian Genocide: Mapping New Terrain With Old Questions," in Adam Jones, ed., *New Directions in Genocide Research*, New York: Routledge, 2012, pp. 198–214.

116 See chapters by van Krieken, Cave, Barta, Zimmerer, and Hitchcock and Koperski in D. Stone, ed., *The Historiography of Genocide*, New York: Palgrave Macmillan, 2010; K. Ellinghaus, "Biological Absorption and Genocide: A Comparison of Indigenous Assimilation in the United States and Australia," *Genocide Studies and Prevention* 4/1, 2009, 59–79; A. Woolford, "Ontological Destruction: Genocide and Aboriginal People," *Genocide Studies and Prevention* 4/1, 2009, 81–97.

117 B. Tovias, "Navigating the Cultural Encounter: Blackfoot Religious Resistance in Canada (c.1870–1930)," in A. D. Moses, ed., *Empire, Colony, Genocide: Conquest, Occupation, and Subaltern Resistance in World History*, New York: Berghahn Books, 2008, pp. 271–95.

118 S. Tarrow, "Bridging the Quantitative–Qualitative Divide in Political Science," In Henry E. Brady and David Collier, eds., *Rethinking Social Inquiry: Diverse Tools, Shared Standards*, Lanham, MD: Rowman & Littlefield, 2004, pp. 171–9.

CHAPTER 3

Critical Genocide Studies

Alexander L. Hinton

Over the last two decades, the interdisciplinary field of genocide studies has dramatically expanded and matured.[1] Genocide studies no longer stands in the shadow of Holocaust studies. It is now the primary subject of journals, textbooks, encyclopedias, readers, handbooks, special journal issues, bibliographies, workshops, seminars, conferences, websites, research centers, government agencies, nongovernmental organizations, international organizations, and a unit at the United Nations. If not yet fully theorized, the discipline is characterized by a number of debates and approaches.

As the outlines of the field emerge more clearly, the time is right to engage in critical reflections about the state of the field, or what might be called critical genocide studies. The goal is not to be critical in a negative sense but to consider, even as a canon becomes ensconced, what is said and unsaid, who has voice and who is silenced, and how such questions may be linked to issues of power and knowledge. It is, in other words, a call for critical thinking about the field of genocide studies itself, exploring our presuppositions, decentering our biases, and throwing light on blind spots in the hope of further enriching this dynamic field.

My use of the term overlaps in many ways with that of A. Dirk Moses,[2] whose important historiography of genocide studies reveals much about the state of the field even if our emphases also differ somewhat: mine is more concerned with the decentering associated with Derridian deconstruction and a Foucauldian archeology of knowledge and his more with critical theory in the tradition of the Frankfurt

School and recent work on empire and world systems theory.[3] A handful of other scholars, such as Anton Weiss-Wendt, Donald Bloxham, Daniel Feierstein, Thomas Cushman, Adam Jones, Mark Levene, and Dan Stone, have also published works that are partly or largely in the spirit of critical genocide studies without using this name. So it seems that perhaps a threshold has been reached where we can speak of a critical genocide studies. My thoughts in this chapter are selective, pointing out some of the domains and directions of a critical genocide studies.

Before beginning, I should note that, sometimes when people hear a term like "deconstruction" or "critical," they dismiss it as "postmodern," "nihilistic," or "relativistic." All of these terms are complex and have their distinct genealogies. My view is that deconstruction is a method of decentering and critique, and such critique, in the sense of critical inquiry, is at the heart of the academic enterprise and should be front and center in the field of genocide studies. Such reflection will only make the field stronger and richer.

My perspective is no doubt linked to my own engagement with genocide studies as I approached it from anthropology, a discipline that had little voice in the field despite offering important insights about genocide. No doubt this is why a critical genocide studies perspective has been a central focus of the Rutgers Center for the Study of Genocide, Conflict Resolution, and Human Rights – even as we have programming on genocide prevention, a topic that is often viewed in opposition to or at least in tension with academic genocide studies let alone critical genocide studies. My own view is that the study of genocide prevention has much to gain from critical genocide studies (and vice versa), but the perceived opposition of academic genocide studies and applied genocide prevention speaks to the "scholar–activist" divide that is part of our origin myth.

THE ORIGIN MYTH

Anthropologists like to examine origin myths, and I am no exception. Ethnicity, we tell our students, is a social category linking a group of people who perceive themselves to share ancestry and identity markers (language, food, dress, religion, and so forth). The sense of ancestry is frequently linked to an origin story, which helps provide a sense of solidarity and belonging as well as difference from other ethnic groups. Ethnic categories are fluid and multiple, thus a person might identify (or be identified) as Chinese, Han, Cantonese, Chinese-American, or American depending on time and place. I will return to this point later.

Many other sorts of groups are also bound by an origin myth, which provides them with a sense of solidarity, belonging, and identity. This includes academic disciplines. In North American anthropology, for example, Franz Boas is venerated as the "father" of the discipline and known, among other things, for refining the anthropological concept of culture and method of participant observation and for challenging the notion of biological race. Introductory students often hear stories about his exploits and efforts to demonstrate that race is a social construction, an endeavor that has continued in North American anthropology into the present.

Within genocide studies, Raphael Lemkin is even more revered as the field's "founding father."[4] Like Boas, he is remembered for his conceptual work (coining and defining the term genocide and writing a history of genocide in the 1940s), life history (including his escape from Poland as World War II began and centering on his life-long quest to criminalize the destruction of human groups), and advocacy (working tirelessly for the passage and then ratification of the UN Genocide Convention, of which he referred to himself as "the founder"). In many respects, he has come to be viewed as the prototypical genocide scholar: academically informed yet politically committed to this pressing social issue – an orientation and a tension that continues into the present. Indeed, the tension between scholarship and activism is the Janus-face of genocide studies, one that continues to inspire and divide scholars, as illustrated by recent controversies over resolutions and the proposed merger of the International Association of Genocide Scholars and International Network of Genocide Scholars.[5] One research direction for a critical genocide studies is to examine the origins of this Janus-face, which has strong roots in modernity, Enlightenment thought, the anti-slavery movement, humanitarianism, and human rights.

The genocide scholar–activist prototype is evident in *Pioneers of Genocide Studies*,[6] an important volume of autobiographical essays written by many of the "first generation" of scholars who helped forge the field of genocide studies in the late 1970s and early 1980s. It also includes an abbreviated version of Raphael Lemkin's unpublished autobiography, *Totally Unofficial Man*. Many of the *Pioneers* essays are striking for their resonance with the Lemkin narrative of finding one's calling and becoming passionately engaged in genocide studies and prevention. While this is no doubt partly the result of the framing questions that were posed to the contributors – the first two questions were concerned with what "led" the author to study genocide and how genocide became "an imperative for you"[7] – it seems likely that they, like many other genocide scholars today, see some of Lemkin's passion in themselves.

Pioneers provides a valuable contribution by chronicling the origins and institutionalization of genocide studies and providing an understanding of some of the varied reasons scholars entered the field. Many had a direct connection to genocide through the Holocaust or Armenian genocide; indeed, a few contributors, like Lemkin, escaped from or even survived Nazi occupation (see the essays by Henry Huttenbach, Robert Melson, and Ervin Staub). Others came to the field more indirectly through the experience of the 1960s, the civil rights movements, and human rights activism. By the early 1980s, several landmark texts began to appear, including Leo Kuper's *Genocide: Its Political Uses in the Twentieth Century*,[8] the first conferences on genocide were held, and an incipient network of scholars was being formed, one that would lead to the creation of the Association of Genocide Scholars, now the International Association of Genocide Scholars, in 1995. The essays in *Pioneers* are illustrative of genocide studies in other ways, exemplifying the field's interdisciplinarity and initial concern with a given set of twentieth-century cases, in particular the Armenian genocide and the Holocaust, with other mentions of cases like Biafra and the Cambodian genocide.

GENOCIDE STUDIES AND THE HOLOCAUST

Pioneers also raises a question: why did genocide studies begin to emerge in the late 1970s? Why not earlier – or even in the immediate aftermath of the passage of the genocide convention, as accusations of genocide began to fly soon thereafter? Raphael Lemkin himself sought to indict the Soviet Union for committing genocide during the break-up of the Baltic states, by kidnapping Jewish children, and by "working Jews to death in drainage projects" in Romania.[9]

While Cold War concerns and politics were involved, this question points toward the other key origin of genocide studies, the Holocaust, an event that shadows the discipline, always there if sometimes backgrounded or taken for granted. The Lemkin origin story is a perfect example. While Lemkin's *Axis Rule in Occupied Europe*[10] focuses on the Holocaust and indeed contains many important legal documents, it is his chapter IX, "Genocide" that gets all the attention in genocide studies. Perhaps the Holocaust would have figured more prominently in this origin story if Lemkin's attempt to push genocide to the forefront of the charges at the Nuremberg trials had been successful. As it was, he left Nuremberg early and devoted his efforts to getting genocide codified in international law. The promulgation of the UN Genocide Convention, not the Holocaust, frequently is viewed as the landmark moment in the genealogy of genocide studies.

This narrative elides the fact that, without the Nazis' attempted annihilation of European Jews and other groups, Lemkin's word might never have made it into the dictionary, the field of genocide studies might not exist, Lemkin might be a forgotten man, and we might very well be talking of "extermination" and crimes against humanity instead of genocide. In other words: no Holocaust (as the Nazi atrocities were later constituted), no Lemkin, no UN Genocide Convention, no genocide studies. To an extent, this argument could be pushed with regard to human rights as well.[11] For these and other reasons, the Nazi effort to destroy the Jews and other groups clearly stands as a watershed event of the twentieth century, one that helped catalyze the human rights regime and the emergence of genocide studies, both of which are closely intertwined.

The origins of the field of genocide studies are also closely tied to another discipline that emerged from the ruins of the Holocaust, Holocaust studies. And even this field only began to emerge following the Eichmann and Auschwitz trials of the 1960s, the publication of Arendt's *Eichmann in Jerusalem*, the 1967 Arab–Israeli War, and increasing efforts at memorialization.[12]

As it grew, Holocaust studies came to be concerned with its own set of issues, including profound questions about uniqueness and representation. In contrast to genocide studies, which has a social science emphasis as I will discuss later, Holocaust studies has been more often linked to the humanities. As the *Pioneers* volume illustrates, a number of the "first generation" of genocide scholars split off from Holocaust studies because of their commitment to comparison, which remains a central theme in genocide studies, and which is often referred to as comparative genocide studies.[13] Indeed, the discipline's predominant social science–positivisitic orientation is frequently directed toward discerning commonalities and general principles about the phenomenon of genocide, a bias that is in keeping with a normative commitment to prevention. (This theme runs through the literature on the Holocaust to a lesser extent, in part because of the uniqueness issue, which orients research toward a single past event.) The field's first introductory text, Adam Jones' *Genocide: A Comprehensive Introduction*,[14] embodies this disciplinary epistemology, as the bulk of the chapters focus on case studies and social scientific findings even as it seeks to decenter some of the field's biases.

DISCIPLINARY ORIENTATIONS, BLIND SPOTS, AND BIASES

The different emphases of Holocaust studies provide one vantage to think critically about and discover new approaches to genocide studies. Indeed, some of the more interesting contemporary work in genocide studies is being done by scholars, in particular historians, like Donald Bloxham, Jacques Semelin, A. Dirk Moses, and Dan Stone, who came to genocide studies from an initial engagement with Holocaust studies. Their work clearly fits into the rapidly emerging sub-discipline of critical genocide studies. As genocide studies has matured and the influence of the "uniqueness" argument has waned within Holocaust studies, genocide studies has, in turn, started to enter into the debates within Holocaust studies. The title of Donald Bloxham's recent book, *The Final Solution: A Genocide*,[15] highlights this point (his chapter in this volume details some of these reactions and debates).

More broadly, a critical genocide studies would be concerned with exploring other fields – including, to name a few, indigenous studies, philosophy, cultural studies, visual and literary arts, semiotics, and critical theory – that have important insights to bring to bear on genocide even as they ask us to rethink the existing assumptions of the field. To be sure, there are some scholars from such disciplines who are active in the field. However, their voices, and the larger insights that may be gleaned from their home disciplines, tend to be more muted than historical and social scientific scholarship in the field.

Yet another fertile direction for research in critical genocide studies comes from scholars working outside of the North American and European regions from where genocide studies first emerged. One illustration of this point is the work of Daniel Feierstein and other Latin American scholars who are questioning the boundaries of genocide studies from an alternative regional and Spanish-language perspective.[16] Such scholarship helps genocide studies interrogate its possible ethnocentric assumptions and discover new ways to envision the field.

THE ANTHROPOLOGY OF GENOCIDE

My own engagement with genocide studies, which began in the early 1990s when, as a graduate student, I began conducting research on the Cambodian genocide and attending meetings of the International Association of Genocide Scholars (IAGS), has in a sense followed these lines. When I attended my first IAGS meeting in 1995, I was surprised to find only one or two other anthropologists in attendance (Robert Hitchcock and Pamela Ballinger if I recall correctly). Genocide studies was also barely on the radar in anthropology, despite the important work that had been done on indigenous peoples.[17] Likewise, some of the relevant concerns and insights of anthropology were completely outside the orbit of genocide studies.

The cultural patterning of violence provides one illustration of this point. Because of their long-standing immersion in and in-depth understanding of given societies, anthropologists are ideally positioned to provide an experience-near perspective on how genocides unfold, how they are understood by both elites and lower-level actors, and how people deal with the experience and aftermaths of genocide. Thus, on the one hand, an anthropological perspective complicates easy assumptions about state/ideology and agency/motivation. To understand motivation and process, then, one needs to comprehend the local understandings that mediate social practices. This can be seen in a variety of domains, ranging from the deliberations of elites to the confines of the torture chamber. The rigid model of state ideology – perpetrator motivation breaks down from this perspective, refocusing our attention on process and context. I have sought to illustrate this point in relationship to the Cambodian genocide[18] even as a small but growing scholarship on genocide has emerged within anthropology, in part due to Bosnia and Rwanda.[19]

On the other hand, an anthropological perspective suggests that we need to broaden our concerns about the aftermaths of genocide. Usually, this issue is largely glossed over with the assumption, yet again linked to the Janus-face of genocide studies, that prevention is the primary normative goal. This certainly is an admirable aim. However, the fixation on prevention may divert our attention away from another critical issue: how people deal with the experience and aftermaths of genocide. A perusal of the key references on genocide show little concern with this issue (an issue discussed in Ernesto Verdeja's chapter in this volume). Aftermath usually equals a concern with denial and legal redress. (Holocaust studies provides another interesting foil in this regard as the field has been deeply concerned with issues of trauma and memory.) Given their on-the-ground interactions with perpetrators and victims, anthropologists have been able to provide a new way of looking at such issues of experience, coping, ritual, and memory. There is even a growing literature within anthropology that seeks to explore the local understandings and social practices that undergird the human rights regime, including transitional justice mechanisms like tribunals.[20] All of this is not to say that we should ignore the issue of prevention but instead cast our gaze on a wider range of "aftermaths." Moreover, prevention is also at stake here since past genocide, including issues of local experience, coping, and memory, is one of the primes for future genocide.[21]

Ethnographic example #1: the Duch trial

To illustrate these points, I want to turn briefly to the fieldwork I have been conducting on the Extraordinary Chambers in the Courts of Cambodia, where the first trial of a senior Khmer Rouge leader has recently concluded. The defendant, Duch (Kaing Kek Ieuv), was the chief of S-21 prison, the regime's central security center where over 12,000 people were incarcerated, many of whom were interrogated and tortured, before being executed.

To many people, Duch is a monster. As a quick Google search will reveal, media accounts often describe Duch as such and the practices that took place under his watch as "savage." At the Tuol Sleng Museum of Genocidal Crimes, located on the S-21 site, I once passed by a photo of Duch and other Khmer Rouge that had been defaced to make them seem demonic.

As opposed to explaining away the actions of perpetrators in such a reductive manner that attributes causality to a naturalized essence of savagery, barbarism, or monstrosity ("Duch carried out X because he is a savage"), we need to try to understand how and why he participated in mass murder. Anthropology is particularly well poised to consider such questions in contrast to other disciplinary perspectives that may start their analysis taking evil – in its Judeo-Christian sense – as a given. The method of cultural relativism helps it do so, as anthropologists try to consider violent acts in terms of the situational knowledge that motivated them. Thus, anthropologists have argued that violent acts such as evisceration or stuffing victims in latrines in Rwanda or IRA assassinations and prison guard brutality do not just make sense to the perpetrators but are structured by moral understandings, abhorrent as they may be to us.[22]

Duch offered answers. During his trial, he explained how he had been drawn to the revolutionary struggle against class oppression and foreign imperialism. He joined the revolution to fight for the liberation of his people, he said. His formal induction into the Khmer Rouge took place on December 5, 1967, when he "stood before the party's flag. I raised my hand to respect and to swear to be sincere to the party, the class and the people of Kampuchea [Cambodia] for my entire life and to serve the party ... [to be willing to] sacrifice anything for the party."[23] He explained that he joined "to liberate the nation, my own people from any oppression. I did not have any intention to do criminal activities."[24]

When he was later asked to run M-13 prison, where torture and executions took place during the civil war, he said that he forced himself to do so out of loyalty and duty – just as he would do in 1976 when asked to run S-21. "I came to hate the excrement," he would say, "but I had to walk in it."[25] Duch said something along these lines to Francois Bizot, a French anthropologist who was imprisoned in M-13 for several months during the civil war before being released.

Duch and Bizot developed a loose rapport and sometimes chatted. At one point, Duch told Bizot that he disliked his work at the prison but had to do it because it was his revolutionary duty. "I had expected to encounter a monster, and inhumane person, but I realized then that things were much more tragic, much more frightening," Bizot explained during his testimony. "I realized that in front of me there was a man who looked very much like many friends of mine, a Marxist, a human being who was a Marxist who was prepared to surrender his life for his country [and] for the revolution. He believed in this cause and the ultimate goal of his commitment and ... the wellbeing of the inhabitants of Cambodia. He was fighting against injustice."[26]

At Duch's trial, Bizot warned against explaining away Duch's motivations in a reductive manner. It would, he stated, "be the greatest possible mistake to turn such monsters into a different category of people, a different species. ... It is necessary to make a distinction between what humans do from what humans are."[27] We must guard against accepting Duch's testimony in any sort of straightforward manner. Nevertheless, it challenges us, as Bizot states, to seek more complicated answers, ones that may very well question our naturalized assumptions about violence. In my own work on perpetrator motivation, I sought to unpack the various layers of meaning that, within a given historical moment and social context, could motivate people to do things they would never have considered doing in other situational contexts.[28] One of the ways anthropologists can contribute to a critical genocide studies, then, is by unpacking these invisible zones of meanings that challenge our assumptions about "the nature" of "good and evil."

Ethnographic example #2: the Khmer Rouge tribunal

An anthropological perspective may also help us think critically about our assumptions concerning the aftermaths of genocide. Many of us, for example, assume that it is impossible for a society to move forward without justice. Indeed, one of the slogans of the Khmer Rouge tribunal is "Moving Forward Through Justice." The newly emerging field of transitional justice is, as the name suggests, often premised on a similar assumption that, in order for societies to "transition" (and I would suggest that the tacit and sometimes explicit suggestion is one of "progress" and "development") from a conflicted past to a better future (here again, the assumption is often one of a neoliberal order defined by justice, the rule of law, and democracy), they must engage in a set of juridical or at least veridical practices.

Not only do transitional justice mechanisms like the Khmer Rogue tribunal supposedly deliver justice and accountability, they also are said to reveal the truth, promote peace and reconciliation, and facilitate healing. An anthropological approach to the tribunal again calls into question such facile assumptions, including the assumption that justice is some sort of universal ideal that all human beings seek. "Justice," like violent practices and all forms of social behavior, is linked to systems of knowledge and practices that take distinct forms in given situations.

This can be demonstrated quite briefly. Twenty years of transitional justice, ranging from a peacekeeping mission and election (along with an accompanying attempt to bring human rights to post-conflict Cambodia) to the tribunal itself, have led to some penetration of ideas like justice into the Cambodian landscape, especially among politicians, the elite, and civil society. Such ideas are nevertheless shaped and molded into local vernaculars, such as Buddhist moral precepts and conceptions. Indeed, Chum Mei, perhaps the most outspoken civil party at the Khmer Rouge tribunal and someone who has been extensively exposed to training workshops, outreach, the trial process itself, and international actors, told me that the tribunal was "Buddhist" since both the court and those who kill and do bad acts will be held accountable.

Chum Mei's comment illustrates how problematic it is to simply assume that Cambodians and people everywhere else in the world want "justice." Chum Mei certainly wants Duch to be tried. He protested vocally when Duch was given what he perceived to be a light sentence (35 years minus 16 years for mitigating factors and time served). But, for him, the process resonates with Buddhist notions of karma and moral sanction. These conceptions are even stronger in the countryside, where villagers have less education and less exposure to global discourses on justice and human rights. Here one also finds people sometimes invoking Buddhist notions of forgiveness and forgetting (lest one lose one's moral compass by becoming overly attached to sentiments such as anger and vengeance). An anthropological approach seeks to bring to light precisely these sorts of obfuscated local understandings that are more or less erased in the arena of international – and, by implication, universal – law and human rights. My current project seeks to unpack such assumptions and consider what the tribunal means in Cambodia. In this way, an anthropological approach again complicates common assumptions about post-genocide response and prevention.

DEFINITION(S)

An anthropological perspective also raises important questions about the issues of definition, one of the central concerns of genocide studies. First there is the semantic question: what does "genocide" mean in different societies where genocide is taking or has taken place? For the term genocide emerged at a given moment in time and in a particular context. What do we miss when we label mass violence "genocide" without seeking to ask what such violence means in given contexts? Adam Jones' introductory text touches on this point, listing different terms.[29] But to truly understand genocide, we need to grapple with local glosses, which may inflect our analysis in new directions and toward previously unrecognized dynamics and meanings. This is all the more critical after-the-fact, given the correlation between memory and genocide.

A second and related question also emerges: what are the categories that the victims and perpetrators use to label and understand one another? This question, which scholars have been grappling with since the early 1980s on an academic level, gained legal salience in the 1990s with the establishment of the International Criminal Tribunal for the Former Yugoslavia (ICTY) and Rwanda (ICTR) and ensuing difficulties in fitting terms like Hutus and Tutsis into the rigid categories of the 1948 United Nations Convention on the Prevention and Punishment of the Crime of Genocide (UNCG). From an anthropological perspective, the reification of race, ethnicity, religion, and nationality, seems both ethnocentric and misleading. To argue that race is "immutable," a key trope of debate when the UNCG was being promulgated (and one that was made when notions of biological race still predominated), is to reassert implicitly an essentialized conception of race that has both been used by perpetrator regimes and long since been shown by people like Franz Boas to be a social myth. Race is a social construction and, like ethnicity, religion, and nationality, is clearly mutable, often highly so. Perhaps one of the more informative illustrations of this point is the not-so-distant assertion that the Irish were a race of savages. Or one can travel to a country like Brazil where racial categories have very different valences. More disturbingly, the UNCG has created a set of privileged protected groups while leaving others unprotected and analytically invisible.

By starting with context, not rigid, pre-existing socio-legal categories, a critical genocide studies may help us understand how a wide variety of identities, including non-Western ones, crystallize (i.e., shift from a more fluid state to one that, at a given moment of time, becomes less fluid, or what I have elsewhere called the "crystallization of difference")[30] in a variety of genocidal situations. From this perspective, the UNCG definition constitutes a historical and social construction that, while having important legal implications, should have been more broadly defined to include the destruction of any sort of group as defined by the protagonists in genocide. Some scholars have usefully proposed something along these lines in terms of definition.[31] But scholarly definitions of genocide tend to be clunky and awkward. There are strengths and weaknesses to a more or less detailed definition.

My own view is that there is also much to be said for definitions that accord with the principle of economy (that less is more) and that open rather than foreclose analysis. While recognizing that all definitions have weaknesses, we might simply define genocide as the more or less coordinated attempt to destroy a dehumanized and excluded group of people because of who they are.

Viewing genocide as "more or less coordinated" allows for the inclusion of cases that range from highly planned, state-sponsored genocides to those that are more haphazard and diffusely carried out. In the latter case, the state's role may have more to do with permissibility than intent (for example, not forbidding or doing nothing about acts of genocide carried out by armed groups on the ground or allowing victim groups to live under conditions of life that lead to their destruction – many Native American genocides fit this situation). The destruction of a group may be in whole or in part.

Such a definition has significant implications, opening the door to cultural genocide, genocide committed by non-state agents, genocide by neglect, and genocide of political, economic, social and other groups as constituted in specific historical and cultural contexts. It also allows us to escape the rash of "-cides," such as politicide, which have been proposed to overcome the gaps in the UN Genocide Convention. We need, in other words, to explore a much wider range of cases, including those where there was a more haphazard attempt to destroy a group or where a group was destroyed over time by more indirect means, including structural ones,[32] or by neglect and indifference. This definition is more in the spirit of Israel Charny's too often dismissed application of the term genocide to almost any targeted civilian group. However, it goes one step further by opening up the possibility that non-civilian groups might be the target of genocide – for example, the attempted mutual destruction of two highly armed protagonists in the course of war, a claim that is close to heresy in the field of genocide studies.

In the end, we might view the above definition as a methodological definition, though of course all definitions have methodological implications. By this I am suggesting that genocide scholars deploy a broad definition for the purposes of analysis, one that allows us to consider the widest range of cases. Whatever bottom-line definition of genocide a scholar selects in the end, a methodological definition would contribute to their research by providing additional case material, including (for those who adhere to a more narrow definition) information on why genocide does not take place in certain situations, an area of study that Leo Kuper so nicely illustrated but that has never been taken up in a significant way by scholars in the field.

A critical genocide studies invites us to take such chances by exploring new areas that have been cordoned off by prevailing assumptions, biases, and gate-keeping maneuvers. For example, one of the critiques of such a definition invokes what might be called the dilution metaphor. If we open the door to such a broad array of phenomena, the argument goes, we "dilute" the meaning and power of the term. Dilution is an interesting term, conjuring up the image of a pure substance being adulterated by an (implicitly contaminating) extraneous element. (It is, ironically, the sort of metaphor that is often linked to genocide.) But who determines what is extraneous? The dilution trope is a gatekeeper notion that asserts case study primacy and relevance on the basis of embodied metaphor, not critical analysis. There is no *a priori* reason why genocide should encompass a smaller set of cases. Indeed, the field of genocide studies might experience enormous growth and vitality by opening the doors to a much broader range of cases. Recent scholarship in critical genocide studies has moved in this direction. A critical genocide studies would be open to exploring what would happen if genocide were to encompass a much broader range of cases, including the many forgotten genocides.[33]

Even if it stayed in the background, the Holocaust very much put its imprint on the UN Genocide Convention and many of the subsequent scholarly definitions that emphasize intent, particularly with regard to the role of the state. And perhaps we have all missed much by focusing so much on the traditional definitions. Recent research in cognitive science, for example, has shown that categorical understanding is much more tied to metaphor, metonymy, and prototype effects.[34] In other words, people think about a phenomenon like genocide using metaphor, metonymy, and prototypes. While this potential shift in the way we think about definition and genocide could be an essay in and of itself, I want here just to note the somewhat obvious point that the Holocaust has long served as the prototype of genocide and Auschwitz as one of its key metonyms. What this means is that, in the back of our minds, many if not most of us have the Holocaust prototype in mind when discoursing about genocide, even if the Rwandan genocide has destabilized this tacit knowledge somewhat.

The uniqueness debate suggests this bias but we find it in many contexts, ranging from issues of definition to canonization. It is also often the case study exemplar that implicitly stands in danger of categorical dilution through association with other, less exemplary examples. The uniqueness debate provides another manifestation of this point. The obvious salience of the Holocaust notwithstanding, there are other possible prototypes and exemplars, such as the massive destruction of largely forgotten peoples, such as the Taino of Hispaniola during the conquest and colonization of the New World or the large number of political groups who perished under Stalin or Mao. What if these cases were the starting points of genocide studies? A critical genocide studies asks us to consider what the entailments of such a rethinking of the concept of genocide might be.

A related decentering comes from a reconsideration of the work of Raphael Lemkin himself. While still heavily influenced by the Holocaust prototype,

Lemkin's conception had a broad historical purview and analytical focus on the different ways in which group life is destroyed, which he viewed as potentially encompassing not just physical but also biological, cultural, and political destruction carried out by state and non-state actors. Over the last decade, there has been a small but growing body of work that conceptualizes genocide from an often Lemkinian perspective, with its long historical purview, interest in antiquity and colonialism, and understanding that genocide may unfold over the course of long periods of time (versus the short duration of most of the case studies upon which genocide studies tends to focus) and through a variety of mechanisms (again, beyond the usual focus on state-sponsored mass murder), including cultural destruction. Accordingly, scholars have begun to consider what were largely forgotten or hidden genocides by increasingly focusing on issues like colonialism, conquest, settler societies, and modernity.[35] This is the work of a critical genocide studies, but there remains much more to do since such cases tend to be relegated to the margins of the genocide studies canon.

Why have we ignored these cases? The reasons are manifold and complex. The Holocaust prototype is one, as it directs our attention toward a certain manifestation of the genocidal process (foregrounding state and ideology). Perceived relevance may be another factor, as scholars have witnessed a number of cases of genocide take place during their lifetimes (even if we have also ignored other contemporary cases, such as the plight of indigenous peoples). There are also more data available about many of these cases, which make research and writing easier. As disciplinary structures of knowledge become ensconced, habit and tradition, including the interests that sustain them, also become a factor in directing our attention to certain cases.

Metanarratives of progress and civilization may also structure our thinking, directing our gaze toward genocidal despots (Hitler, Pol Pot, Milošević, Bashir) and authoritarian regimes. The language of the UN Genocide Convention codifies this, stating that genocide is "condemned by the civilized world." (Lemkin himself frequently used this register.) Such language implies that genocide is only carried out by barbarians and savages, an understanding condensed by symbols such as the shrunken head of Buchenwald that was exhibited at Nuremberg. While genocide is brutal and to be condemned, it is also something that is closely intertwined with modernity and even democracy.[36] The discipline's long-standing neglect of Native Americans, slavery, and indigenous peoples illustrates this point.[37]

Critical genocide studies asks us to consider why scholars have looked away from such issues. One reason may well be a "liberal" tendency[38] among genocide scholars to seek "progress" and, as the UN Genocide Convention states, "to liberate mankind from such an odious scourge." We return to the Janus-face of the discipline. A critical genocide studies does not demand we give up this objective, but instead think critically about its genealogy/framings and our potential conceptual biases and thereby find new ways to approach the problem. For example, how does the "savage"/"barbaric" other we construct in our analyses also construct, through inversion, an image of ourselves as modern, developed, and civilized? What do we miss by such identifications? One answer is that our gaze may too easily be directed away from the relationship of genocide and modernity and toward explanations that smack of ethnic primordialism, stage theory (an implied progression from a state of savagery to civilization), atavism (the Nazis as a throwback), or biological/psychological reductionism (our "barbaric" or "sadistic" "nature" – think of *Lord of the Flies* and *Psycho*).

CANONIZATION

Such decenterings ask us to think critically about the canons that have emerged in genocide studies. To date there has been a strong bias toward a canon that unfolds roughly along the lines set out in Table 3.1.

Table 3.1 The genocide studies canon

Prototype	*Holocaust*
The triad	Holocaust
	Armenian genocide
	Rwanda
Twentieth-century core	Holocaust
	Armenian genocide
	Cambodia
	Rwanda
	Bosnia
	Darfur (twenty-first century)
	Indigenous peoples (taken as a whole)
The second circle	East Pakistan
	Guatemala
	Herero/Namibian
	Kosovo
	Kurdish
	Carthage
	Settler genocides
	Ukrainian/Soviet
The periphery	Indonesia
	Argentina
	Specific cases of indigenous peoples
	Genocides of antiquity
	Assyrian and Greek cases
	East Timor
	Burundi
	Maoist China
	Democratic Republic of the Congo
Forgotten genocides	Multitude of more or less invisible/hidden/forgotten cases

With certain exceptions, the bulk of scholarship in the field of genocide studies, especially from 1980 through the 1990s, has focused on the twentieth-century core, with the Holocaust both foregrounded and backgrounded in the ways discussed above. Like all canons, there has been some internal fluidity over which groups are included (for example, the beginnings of a shift of the Ottoman Assyrian and Greek genocides from the status of invisible/forgotten genocides to the periphery or perhaps even second circle, mirroring a similar shift that took place earlier in the canonization of the Herero/Namibian case, which has risen into the second circle or perhaps even the twentieth-century core).

The above model is, of course, an ideal type but it points toward some of the disciplinary biases that have emerged in the field. For instance, while cutting against the grain in many ways and discussing the periphery or even forgotten genocides at times, Adam Jones' introductory text still gives primacy to the twentieth-century core.[39] A similar statement could be made about readers and edited volumes in the field.[40] A critical genocide studies asks us all to consider how such biases have shaped our own research and teaching and, through decentering, re-vision our field of study.

As this discussion suggests, issues of definition and canonization are not value neutral but also linked to issues of power and knowledge. Why, we must ask, is it that certain cases of genocide are forgotten? The literature on denial (which has its own Janus-face of ensuring historical accuracy about horrible events but potentially diminishing debate) has grappled with this question. But we also need to consider why we focus on certain cases and topics and what sorts of inclusions and exclusions ensue. What is left invisible to us and what can we do to cast light on what has formerly been opaque? Given the ongoing politicization of our topic, how might we be influenced by given interests and agendas? Why, we need to ask, are certain cases forgotten, remembered, recognized, or even intentionally hidden in the sense of being written out of history? For our discipline to flourish, we need to consider a wide range of such questions, to decenter and rethink our taken-for-granted assumptions and biases, to seek out new ways to approach the field, to engage in critical genocide studies.

NOTES

1 I would like to thank Nicole Cooley, Joyce Apsel, Ernesto Verdeja, Sam Totten, Henry Theriault, and A. Dirk Moses for their comments and suggestions on this chapter.

2 A. D. Moses (2008) "Toward a Theory of Critical Genocide Studies," *Online Encyclopedia of Mass Violence*. Available HTTP: http://massviolence.org/Toward-a-Theory-of-Critical-Genocide-Studies (accessed July 5, 2011).

3 But see A. D. Moses, "Conceptual Blockages and Definitional Dilemmas in the 'Racial Century': Genocides of Indigenous Peoples and the Holocaust," *Patterns of Prejudice* 36/4, 2002, 7–36; A. D. Moses, "Raphael Lemkin, Culture, and the Concept of Genocide," in Donald Bloxham and A. Dirk Moses, eds., *The Oxford Handbook of Genocide Studies*, New York: Oxford University Press, 2010, pp. 19–41; A. D. Moses and D. Bloxham, "Genocide and Modernity," in D. Stone, ed., *The Historiography of Genocide*, Houndmills, UK: Palgrave Macmillan, 2008, pp. 156–93.

4 The focus on Lemkin has increased dramatically over the last decade, in part because of the publication of Samantha Power's best-selling *"A Problem from Hell": America and the Age of Genocide* (New York: Basic Books, 2003). Before the millennium, Lemkin's work was appreciated by first-generation genocide scholars but he had not yet attained the status of founding father, a fact that illustrates how knowledge is produced within academia (Joyce Apsel, personal communication). There is also a strand of critical genocide studies that uses Lemkin's historical work to reconsider the field's traditional emphases. See, for example, J. Zimmerer and D. Schaller, eds., *The Origins of Genocide: Raphael Lemkin as a Historian of Mass Violence*, London: Routledge, 2009.

5 See, for example, G. Beckerman, "Top Genocide Scholars Battle over How to Characterize Israel's Actions," *Forward: The Jewish Daily*, February 16, 2011. Online. Available HTTP: www.forward.com/articles/135484/ (accessed February 21, 2011).

6 S. Totten and S. L. Jacobs, eds., *Pioneers of Genocide Studies*, New Brunswick, NJ: Transaction Publishers, 2002.

7 Ibid., p. xiv. See also A. D. Moses, "The Field of Genocide Studies," in A. Dirk Moses, ed., *Genocide: Critical Concepts in Historical Studies*, Abingdon, UK: Routledge, 2010, pp. 1–23.

8 L. Kuper, *Genocide: Its Political Use in the Twentieth Century*, New Haven, CT: Yale University Press, 1983. See also I. W. Charny, *How Can We Commit the Unthinkable? Genocide, The Human Cancer*, Boulder, CO: Westview Press, 1982.; I. L. Horowitz, *Taking Lives: Genocide and State Power*, revised edition, New Brunswick, NJ: Transaction Publishers, 2002; J. N. Porter, *Genocide and Human Rights: A Global Anthology*, Washington, DC: University Press of America, 1982.

9 *Washington Post*, "U.N. Genocide Action Sought on Red Bloc," January 18, 1953: M3.

10 R. Lemkin, *Axis Rule in Occupied Europe: Laws of Occupation, Analysis of Government, Proposals for Redress*, Washington, DC: Carnegie Endowment for International Peace, Division of International Law, 1944.

11 See, for instance, J. Donnelly, *International Human Rights*, Boulder, CO: Westview Press, 2006.

12 D. Levy and N. Sznaider, *The Holocaust and Memory in the Global Age*, Philadelphia, PA: Temple University Press, 2006. See also A. D. Moses, "The Holocaust and Genocide," in Dan Stone, ed., *The Historiography of the Holocaust*, Houndmills, UK: Palgrave Macmillan, 2004, pp. 533–55.

13 See S. Straus, "Second-Generation Comparative Research on Genocide," *World Politics* 59, 2007, 476–501.

14 A. Jones, *Genocide: A Comprehensive Introduction*, 2nd edition, New York: Routledge, 2011.

15 D. Bloxham, *The Final Solution: A Genocide*, New York: Oxford University Press, 2009. See also the recent exchange on Bloxham's book in the May 2011 issue of the *Journal of Genocide Research*.

16 See, for example, Marcia Esparza, Henry R. Huttenbach and Daniel Feierstein (eds.), *State Violence and Genocide in Latin America: The Cold War Years* (New York: Routledge, 2009); Daniel Feierstein, *El Genocidio Como Práctica Social: Entre el Nazismo Y La Experjencia Argentina* (TLalpan, Mexic 2008); *Revista de Estadios Sobre Genocidio*.

17 See A. L. Hinton, ed., *Annihilating Difference: The Anthropology of Genocide*, Berkeley: University of California Press, 2002. See also Hitchcock and Totten (2011).

18 A. L. Hinton, *Why Did They Kill? Cambodia in the Shadow of Genocide*, Berkeley: University of California Press, 2005.

19 A. L. Hinton and K. Roth, eds., *Annihilating Difference: The Anthropology of Genocide*, Berkeley: University of California Press, 2002.

20 See A. L. Hinton and K. L. O'Neill, eds., *Genocide: Truth, Memory, and Representation*, Durham, NC: Duke University Press, 2009; A. L. Hinton, ed., *Transitional Justice: Global Mechanisms and Local Realities after Genocide and Mass Violence*, New Brunswick, NJ: Rutgers University Press, 2010; and V. Sanford, *Buried Secrets: Truth and Human Rights in Guatemala*, New York: Palgrave Macmillan, 2003.

21 See S. Totten and R. Ubaldo, eds., *We Cannot Forget: Interviews with Survivors of the 1994 Genocide in Rwanda*, Piscataway, NJ: Rutgers University Press, 2011; and other interviews with survivors and memoirs.

22 C. C. Taylor, *Sacrifice as Terror: The Rwandan Genocide of 1994*, London: Berg Publishers, 1999; A. Hinton, *Why Did They kill?*

23 Transcript of Proceedings – "Duch" trial, August 31, 2009, trial day 67. Phnom Penh, Cambodia: Extraordinary Chambers in the Courts of Cambodia, p. 18 (hereafter "Duch trial, D4").

24 Duch trial, D4: 49–50.

25 Ibid., D4: 67–8, 79.

26 Ibid., D6: 71.

27 Ibid., D6: 73.

28 Hinton, *Why Did They Kill?*

29 Jones, *Genocide: A Comprehensive Introduction*, pp. 23–4.

30 See Hinton, *Why Did They Kill?*

31 See F. Chalk and K. Jonassohn, *The History and Sociology of Genocide*, New Haven, CT: Yale University Press, 1990.; H. Fein, "Genocide: A Sociological Perspective," *Current Sociology* 38/1, 1990, 1–126.

32 See, for example, Jones, *Genocide: A Comprehensive Introduction*, on structural genocide, or the chapter by Sheri Rosenberg and Everita Silina in this volume.

33 See, for example, D. Bloxham and A. D. Moses, eds., *The Oxford Handbook of Genocide Studies*, New York: Oxford University Press, 2010.; B. Kiernan, *Blood and Soil: A World History of Genocide and Extermination from Sparta to Darfur*, New Haven, CT: Yale University Press, 2007; R. Lemarchand, ed., *Forgotten Genocides: Oblivion, Denial, and Memory*, Philadelphia: University of Pennsylvania Press, 2011.

34 G. Lakoff, *Women, Fire, and Dangerous Things: What Categories Reveal about the Mind*, Chicago: Chicago University Press, 2007.

35 See, for example, Z. Bauman, *Modernity and the Holocaust*, updated edition, Ithaca, NY: Cornell University Press, 2000; Hinton, *Annihilating Difference*; Kiernan, *Blood and Soil*; M. Mann, *The Dark Side of Democracy: Explaining Ethnic Cleansing*, New York: Cambridge University Press, 2005; Moses, "Toward a Theory of Critical Genocide Studies"; A. D. Moses, ed., *Genocide and Settler Society: Frontier Violence and Stolen Indigenous Children in Australian History*, New York: Berghahn, 2004; A. D. Moses and D. Stone, eds., *Colonialism and Genocide*, New York: Routledge, 2007; A. D. Moses, ed., *Empire, Colony, Genocide: Conquest, Occupation, and Subaltern Resistance in World History*, New York: Berghahn, 2008; M. Levene, *Genocide in the Age of the Nation State, Vol. I, The Meaning of Genocide*, New York: I. B. Tauris, 2005; M. Levene, *Genocide in the Age of the Nation State, Vol. II, The Rise of the West and the Coming of Genocide*, New York: I. B. Tauris, 2005. See also the early volumes by Bauman, *Modernity and the Holocaust*; see also Chalk and Jonassohn, *The History and Sociology of Genocide*; and W. Churchill, *A Little Matter of Genocide: Holocaust and Denial in the Americas, 1492 to the Present*, San Francisco, CA: City Lights Books, 1997. For a recent argument that the UN Genocide Convention is more elastic than typically recognized, see S. P. Rosenberg, "Genocide Is a Process, Not an Event," *Genocide Studies and Prevention* 7/1, 2012, 16–23.

36 Bauman, *Modernity and the Holocaust*; Mann, *The Dark Side of Democracy*.

37 J. H. Bodley, *Victims of Progress*, 3rd edition, Mountain View, CA: Mayfield, 1990; Churchill, *A Little Matter of Genocide*; W. L. Patterson and P. Robeson, eds., *We Charge Genocide: The Historic Petition to the United Nations for Relief from a Crime of the United States Government Against the Negro People*, New York: International Publishers, 1970.

38 Moses, "Toward a Theory of Critical Genocide Studies."

39 In a February 15, 2011 lecture at the Rutgers Center for the Study of Genocide, Conflict Resolution, and Human Rights titled "Studying Genocide, Preventing Genocide," Adam Jones noted the dilemmas inherent in selecting cases and the dangers of canonization. His own efforts at grappling with these problems are illustrated in differences between the first and second editions of his books, with the first edition chapter "The Armenian Genocide" being recast as "The Ottoman Destruction of Christian Minorities" in the second. Similarly, he expanded the first edition chapter "Stalin's Terror" to "Stalin and Mao" in the second edition. He noted that he deliberately attempted to weave in a number of cases, ranging from attacks on witches to post-US-invasion Iraq, to cut against the grain of canonization.

40 But see Chalk and Jonassohn, *The History and Sociology of Genocide*, for an early exception.

CHAPTER 4

Holocaust Studies and Genocide Studies

Past, present, and future

Donald Bloxham

This chapter explores ongoing tensions between Holocaust studies and genocide studies; it also discusses possibilities for synergy, especially the scope for the comparativist to capitalize on what already exists latently within the historiography and history of the Holocaust. I was prompted to sustained reflection on relations between the two fields by the (ongoing) controversies following the publication of my work *The Final Solution: A Genocide* (2009) and repeatedly voiced criticisms by historian Omer Bartov in particular.[1] Bartov's views constitute an important litmus test of the interaction between the fields because he has previously been one of the more conceptually adventurous Holocaust scholars.

Bartov's criticism of *The Final Solution: A Genocide*, Timothy Snyder's *Bloodlands: Eastern Europe between Hitler and Stalin* (2010) and the works of A. Dirk Moses and Mark Mazower reveal a considerable hostility towards placing the Holocaust in a wider history of genocidal violence. That criticism includes imputing political biases and agendas.[2] Snyder and I also come under critique from Yad Vashem's Robert Rozett, in an article whose tone is fortunately more moderate than its emotive title "Diminishing the Holocaust: Scholarly Fodder for a Discourse of Distortion."[3] All four aforementioned scholars – Bloxham, Mazower, Moses, and Snyder – are also criticized by Yad Vashem's senior historian, Dan Michman. The critique appears in a paper with the heading "The Jewish Dimension of the

Holocaust in Dire Straits: Current Challenges of Interpretation and Scope."[4] This heading indicates a lack of sense of proportion, indeed realism, given the many Holocaust museums and memorial days, the tens of thousands of recorded or published survivor testimonies, the existence of a Task Force for International Cooperation on Holocaust Education, Remembrance and Research (ITF), and of course a vast, growing historiography.

Michman has already expressed concern over what he calls the politicization of genocide studies – with the implication that Holocaust studies is not politicized – and shares Bartov's express concern with, inter alia, that strand of genocide studies that places the Holocaust in relation to Europe's crimes of colonialism outside Europe. He writes that this historiographical strand "lessens – or even (sometimes intentionally!) – downplays the scope and enormity of the Nazi anti-Jewish project," without substantiating his allegations of intent. At the same time he announces that Yad Vashem's library is augmented by 4,000 Holocaust-related titles per year, which brings into question why he feels that a handful of recent works will fundamentally alter the way in which the Holocaust is or "should be" perceived.[5] This response may be caused by fear of a repositioning of the Holocaust in the intellectual firmament. Indicatively, the tellingly-titled journal *Holocaust and Genocide Studies* faces more market competition from newer journals that only have the "G-word" in the title. Perhaps some scholars who once felt confident about the relative status of the Holocaust are worried as students of other genocides approach the subject from very different perspectives that reflect the wider historiographical and socio-cultural developments of the past 30 years. Those students engage with study of the Holocaust, if at all, on their own terms. Some studies analyze the Holocaust with paradigms created in the study of other genocides, and to some extent subsume it within broader patterns involving other genocides.[6]

Therefore, one springboard for my chapter is the old debate around the relationship between the Holocaust's specificity and its universality as that plays out in the relation of different genocides to one another. Considering that debate leads to examining other cross-cutting relationships between Holocaust studies and genocide studies, namely relations between analysis and commemoration, and contemplation and activism. Overall, the future of cross-fertilization between Holocaust studies and genocide studies is quite bright, provided that cross-fertilization is taken to mean something more like osmosis than assimilation and provided that some of the barricades left in place from the battles of earlier generations of scholarship can be moved to the sidelines rather than reinforced. *In purely intellectual terms*, what is at issue is another case study of a generic relationship – at once irresolvable, if one is looking for some decisive formula, but fruitful and mutually informative – between the specific and general study of related phenomena in the realm of human affairs. Phrased thus, there is no question of one side or the other being considered an objective "problem" or a "remedy," only differing foci of intellectual interests, each of which reciprocally thickens our understanding. Yet this appeal to the norms and normal development of traditional history and social science downplays the very real emotional and ethical concerns that underpin the interest of the human, different humans, and different groups of humans, in wrestling with the past. Emotional and ethical issues certainly pertain to a particularly intense degree in the study of the perpetration and experience of mass murder, and so special caution is needed.

The relationship between Holocaust studies and genocide studies is asymmetric in four ways. The first three are contingent. They are: first, the advanced scholarly state of Holocaust studies relative to genocide studies; second, the context of relatively great public awareness of the Holocaust as compared to other genocides, including other genocides perpetrated by Nazi Germany; and third, the fact that the core of Holocaust studies has tended to be the investigation of events by historians, whereas genocide studies has largely been constructed by social and political scientists with their different balance of interest in the general versus the particular. The third way is related to the fourth, which is that genocide studies by definition seeks to incorporate the study of the Holocaust while the reverse is not true. That asymmetry is permanent.

The self-defined brief of genocide studies to be more general in scope than Holocaust studies has wide ramifications. This is not to say that there has not long been a generalizing trend in the study of the Holocaust, whether via Raul Hilberg's depiction of the Final Solution as a bureaucratic crime, Hannah Arendt's observations on the banality of evil, Zygmunt Bauman's *Modernity and the Holocaust*, or Christopher Browning's study of the *Ordinary Men* involved in mass murder during the discharge of their policing responsibilities.[7] But it is noteworthy that these are perpetrator-centric works. Writing in 2005, Anita Shapira observed the difference when the focus is on the victims:

> If the actions of the evildoers are foregrounded, then it is but a short leap to examining the question of evil more generally in philosophical and universal terms. If the spotlight is on the suffering of the Jews as real flesh-and-blood human beings, not as a more abstracted generalization in the sense of "victims", then the Holocaust is a unique event, "Jewish" in its very pith and essence.[8]

As ever, one could hedge and qualify. For instance Yaacov Lozowick's work *Hitler's Bureaucrats: The Nazi Security Police and the Banality of Evil* is a study of perpetrators that concludes with an anti-Arendtian injunction about "listening to the screams" of the victims by way of furthering the argument that the perpetrators of Adolf Eichmann's office acted necessarily and sufficiently out of anti-Jewish hatred, as opposed to some generalized set of modern behavioral norms.[9] Saul Friedländer's two volume *Nazi Germany and the Jews* blends the high narrative of the Final Solution and some of its highest-ranking orchestrators with the experience of the victims as depicted through select testimonies, and binds the two together via the causal role of a perpetrator ideology of "redemptive antisemitism."[10] Equally there are analyses of victims' experiences and memoirs that compare between genocides. But Shapira's point remains important in undermining any prognosis on the shared future of Holocaust and genocide studies that obscures the fact that within Holocaust studies, as within genocide studies, there are very different paradigms of understanding. This is not a question of Jewish intellectuals versus non-Jewish intellectuals. After all, only one scholar so far named – Browning – is non-Jewish, and as Shapira indicates the universality–specificity debate has remained a live one in Israel at least since Arendt's volume. At issue is on one hand a clash of disciplinary–philosophical perspectives – of the aforementioned "generalizers," Browning is the only historian, and beyond *Ordinary Men*, he has expended huge effort in investigating Nazi Jewish policy in its specificity. On the other hand, we witness the clash of something like deep and competing intuitive preferences or needs that, as Berel Lang points out, are probably impossible to reconcile in their starkest forms.[11]

One response to the inherent asymmetry of Holocaust and genocide studies is that such synthesis as occurs between the fields should never be forced: genocide studies cannot be rapacious. Scholars of individual genocides – I am thinking primarily of the Holocaust, but it of course applies to scholars of other genocides too, though many and perhaps most of those already feel reasonably comfortable working under the "genocide studies" umbrella – should never be put under any pressure to do anything other than follow their personal concerns through. This rather obvious point merits reaffirmation because of the long and grotesque history of a Christian Occident that regularly warned its internal Jewish "other" against any sort of seeming "ostentation," including in the recording of Jewish suffering at the hands of that wider society. The preparedness of European states to confront the record of the World War II era, which in its antisemitic violence is much more than a Nazi/German issue, will remain an important index of majority–Jewish relations and of state contrition.

The freedom to examine whatever and however one wants should be a thoroughgoing freedom, which entails not having its *conclusions* pre-empted by anyone else, whether of universalist or particularist persuasion. I am thinking for instance of Yehuda Bauer's statement that:

> universalising statements [regarding the Holocaust] seem to me to be, on the Jewish side, attempts by their authors to escape their Jewishness. They are expressions of a deep-seated insecurity; these people feel more secure when they can say "we are just like all the others." The Holocaust should have proved to them that the Jews were, unfortunately, not like the others. Obviously it did not.[12]

Furthermore, as with the liberal philosophical convention, freedom is unlimited except at that point at which it imposes upon others. I refer by example to the rhetoric of "uniqueness" that finds its way into Shapira's analysis. The reason that this rhetoric irritates – let us be frank, the reason it offends – many scholars and indeed victims of other genocides is that "uniqueness" in the sense meant can only do its work by establishing the significance of the Holocaust by extrinsic means. It works by contrasting, by setting the Holocaust *in relation to other genocides*, even as the scholars of the Holocaust (or their readers) in Shapira's example purport to be examining something in and for its own sake and intrinsic meaning. The claim is particularly problematic given the aforementioned contingent state of affairs whereby the Holocaust has such popular prominence relative to knowledge and understanding of other genocides, and whereby, by extension, irrespective of the growth of academic and activist genocide studies, pronouncements about the Holocaust affect public comprehension of genocide much more than vice versa.

THE UNIQUENESS ISSUE REVISITED – IT IS HOPED FOR THE LAST TIME

The issue of uniqueness and what it entails is important to the remainder of my argument, so I shall be as clear as possible. I do not presume to speak for genocide scholars other than myself, though I suspect that I do speak for quite a few of them, when I say that I have always recognized the extremity of the Holocaust relative to other genocides of which I am aware, the extreme fervor of the Nazi pursuit of Jews across national boundaries, and the totality of the desire – after a certain point of radicalization had been reached during World War II – to murder all Jews on whom hands could be laid. And I think it impossible not to conclude that the extent of the "final solution" was, various modalities of partially contingent radicalization permitting, shaped by an antisemitism that was colored by a different element over and above the racism and ethno-nationalism that explains the murder of other groups by Nazi Germany – that element being the view of "the Jews" as an implacable, collective world enemy. What I do object to is the way that empirical differences such as these have been used to mandate quasi-philosophical claims about the radical difference of the Holocaust *in toto*. The cumulative *effect* of much that has been written and said about the Holocaust in relation to *all* other genocides, Nazi or non-Nazi, is to create a hierarchy that hinders the integrated study of genocides. (It is important to emphasize that this is a discussion about the "cumulative effect" of this scholarly hierarchization rather than the "intent." Some of the hierarchizing may have been deliberate, but much – certainly more – has not.) For substantiation of the implicit hierarchization, readers are referred to A. Dirk Moses' seminal article on the subject.[13] By "unique" is meant not the mundane uniqueness of every historical event, but a special quality whereby the particular characteristics of the Holocaust are promoted to the exclusion of its commonalities with other genocides, and whereby comparative studies – which is concerned with similarities as well as differences – is therefore a distorted pursuit.

Let us be in no doubt that the language of uniqueness is universalist, both in the positive sense of being a demand for universal attention on the basis of some specific claim, and in the negative sense of claiming that every other ostensibly comparable event is categorically different in some essential way. Here, as is often the case with universal statements, it carries the baggage of particularism and is even phrased by Shapira as particularist, which provides just one instance of a more general, vitiating confusion in the fields of Holocaust and genocide studies of partly overlapping, partly discrete philosophical, analytical, representational, moral and political criteria.

Not the least potentially confusing is the claim that the Holocaust's extreme particularity renders it universally relevant, with few questions asked about how that ostensibly paradoxical relationship works. To the extent that there is genocide scholarship that deliberately or incidentally downplays the "scope and enormity of the Nazi anti-Jewish project," in Michman's words (where "enormity" begs the question of which contrasted genocide is not possessed of enormity; the mind turns to Colin Tatz's recent suggestion that we establish a "Richter scale" of different genocides),[14] there is far more that seeks to come good on one of the loudest clarion-calls of campaigns for Holocaust awareness. If, as we are so often told, the Holocaust is of general relevance, as I believe it to be, then surely one vital way of illustrating this relevance is to tie it in to some extent with broader trends in world history. The crux of the matter is: to what extent?

Since precise judgments of extent and of which broader historical trends to integrate will vary from scholar to scholar, here is where the interpretative controversy is likely to occur. The comparative scholar whose interest is in both similarity and difference will be disloyal to her undertaking if she renders that "extent" total in the case of the Holocaust or any other genocide or genocide-like occurrence, since all will have both general and particular features. Those who examine the Holocaust under, say, the rubric of colonialism are only necessarily in error when they claim colonialism is the only relevant context, not when they claim that it is relevant, but that goes for any claim about contextualization. Contextualization is not a zero-sum game and the only thing that can definitively be said about the causation of any historical event is that it will be multicausal. The strength of relevance of any given context is something that is then argued rather than asserted or counter-asserted, and in the counter-argument there is a difference between arguing that a context is irrelevant and arguing that it is not the only or primary context. While my writings have not been especially prominent in arguing the colonial connection, I accept the force of the arguments for its relevance. Like Michman, and I believe many (most? nearly all?) of the proponents of the colonialism connection, I do not think it can explain every aspect of the Holocaust. But the only necessary outcome of that recognition is to reiterate that the Holocaust was multicausal. Equally, the Holocaust scholar who proclaims the Holocaust's general relevance but then resents attempts to think about it in settings additional to those he is comfortable with, say the context of Nazi or German antisemitism, is trying to have his cake and eat it.

Less ink is spilled these days than a few decades ago on uniqueness but its ongoing place in the "common sense" of Holocaust studies is illustrated by its effective restatement by Michman (in the aforementioned lecture) and other prominent scholars.[15] Challenges to the idea of uniqueness have brought forth not abandonment but reassertion of the claim,[16] and of course the scholarly impetus given over decades to the claim has fed enduring popular and interest-group discourse. A recent example is illustrated in the controversies over the relationship between Holocaust commemoration and the representation of other genocides and general human rights education in the yet-to-be-opened Canadian Museum for Human Rights (CMHR).[17] Many scholars of other genocides certainly still live under the sign of uniqueness by contesting it or – misguidedly – attempting to make "their" genocides look exactly "like" the Holocaust in order to gain the basic recognition that many of them still lack.[18] It is, after all, a conversation into which they have been drawn by earlier and similar claims.

Insofar as "uniqueness" has become common sense within Holocaust studies and many popular spheres, it does not need to be explicitly invoked, and proponents can even disavow the name while tacitly subscribing to the idea of the Holocaust's special difference. They may use euphemisms or near-synonyms such as the Holocaust's "centrality" (Omer Bartov, Doris Bergen),[19] "singularity" (David Cesarani),[20] "unprecedentedness" (Yehuda Bauer, the Stockholm Declaration),[21] "particularity" (Dalia Ofer),[22] or its "paradigmatic" status (Zev Garber, the ITF).[23] Many of these terms, like "uniqueness," and other words such as "specificity" and "historicity," have perfectly mundane lower-case usages that problematically obscure the upper-case theological usage for which they are frequently deployed. Yehuda Bauer's concept of the Holocaust as "unprecedented" has the same performative function as "uniqueness." Just as every event is in some way unprecedented, it is also in some way unique, so unless unprecedented has a special meaning over and above its mundane use, Bauer intends to say nothing by calling the Holocaust unprecedented – which is of course not what he intends to say. The Holocaust's unprecedentedness places it in a unidirectional relationship with other genocides: it is separated from anything before it or simultaneous to it, and should any future genocide occur that is recognized to have all of its features, then that genocide will have the Holocaust as its precedent, and the Holocaust will accordingly still have some sort of representational primacy. Likewise consider "centrality": if the Holocaust is at the center of a discourse, other genocides will be towards or at the periphery. Given the significance of Uniqueness talk, it is beholden on all scholars who use what may be taken for a synonym to make their subject position clear. This will provide scholars who think Uniqueness an obstacle to scholarship a basis to know whom to disagree with, and who is just inadvertently using ambiguous terms (as some of the above scholars may be).

REPRESENTATION BETWEEN COMPARISON AND COMMEMORATION

A recent example of some of the conceptual confusions abroad in this area was reflected in Omer Bartov's response to my work, in particular, my book *The Final Solution: A Genocide*. He inquired after the moral content of the final sentence of the book's introduction. This sentence reads, "the intellectual purpose of looking at the full range of people and peoples killed and expelled for political reasons in the broadest sense in and around the Nazi period is complemented by the conviction that recognition of their often undescribed fates is itself a moral statement."[24] In chastising me for lack of "empathy" with the victims of the Holocaust (in the same part of the introduction it is clearly stated that the volume will not be examining victims' perspectives), Bartov thinks there is something *morally wrong* with my position. There is an additional matter in the mix, to which I shall return shortly: my assertion that in the most prominent instances of the historiography where the history of victims and perpetrators has been combined, the victims have often been largely restricted to Jewish victims of Nazi Germany.

Clearly, Bartov's charges are in contradiction with my earlier work: a volume co-authored with Tony Kushner gave extensive consideration to survivor testimony, while my first book, on the Nuremberg trials, pointed to the problems of excluding victim testimony in specific interpretative contexts.[25] For the moment, what is important is that it becomes clear that my alleged error is not one of category, but of judgment within category. Bartov goes so far as to use the uniquely morally invested expression "never again" in the final sentence of his critique in reference to works like mine that do not address victims' experiences of genocide.[26] Bartov's language here is moralistic, that is, conveying a belief that there is only one definitive moral perspective irrespective of context, which contrasts with a language of moral debate. His "never again" shows explicitly that he thinks there is only one morally correct way to approach the study of any given genocide, so he makes of his own position an absolute moral yardstick. He explicitly disavows the very sort of perpetrator-centric work on which he built his reputation and gained a platform. He writes,

> No amount of contextualization and comparison can compensate for a view from below and from within … [t]he witnesses of [genocides] will bring out the uniqueness of their experiences as individuals, as members of communities, of groups, of nations – an individual experience that was denied them by the killers and that finds no room in the broad sketches of comparative genocide studies and the generalized overview of events. Since the goal of genocide is to destroy groups as such, it behooves the historian to rescue these groups from oblivion, even if only in history and memory. And for that we must listen to the survivors of genocide, not least because invariably they demand to be heard.[27]

Bartov's position in some ways replicates that of the vastly influential Saul Friedländer. In broad terms, Friedländer's argument is that listening to the victims' voices is a way of breaking through the totality of perpetrator ideology, preventing the perpetrators from providing *the* abiding representation of the victims, but also exposing the spurious analytical "objectivity" and abstraction of traditional historiography. I do not have space here to do justice to the sophistication of Friedländer's argumentation and the significance of his corpus, of which *Nazi Germany and the Jews*, the crowning achievement, has become one of the half dozen or fewer seminal texts in the field. Let it suffice to say that I do not question its integrity or coherence, only the breadth of its applicability and the weight of some of the critiques that he has made of alternative kinds of scholarship. He has criticized "the (mostly involuntary) smugness of scholarly detachment and 'objectivity,'" while in his famous 1982 book *Reflections on Nazism: An Essay on Kitsch and Death*, he wrote that the norms and tone of traditional detached analytical historical writing place the writer and reader "in a situation not unrelated to the detached position of an administrator of extermination. Interest is fixed on an administrative process, an activity of building and transportation, words used for record-keeping. And that's all."[28] There is a fairly straight line from Friedländer's judgment to Bartov's assertion that perpetrator-centric approaches become "complicit in the depersonalization, not to say dehumanization of the victims sought by the perpetrators."[29] Likewise Alexandra Garbarini has criticized Dan Stone and others for deciding to focus on perpetrators, and concludes with a rhetorical gambit that stigmatizes such work. She writes that the activism of genocide prevention (traditionally focused on perpetrators), "does not necessarily follow from people getting in touch with their own ability to violate others' human rights. It may just as much follow from people understanding those whose rights have been violated."[30] Note the different phraseology and subject–object relationships. In the second sentence, it is a matter of scholars *understanding those who have been violated*. This is entirely unobjectionable. In the first sentence, however, it is scholars *accessing (embracing?) their own ability to violate* – not *trying to understand those who violate*. (The commonest use of "getting in touch with" pertains to one's emotions, hence the uncertainty as to whether it means accessing or embracing here.) By such accounts, all who focus on the perpetrators and perpetration of genocide stand accused of having some positive relationship to perpetration.

What is ultimately at stake is the validity of a plurality of approaches. Bartov, like Michman, writes as if supposing that there is only one book that readers will read on the Holocaust. This is the only way I can make sense of his zero-sum approach to what any individual book does. Friedländer calls his history of the Holocaust "integrated," and I think the best way of opening up the issue is to consider the status of that word, just as I sought to challenge any particular ownership of it in the introduction to my work *The Final Solution: A Genocide*.[31] Its obvious implication is that different approaches are not integrated, which begs a raft of questions in the analytical and critical philosophy of history. What of accounts that seek to: render a fully gendered account of the genocide; combine the story of the murder of the Jews with policies against other Nazi victim groups, or the course of the war, or the life and crimes of "Germany," or "fascism," "racism," "colonialism," and so on? Does morality inhere in one's investigative subject matter or the reasons one selects a subject matter and then goes on to study it, whatever it may be?

Perhaps this question cannot be answered in a theory-neutral way, one free of presuppositions disposing the respondent to favor one answer. There is simply no set, monolithic context with reference to which different discursive decisions can be measured against each other. Recall that in the 1980s one strand of German historiography was criticized for focusing on the commemoration of the German-Jewish victims, and thereby, allegedly, abrogating the moral, national responsibility of confronting perpetratorhood.[32] Given competing demands, assessments of morality cannot be separated from the precise intellectual function of the inquiry and the intellectual backdrop against which the function is deemed necessary. This comment reflects the recognition that no one can write *histoire totale*, combining all possible perspectives and addressing all salient moral concerns. Each author has to choose and justify his or her focus and at the same time acknowledge that there will be exclusions that others can address. Equally, therefore, no book should proclaim its own approach as *the* way forward, because the way forward will always be changing.

Adopting the pluralist principle as a general one would also forestall the implicit response I made to Friedländer in my book's introduction, in reference to his critique of other sorts of scholarship. Friedländer's second volume, *The Years of Extermination*, includes analytical justifications for avoiding any extensive discussion of non-Jewish victims of Nazi Germany, referring to the different positions of e.g. Slavs and Romanies in the ideological firmament of the perpetrators. It is perfectly legitimate to make such distinctions, just as it is to emphasize the commonalities across the Nazi policies of destruction. Yet the book ends with an explicit embrace of a memorial function: the very final words of the second and final volume effectively dedicate the book to "the indelible memory of the dead." Which dead is obvious: since millions of victims of the Nazis have been excluded from the account on analytical grounds, they are not available to be considered on commemorative grounds. Likewise, Yaacov Lozowick's call to listen to the screams of the victims does not generally extend further than the Jewish victims of the Nazi security police. Boaz Cohen, while stressing the importance of incorporating the study of victims and applauding those scholars who have, does not consider any other group than Jewish victims. Alexandra Garbarini rightly calls for the experiences of Jewish victims to be integrated in all sorts of national and transnational frameworks during World War II, but does not consider that one such framework could be that of the experiences of other victim groups of Nazi Germany.[33] These are considerations with moral content, since we are dealing with inclusions and exclusions in what Bartov calls "history and memory." A relationship between analysis and commemoration is also present in Guenter Lewy's pointedly-entitled *The Nazi Persecution of the Gypsies*. Lewy's determination to show that what befell Europe's Roma and Sinti was not genocide is coterminous in his writing with saying it was not the same as the "final solution of the Jewish question" – a conflation that seems to characterize his work on other "genocides" too, even when, as in this case, he might have paid more attention to similarities alongside differences. The memorial salience of the sharp distinction is made clear when in his final pages he uses this analytical distinction to argue against those scholars and members of Romany communities who argued for greater attention to the Porrajmos, or Romany genocide, in the US Holocaust Memorial Museum.[34]

It would be helpful to have a more detailed examination of the relationship between analytical distinction and commemorative distinction, since it seems that this has been elided in the study of our memorial culture as a whole, even as the relationship has played an important role in the world of commemoration. The same move from analytical distinction to commemorative function was made in the decision in Berlin to create a "Memorial to the murdered Jews of Europe," and in the United Kingdom to create a Holocaust memorial day rather than a day to commemorate all the victims of Nazism (or genocide more generally). Unremarked is the irony whereby a perpetrator-centric analytical fact – the peculiarly fervent and extensive Nazi pursuit of Europe's Jews – mandates a particular commemorative decision on behalf of a whole national community (German or British here). One implication, whether intended or not, is that certain victims are more important to commemorate than others on the basis of the view of those victims held by the Nazis. The only way of explaining such a situation would be that since the Nazis sought to utterly destroy world Jewry then there is a particular commemorative responsibility in the question of Jewish victimhood in order to negate the Nazi project. But that would only make sense if the Nazis had succeeded in utterly destroying European or "world Jewry," which they did not. As it stands, in both monument and memorial day victims like Romanies, who were marginal in Nazi-German eyes yet still murdered by them in the hundreds of thousands, are left marginal in the politics of commemoration too, at best cast along with others in the semi-darkness that is the miscellany of "other victims." This simply does not seem right for a number of reasons, not least the distastefulness of allowing expressed Nazi genocidal priorities to dictate our memorial sensibilities.

Annegret Ehmann observes that exclusivism around the Holocaust has also entered schoolbooks. It is expounded, for example, by a bilingual French–German high school history textbook. The chapter dealing with the memory of World War II and the obligation of remembrance is devoted exclusively to the "commemoration of the Shoah." Both text and pictures refer only to the world's new Holocaust memorials, at Yad Vashem and in Paris, Washington DC, and Berlin. The only authentic memorial site depicted is Auschwitz, represented by a small photo with a description questioning Polish memorial politics and mentioning, in half a sentence, an exhibition about the "genocide of Sinti and Roma" that has been mounted at the death camp museum since 2001. While the volume covers the era from 1814 to 1945, the genocide of the Armenians 1915–17 under Ottoman rule is not mentioned at all.[35]

It seems that we still have a long way to go in promoting awareness of the extent of Nazi genocide. As things stand, prescriptions against comparative study end up reading like recommendations for an "each to his own" study of individual genocides in isolation, with the chips falling where they may in terms of general understanding of the phenomenon, ignoring the existing disparities in public awareness of different genocides.

A key difference between works such as Friedländer's *Nazi Germany and the Jews* and the national and international memorial decisions is that in national memorial cultures there is a much more circumscribed space than amid the discursive multiplicity of professional historiography. The state is capable to a much greater degree of policing memory in its formalized memorial procedures than in the activities of scholars within its universities. The significance of Friedländer's analytic decisions and narrative priorities is simply to remind us that every version of "integration" brings not just different intellectual costs and benefits but also different discursive inclusions and exclusions. My insertion of the Holocaust into the history of the perpetration of a multiplicity of genocides and ethnic cleansings was an attempt to integrate the Holocaust along a different axis of integration to that approach integrating the story of perpetrators and Jewish victims.

TWO SORTS OF RESPONSE: CONTEMPLATION AND ACTIVISM

If we accept that there are no universal or timeless givens about how to approach this or any genocide, then we are left only with context-appropriate approaches. Evolving contexts raise new demands on us to do justice to the silent, to balance what has been emphasized with what is neglected, and so forth. Rather than unhelpfully creating an absolute polarity here, it may be helpful to place Friedländer's agenda in historical context, seeing it not as an absolute imperative but as a key corrective at a specific historiographical juncture.

Holocaust studies and contemplation

That juncture included the German "historians' debate" (*Historikerstreit*) of the 1980s.[36] The debate rightly set alarm bells ringing about the misuses of particular contextualizations and "normalization" of the Holocaust because these were clearly in the line of mitigatory pleas designed to alleviate German guilt and clear the way for the creation of an identity unburdened by the past. Against this context, Martin Broszat's idea of "historicizing" or "historizing" the history of National Socialism seemed problematic, although it should be emphasized that Broszat was not one of the protagonists in the more overtly politicized aspects of the debate and Friedländer acknowledged that his motives were honorable.

One of Broszat's recommendations was to incorporate the experience of the 'Third Reich' into *Alltagsgeschichte* – the history of the everyday life of ordinary Germans, which entailed a balance of change and continuity before, during and after the 1933–45 period. But that approach excluded the experience of a persecuted minority who were systematically ostracized from the wider community, a community for which 1933 represented a fundamental caesura. Broszat was also a practitioner of a particular form of historiography of Nazi Germany and the "final solution." That historiography seemed to have become overly preoccupied with the workings of bureaucratic perpetrator institutions, and a dry "functionalist" analysis, at the expense of examining ideology and what was actually done – and how and to whom – in the name of that ideology. That too was part of the backdrop for Friedländer's agenda.

Friedländer's work is one of the most significant statements in a strand of historiography concerned with a *contemplative morality*, that of *representation*. Friedländer's approach was addressed to the integrity of the historical memory of the murder of the Jews as more than just an abstract intellectual, causal problem to be explained (and in some cases explained away) in a fashion that approached neither the horrific–tragic nature of events nor the vital question of significance, and that did not take account of the victims' experiences. This agenda was all the more pressing since, while the 1980s saw a significant rise in public interest in the Holocaust across the Occident, it was not that long since the subject had to be dragged to the attention of mainstream historiography and national memory after a post-war period in which neither historians nor states had taken much cognizance of it.

Genocide studies and activism

There is a very different context for my work and that of others in my cohort. My undergraduate and postgraduate study took place in the 1990s, a decade of booming Holocaust awareness and of genocide and ethnic cleansing in Rwanda and Yugoslavia. Indeed, the Rwandan genocide occurred towards the end of my final year as an undergraduate (1993–4), the year of the release of *Schindler's List* and the establishment of the International Criminal Tribunal for the former Yugoslavia. My most in-depth course of study was a year-long "special subject" entitled "Shoah: the murder of European Jewry," taught by the medievalist Colin Richmond.

My undergraduate dissertation was a comparison of the Armenian genocide, the Cambodian genocide(s) and the Holocaust. Interested in the Holocaust, other genocides and the punishment of war criminals, late in 1994 I began my doctoral studies on the post-World War II tribunals set up for the prosecution of "Axis criminality," and looked specifically at the punishment of Holocaust perpetrators and how their crimes were represented through the legal prism and the political discourse surrounding the trials and subsequent early release schemes. This became my first book. My second was on the Armenian case, its origins, course, and afterlife amid the politics of "recognition" and denial.[37]

My work, like others of my generation, is written in light of what Friedländer and a great number of other Holocaust scholars have written, and in light of the cultural "common sense" to which they have contributed in regard to the murder of the Jews and other genocides, whether those other genocides were perpetrated by the Nazis or not. There is at present an environment where studies of witness testimonies are rich and manifold, and where the interdisciplinary scholarship on all aspects of the representation of the Holocaust surely exceeds in size the empirical work on the perpetration and processes of the Final Solution.

Today, there is also another tradition from Friedländer's, one that could broadly be described as genocide studies, something which, when I began, was relatively unusual for a historian, though is less so now. That strand of inquiry has as one of its characteristics, though certainly not its sole preserve, a more *activist morality*, one of *prevention*. Prevention does not necessarily mean the sort of armed intervention occasionally seen in recent decades. Like historian Mark Levene, I think of prevention as engaging the underlying problems of a competitive, resource-hungry international state system in which peoples are divided into trustworthy and untrustworthy, productive and debilitating, especially but not always along pre-existing ethnic lines. In this light, prevention works at the level of recalibrating general political and economic norms.

Genocide studies has always been concerned, as the title of the UN convention suggests, with the prevention and punishment of genocide, and therefore with patterns of perpetration and perpetrator motivation, and bystanding and intervention. The rationale is that the perpetrators and bystanders are the ones who make genocide happen, or allow it to happen. One of the central methodologies of this scholarship has been the comparison of genocide at the level of causation, meaning primarily the patterns and motives of perpetration, in order to establish patterns in the interests specifically of prediction, but more generally to promote understanding of the causes of a horrific, recurrent phenomenon. For example, Alexandra Garbarini forgets the comparative aspect along with the multiplicity of victim groups as she challenges perpetrator-centric scholars on the activism issue.[38] Insofar as this comparative work extends to the Holocaust, it is of a very different sort than that practiced in the *Historikerstreit*, which clarified the outer moral parameter of discourse around the Holocaust and illustrated the illegitimate use of comparison. But the *Historikerstreit* was a contingent, not inevitable expression of the incorporation of the Holocaust into broader currents of historical inquiry. As long as comparative or contextual approaches do not serve to mitigate or excuse, then there is no limit in principle to their scope and nature.

In genocide studies the etic tradition – with its use of analytical categories that belong to the community of researchers and that are developed from "external" study of broader historical processes – is stronger than the emic tradition of "insider" study that deploys the terms of the self-understanding of studied actors. This need not always be the case, and it is eminently possible to fuse emic and etic analysis,[39] and to attempt very different things within each analytical tradition. It is also vital to stress that neither the emic nor etic approach is intrinsically superior, and that neither the contemplative nor the activist orientations with which these differing approaches may sometimes (not always!) be correlated is intrinsically more important. In an ideal world contemplative/commemorative and activist orientations would be mutually supportive. Yet, there is not always a synergy, as is vividly illustrated in the conflict between proposed commemorative and educational/activist functions for the Canadian Museum for Human Rights.[40]

At the outset of any broad-brush discussion of Holocaust historiography or any other historiography, a required caveat is that the historiography is not homogeneous in nature or thrust. A more advanced Holocaust scholarship has highlighted fruitful avenues of research for scholars of other genocides, and some scholars who were stimulated by the Holocaust have pioneered the study of other genocides.[41] There is no doubt that historiographical advances in Holocaust studies have hitherto benefited genocide studies more than the other way around. As genocide studies develops, the comparative historiographical process can also work in reverse, with the study of other genocides informing that of the Holocaust. For instance, one can detect a connection between the growing interest in the hands-on, neighbor-on-neighbor violence of the Holocaust in the killing fields of Eastern Europe (particularly eastern Poland, the Baltic states, Belarus, and Ukraine) in the 1990s and the similar violence of the Rwandan and Yugoslavian genocides of the same decade.[42] Study of the sexual violence of those recent genocides has also gone alongside a growing interest in the issue in the Nazi period.

So, clearly, there need be no tension between Holocaust studies and genocide studies. The relationship is a contingent and changing one rather than an intrinsic one. It has no inbuilt trajectory either of exclusivity or inclusivity. The asymmetry of the relationship in the spheres of historiography and popular consciousness does not flow *necessarily* from any objectively special quality of the Holocaust, but rather from the fact that the Holocaust was the first genocide to be given extensive scholarly and popular exposure, the relatively large number of survivors and their testimonies in the countries and languages of the places that have also spawned genocide scholarship, and so on. Conversely, there is nothing specially strange about the way that the Holocaust has achieved such prominence given the circumstances just described. Whether or not we adhere to the notion of a "Holocaust industry," had another genocide contingently first risen to prominence, I have no doubt that it too would have spawned both guardians of its particularity and proselytizers of its universal relevance alongside scholars and activists with a more ecumenical interest in the generic phenomenon of genocide. Thus, there is the multidirectionality of memory, to use a term coined by Michael Rothberg.[43] There is absolutely nothing unusual in the existence of some proprietorship around the memory and perceived integrity of a vastly traumatic historical event. The Armenian genocide is another case in point, with some competition as well as cooperation among heirs of the different victim groups of the late Ottoman Empire – Armenians, "Assyrians," Pontic and other Anatolian Greeks, even Kurds – for recognition of their fates.[44]

As regards Holocaust historiography, beyond the matter of genocide hierarchization and memorial inclusivity/exclusivity, there are real political implications to emphasizing differences and de-emphasizing similarities, especially at the level of perpetrator ideology. Here the preventionist strand of genocide studies with its emphasis on lessons for action finds itself at loggerheads with the representational strand with its emphasis on historical specificity. It is the real or perceived differences between the Holocaust and other cases of mass murder at the level of motivation that has allowed leading lights of the international community to legitimate non-intervention in cases like East Pakistan, Rwanda, and Yugoslavia in the first instance, in part on the basis that they are manifestations not of some unilateral, utopian desire to exterminate but the result of bilateral "tribal atavism" and the like. Analogous "civil war" argumentation is also seized upon by the government of Turkey (and some non-Turkish historians) in justification of its refusal to recognize the Armenian case as genocide, and by Sudan in the Darfur case.[45]

Part of the preventionist agenda may be the simple reportage of mass atrocities that are held as politically controversial, in order to speak truth to power – and this whether or not the events qualify strictly for the "G-word." My experience writing on the Armenian genocide tells me how important it is for the former victim community to hear described the responsibility of the perpetrators, given that the heirs of the perpetrators are the deniers. Many other genocides have been the subject of far more successful politicized scholarship than that of Holocaust deniers and revisionists, as such "scholarship" seeks to deny or obscure (or, equally, exaggerate or instrumentalize) them. Some have been so successfully confined to oblivion or to the margins that the former perpetrators need not bother denying them at all. Consider my own country, the UK, with its airbrushed history of genocide in Tasmania.

Indeed, the admirable current institutionalized sensitivity to the Holocaust contrasts with institutional responses to other genocides. This is no mere coincidence, since institutionalization entails a certain depoliticization, a strict delineation of commemorative and activist responses – as if responding to genocide, and choosing which to commemorate, could ever be other than political. Part of the "depoliticization" stems from the Holocaust's being "safely" in the past. When it was happening the attitude of the United States and Britain at least was tellingly different. Another reason, one that is more thematically bound than chronologically bound, is that in important senses the Holocaust has been politically hived-off from other more "controversial" forms of genocide. For countries like Britain and the United States "controversial" also denotes genocides that happened in the course of the establishment or imperial expansion of their own state. These genocides, that is, challenge their own national narratives of tolerance and beneficence. Placing the Holocaust in a special category among genocides may be very convenient for some states, holding up a mirror to their own virtue in the contrast to Nazi Germany while impeding the contemplation of genocide (other than a select few cases) as a generic issue. It is also telling that in Britain's Holocaust memorial days no attention has been paid to the deep British history of antisemitism – one of the really painful British national connections with the fate of the European Jews. It may be that the organizers of Britain's Holocaust day have opted for the easy way out.[46] Only in an attenuated way can *this* sort of commemoration of the Holocaust be celebrated, since it functions to avoid some of the toughest questions relating to the Holocaust and other genocides, even while, absolutely legitimately and happily, recognizing the intrinsic significance of the Holocaust.

THE INTELLECTUAL POSSIBILITIES OF COMPARISON

As Mark Mazower put it some time ago, there may be

> a widely-held unspoken assumption that the mass killing of African or American peoples was distant and in some senses an "inevitable" part of progress while what was genuinely shocking was the attempt to exterminate an entire people in Europe. This assumption may rest upon an implicit racism, or simply upon a failure of historical imagination; it leads, in either case, to the view that it was specifically with the Holocaust that European civilization – the values of the Enlightenment, a confidence in progress and modernization – finally undermined itself.[47]

Along with the work of Jürgen Zimmerer, remarks such as these have stimulated Omer Bartov's retort that the "differences between what happened in Poland in 1939–44 and, say, German Southwest Africa in 1904, are so vast that putting them both in the same explanatory framework of genocidal colonialism does not appear particularly useful."[48] Now of course Bartov is entitled to his views, but he cannot merely decree that there is no relevant connection without engaging with the intellectuals who have made the case over the last 60 years and more, from Aimé Césaire and in a different way Hannah Arendt, through Woodruff D. Smith, to Zimmerer, Dirk Moses, Wendy Lower, David Furber, and Dan Stone; none has created a complete co-identity of the Holocaust with any other genocide.[49]

Bartov would also be within his rights to argue that other instances of genocide closer to "home" geographically and chronologically than the Southwest Africa case are irrelevant to conceptualizing or contextualizing the Holocaust, but then we are entitled to ask where he draws the line. If he remains true to his belief that demarcation should be provided by Nazi-German utopian antisemitism alone, he will find that a significant part of what is traditionally thought of as the Holocaust does not actually fit such a binary worldview. How would such a worldview accommodate the murder of Bessarabian, Bukovinian and Transnistrian Jewry, most of whom were killed by and on the initiative of the Romanian state itself? Or the Hungarian murder of Jews alongside Serbs in Novi Sad in January 1942 and the murderous Hungarian labor battalions, and the Jews evicted to their deaths in 1941 from the Subcarpathian Rus region that Hungary took from Slovakia? Or the killings not just of hundreds of thousands of Serbs by the Ustasha regime but of up to 20,000 Jews, many more than those deported to German hands and Auschwitz? Or Slovakia's eagerness in 1942 to divest itself of Jews that it itself had impoverished and marginalized? Or the enthusiasm of French civil servants and policemen in handing over Jews without French citizenship? To the mix we might add Lithuanian, Latvian, and Ukrainian nationalists who provided many, many thousands of collaborators and perpetrators, without whom the "final solution" simply could not have achieved the dimensions it did in the Soviet territories. Now of course these episodes *are* generally included in conceptualizations of the Holocaust, which means that we have already gone beyond the Nazi–Jewish nexus, beyond Friedländer's titular *Nazi Germany and the Jews*, and beyond a German "redemptive antisemitism." And *we have illustrated in the process that the historian of the Holocaust is already a comparative historian of what are partly separate genocidal stories* written by states and social groups with their own variants of antisemitism and their own political and geopolitical priorities. This is a vital consideration when considering synergies between the fields of Holocaust and genocide studies.

Further, I would argue, if we are to understand the multinational nature of the perpetration as well as the international experience of Jewish victimhood, we need to look to why so many states and peoples turned on their "inner enemies" at this point. Jewish policy was one particularly widespread part of a broader set of demographic concerns that had become acute across recent generations, as the peoples of eastern, southeastern and east-central Europe tried more and less successfully to smash their way to nation-state status out of the bodies of declining dynastic empires, and reconfigure the political space of half a continent, the half where by far the most people lived. Demographic warfare was an expression of the quest for ethnic majoritarianism or exclusivity and the "nationalization" of economies. Jews had become particular targets of these developments in many places well before the Nazi rise to power, but they were not alone. Ustasha anti-Serb violence was more extensive than anti-Jewish violence; Ukrainian nationalist participation in the genocide of the Jews cannot really be understood without the context of a Ukrainian nationalist struggle that targeted Poles too (and vice versa); and so on. Like Germany, the wartime Slovakian, Croatian, Romanian, and Hungarian regimes murdered or deported for murder Romanies as well as Jews.

As to yet other victim groups, it is now a commonplace that the killing technology and human expertise used in the early gassing facilities for Jews and others was first developed in the murder of Germany's mentally and physically handicapped. But the connections do not stop there, because the treatment of institutional patients in the 1930s was the first experiment with the contained starvation of "inferiors" under German control. That system would be exported eastwards after 1939 and again from June 1941 when ghettos were established for Polish and Soviet Jews and when Soviet prisoners of war were incarcerated and effectively murdered in their millions. Other paths are somewhat better trodden in the historiography: the relationship between general demographic engineering in Poland in 1939–41, involving huge numbers of Poles and ethnic Germans, and the development of the specific subset of demographic policy that was Nazi *Judenpolitik*. The specialist literature on perpetration, much available in the German language only, has also revealed the way in which the military "anti-partisan" campaign included the murder of both Slavs and Jews. Many of the concentration camp guards learned their murderous trade brutalizing political opponents and "asocials" from 1933 onward. In short, integration of Nazi policy towards victim groups is not only intrinsically important; it will benefit the study of the Holocaust just as it itself should benefit from the study of the Holocaust.

My book *The Final Solution* sought to do three things, working backwards, as it were, from the Holocaust, which, as I put it on the first page of my introduction, was to be at the center ground of the book. First, the work attempted to embed the Final Solution in a wider history of Nazi genocide and the demographic, ideological and geopolitical agendas of the Nazi-German state. Second, it tried to embed that German story within the history of a wider Europe that not only provided willing murderers of Jews but of a range of other groups deemed dangerous or simply "other." Third, it traced this conjunction of primarily ethnic and ethno-religious violence back to some of its proximate origins in Europe's late nineteenth-century history. The volume then tried to draw out and extend across time some of the comparative and contextual considerations already inherent in Holocaust historiography; and to draw some of these to their logical conclusion.

TO THE FUTURE

Clearly, a number of the controversies about *The Final Solution* outlined in this chapter reflect ongoing tensions and different perspectives between how studies of the Holocaust and genocides are written and interpreted. It would be wrong to dismiss the fears of Michman, Bartov and others. In the view of most but not all comparative genocide scholars, and certainly a large number of Holocaust scholars too, the Holocaust is one genocide among many, each with its own particular and general characteristics. It cannot be stressed enough that this view only entails a shift in the relative status of the Holocaust, not its absolute status. The Holocaust's intrinsic significance is indeed absolute, but so is the significance of every other genocide and genocide-like event. Relationships can be established between different genocides both historically and historiographically but these are not hierarchical relationships nor absolute equations; rather, they are relationships of conceptual, contextual, phenomeral, or causal family resemblance (historically speaking) and mutual illumination (historiographically speaking).

Quite rightly, none of these considerations establishes an inherent superiority, ethically or otherwise, of genocide studies over Holocaust studies. Not only is neither monolithic, each has a range of different purposes with their own internal integrity. Some of the purposes of each partly overlap with some of the purposes of the other. And whatever its remit, genocide studies runs up against analogous conceptual obstacles to that embodied in the rhetoric of Holocaust uniqueness – it is just that the obstacles are encountered at a point commensurate with the broader range of phenomena that genocide studies takes as its business to explore. I refer to the at-once inclusive and exclusive dividing line drawn by the applicability or otherwise of the "G-word."

Genocide studies cannot be said to have ducked the challenge prompted by definitionalism. A large (perhaps too large) proportion of its output is concerned with exegesis of the United Nations definition, legal judgments pursuant to it, and the proposal of separate definitions consistent with the premise that genocide is a social scientific term as well as a legal term. That said, there is a difference between on the one hand creating abstract definitions and on the other hand ruling any given concrete case, beyond a handful of universally accepted instances of genocide, to one or the other side of the definitional divide (see, for instance, Alexander Hinton's chapter in this volume). If we conjoin the political and emotive utility of the G-word, the fear of genocide scholars of appearing as "deniers" if they rule out given cases, and the increasingly sophisticated arguments for broader application, there is an almost built-in expansion to the remit of genocide studies at the level of socio-historical investigation if not at the level of courtroom judgment. This expansion will underline quite how frequent genocide has been in human history, but beyond a point it may render "genocide" if not an empty then certainly a too-capacious signifier, detracting from its intellectual utility and conceptual coherence, on the pragmatic premise that any given concept is only useful if it has some capacity to differentiate meaningfully. How far the process of expansion will go is anyone's guess, and I have no stake in the matter since I subscribe to the corollary of the pragmatic view – namely that once one concept has exhausted its utility, others will emerge in its place. Genocide studies will mutate in accordance with the needs of the moment, just as Holocaust studies will. One possible result of its mutation would be the creation of new forms of temporarily manageable sub-divisions of the concept "genocide." It would be ironic and frustrating, but not surprising, were this to result in some new formulation of different sub-categorizations of genocide to which some implicit hierarchy could be argued to correspond!

Along a different axis, that of disciplinary integration, the establishment of genocide as a legitimate, "mainstream" subject of interest within various specializations may mean its partial incorporation or even assimilation as those disciplines accept and in turn remold it. This process of remolding may be particularly significant in fields like international law, where acquaintance with the disciplinary concepts and idioms is more important than deep knowledge of historical events. Thus, for instance, area studies specialists with an interest in genocide have some significant advantages over genocide studies generalists, because of their linguistic skills and acquaintance with regional histories, archives and peoples. The area studies factor is of added importance when we consider the strong policy orientation of some genocide scholarship, given that since 1945 genocide has tended to occur outside the "West" from which most comparative genocide scholars spring. And it will presumably continue to occur disproportionately outside the West, especially in those poorest areas of the world least prepared infrastructurally for, and likely to be most affected by, the coming wars of resource scarcity and population movements (both refugees and internally displaced) that will accompany anthropogenic climate change. Civil wars, insurgency and counter-insurgency campaigns, state-induced or state-exacerbated famines, and the "structural violence" of developmentalism and environmental degradation each overlap to a lesser or greater extent with changing ideas of what genocide is.

Whatever the future of "genocide" as a subject of interest, comparison as a method of study will remain. With it, especially for the historian–comparativist, will endure an interest in the intersection of the general and the specific in the human experience.

NOTES

1 O. Bartov, "Locating the Holocaust," *Journal of Genocide Research* 13/1, 2011, 121–9; O. Bartov, "Genocide and the Holocaust: What Are We Arguing About?: Leo Kuper: *Genocide* (1981)," in Uffa Jensen, Habbo Knoch, Daniel Morat and Miriam Rürup, eds., *Gewalt und Gesellschaft: Klassiker modernen Denkens neu gelesen*, Göttingen, Germany: Wallstein, 2011, pp. 381–93. Variants on the same theme were also given as keynote lectures at two conferences: the "Lessons and Legacies" conference of November 2010 and the Wiener Library/Kingston University conference on the Holocaust and Genocide of June 2010, the latter paper also entitled "Genocide and the Holocaust: What Are We Arguing About?" – I thank Omer Bartov for the script of the conference paper, which I henceforth refer to as "Genocide and the Holocaust."

2 See previous note, plus Bartov's review of T. Snyder, *Bloodlands: Europe Between Hitler and Stalin*, New York: Basic Books, 2010, in the *Slavic Review* 7/2, 2011, 424–8. Various of Moses' works are listed below; Mazower's *Hitler's Empire*, London: Penguin, 2008 is critiqued.

3 R. Rozett, "Diminishing the Holocaust: Scholarly Fodder for a Discourse of Distortion," *Israel Journal of Foreign Affairs* 6/1, 2012, 53–64.

4 At the University of Florida Conference "Rewriting the Jewish History of the Holocaust," March 17–19, 2012, program at http://web.jst.ufl.edu/pdf/conference-Poster.pdf. I thank Professor Michman for subsequently providing me with a text of his paper.

5 See his review of T. Lawson, *Debates on the Holocaust*, Manchester, UK: Manchester University Press, 2010. Online. Available at www.history.ac.uk/reviews/review/1160. Accessed May 15, 2012. For references to relevant literature on the colonial connection, see note 49 below.

6 See for example the editor's introduction to A. D. Moses, ed., *Empire, Colony, Genocide*, New York: Berghahn, 2008.

7 R. Hilberg, *The Destruction of the European Jews*, 3 vols, New York: Holmes and Meier, 1985; Z. Bauman, *Modernity and the Holocaust*, Ithaca, NY: Cornell University Press, 1989; H. Arendt, *Eichmann in Jerusalem: A Report on the Banality of Evil*, Harmondsworth, UK: Penguin, 1994; C. Browning, *Ordinary Men: Reserve Police Battalion 101 and the Final Solution in Poland*, New York: HarperCollins, 1993.

8 A. Shapira, "The Eichmann Trial: Changing Perspectives," in David Cesarani, ed., *After Eichmann: Collective Memory and the Holocaust since 1961*, London: Routledge, 2005, pp. 18–39, here 23.

9 Y. Lozowick, *Hitler's Bureaucrats: The Nazi Security Police and the Banality of Evil*, New York: Continuum, 2002, conclusion.

10 S. Friedländer, *The Years of Persecution: Nazi Germany and the Jews: 1933–1939*, New York: HarperCollins, 1997; S. Friedländer, *The Years of Extermination: Nazi Germany and the Jews: 1939–1945*, New York: HarperCollins, 2007.

11 B. Lang, *Post-Holocaust: Interpretation, Misinterpretation, and the Claims of History*, Bloomington: Indiana University Press, 2004, p. 102.

12 Y. Bauer, "A Past That Will Not Go Away," p. 17, cited in A. D. Moses, "Conceptual Blockages and Definitional Dilemmas in the Racial Century: Genocide of Indigenous Peoples and the Holocaust," *Patterns of Prejudice* 36/4, 2002, 14–15.

13 A. D. Moses, "Conceptual Blockages," p. 9.

14 C. Tatz, "Genocide and the Holocaust: The Need for a Richter-Scale," keynote lecture at the conference "The Holocaust and Legacies of Race in the Postcolonial World, 1945 to the Present," University of Sydney, April 10–12, 2012.

15 For instance, see the "Research Forum – Holocaust and Genocide," *Dapim* 25, 2011, 301–69.

16 See Bartov, "Locating the Holocaust," and Eric Ehrenreich's review of my book in the *American Historical Review* 115/4, 2010, 1244–5.

17 A. D. Moses, "The Canadian Museum for Human Rights: The 'Uniqueness of the Holocaust' and the Question of Genocide," *Journal of Genocide Research* 14/2, 2012, 215–38.

18 Generally, see D. Moshman, "Conceptual Constraints on Thinking About Genocide," *Journal of Genocide Research* 3/3, 2001, 431–50. For the politics of comparison and the Armenian case, D. Bloxham, "The Organization of Genocide: Perpetration in Comparative Perspective," in Olaf Jensen and Claus-Christian Szjenmann, eds., *Ordinary People as Mass Murderers: Perpetrators in Comparative Perspective*, London: Palgrave, 2008, pp. 185–200.

19 Bartov, "Locating the Holocaust," p. 122; D. Bergen, "Challenging Uniqueness: Decentering and Recentering the Holocaust," *Journal of Genocide Research* 13/1-2, 2011, 129–34.

20 D. Cesarani, "Does the Singularity of the Holocaust Make It Incomparable and Inoperative in Commemorating, Studying and Preventing Genocide? Britain's Holocaust Memorial Day as a Case Study," *Journal of Holocaust Education* 10/2, 2001, 40–56.

21 Y. Bauer, "Genocide Prevention in Historical Perspective," *Dapim: Studies on the Shoah* 25, 2011, p. 319; *The Stockholm International Forum on the Holocaust: A Conference on Education, Remembrance and Research*, Stockholm, Sweden, January 26–28, 2000, proceedings (Stockholm: Regeringskansliet, 2000), p. 3, cited in A. Ehmann, "Is the Holocaust a Unique and Unprecedented Tragedy? On Holocaust Politics and Genocide," *Dapim: Studies on the Shoah* 25, 2011, p. 348.

22 D. Ofer, "Israel," in David S. Wyman and Charles H. Rosenzveig, eds., *The World Reacts to the Holocaust*, Baltimore, MD: Johns Hopkins University Press, 1996, 836–924, here 885.

23 Z. Garber, *Shoah, the Paradigmatic Genocide: Essays in Exegesis and Eisegesis*, Lanham, MD: University Press of America, 1994; Task Force for International Cooperation on Holocaust Education, Remembrance, and Research, ed., "Holocaust, Genocide, and Crimes Against Humanity," Online. Available at: www.hedp.org.uk/_files/Documents/holocaust_genocide_and_crimes_against_humanity.pdf. Accessed May 12, 2012.

24 Bartov, "Locating the Holocaust," p. 121.

25 D. Bloxham and T. Kushner, *The Holocaust: Critical Historical Approaches*, Manchester, England: Manchester University Press, 2005; D. Bloxham, *Genocide on Trial: War Crimes Trials and the Formation of Holocaust History and Memory*, New York: Oxford University Press, 2001.

26 Bartov, "Locating the Holocaust," p. 129.

27 Ibid., 128–9.

28 Friedländer, *The Years of Extermination*, p. xxvi; Friedländer, *Reflections of Nazism: An Essay on Kitsch and Death*, New York: Harper and Row, 1984, pp. 90–1.

29 Bartov, "Locating the Holocaust," p. 128.

30 A. Garbarini, "Reflections on the Holocaust and Jewish History," *Jewish Quarterly Review* 102/1, 2012, 90. Dan Stone's book is *Histories of the Holocaust*, Oxford: Oxford University Press, 2010.

31 As indicated by its appearance in scare-quotes on the final page of my book's introduction.

32 M. Richarz, "Luftaufnahme – Die Schwierigkeiten der Heimatforscher mit der jüdischen Geschichte," *Babylon* 8, 1991, 27–33.

33 Y. Lozowick, *Hitler's Bureaucrats: The Nazi Security Police and the Banality of Evil*; B. Cohen, "Jewish Studies," in Jean-Marc Dreyfus and Daniel Langton, eds., *Writing the Holocaust*, London: Bloomsbury Academic, 2011, pp. 108–24; Garbarini, "On the Holocaust and Jewish History."

34 G. Lewy, *The Nazi Persecution of the Gypsies*, Oxford: Oxford University Press, 2000, pp. 226–8. See reviews in *Journal of Contemporary History* 37/2, 2002, 275–92; *Journal of Genocide Research* 3/1, 2001, 79–85, and especially the latter on the relationship between analysis and the politics of commemoration. Also G. Lewy, *The Armenian Massacres in Ottoman Turkey: A Disputed Genocide*, Salt Lake City: University of Utah Press, 2005; G. Lewy, "Can There Be Genocide Without the Intent to Commit Genocide?" *Journal of Genocide Research* 9/4, 2007, 661–74. See also the responses to the final piece that appear in the same journal issue. On the observation that Lewy seems to be making the Holocaust the paradigm of genocide, see Hans-Lukas Kieser's review article on Armenian genocide scholarship in H. Kieser, *Vierteljahreshefte für Zeitgeschichte – Rezensionen in den sehepunkten* 7, 2007, 29.

35 A. Ehmann, "Is the Holocaust a Unique and Unprecedented Tragedy," p. 349. The books she cites are apparently: G. Le Quintrec and P. Geiss, eds., *Histoire/Geschichte, Europa und die Welt seit 1945*, Stuttgart, Leipzig: Ernst Klett Schulbuchverlage, 2006; D. Henry, G. le Quintrec and P. Geiss, eds., *Histoire/Geschichte. Europa und die Welt vom Wiener Kongress bis 1945*, Stuttgart, Leipzig: Ernst Klett Schulbuchverlage, 2008.

36 J. Knowlton and T. Cates, eds., *Forever in the Shadow of Hitler? Original Documents of the Historikerstreit, The Controversy Concerning the Singularity of the Holocaust*, Atlantic Highlands, NJ: Humanities Press International, 1993.

37 D. Bloxham, *Genocide on Trial: War Crimes Trials and the Formation of Holocaust History and Memory*, New York: Oxford University Press, 2001; D. Bloxham, *The Great Game of Genocide: Imperialism, Nationalism and the Destruction of the Ottoman Armenians*, New York: Oxford University Press, 2005.

38 See note 30.

39 M. Morris, K. Leung, D. Ames and B. Lickel, "Views from Outside and Inside: Integrating Emic and Etic Insights about Culture and Justice Judgment," *Academy of Management Review* 24/4, 1999, 781–96.

40 A. D. Moses, "The Canadian Museum for Human Rights." For my original elaboration of the contemplative/commemorative versus activist dichotomy, see my response to Bartov and others, D. Bloxham, "Discussing Genocide: Two Moralities and Some Obstacles," *Journal of Genocide Research* 13/1, 2011, 135–52.

41 Editors' introduction to D. Bloxham and A. D. Moses, eds., *The Oxford Handbook of Genocide Studies*, Oxford: Oxford University Press, 2010, p. 5.

42 This point cannot be empirically proved but nevertheless it seems probable. For a sample of the literature de-emphasizing "Auschwitz" in the "final solution," see the essays on Eastern Europe in U. Herbert, ed., *Nationalsozialistische Vernichtungspolitik 1939–1945: Neue Forschungen und Kontroversen*, Frankfurt am Main: Fischer, 1998.

43 M. Rothberg, *Multidirectional Memory: Remembering the Holocaust in the Age of Decolonization*, Stanford, CA: Stanford University Press, 2009

44 See C. Gerlach, *Extremely Violent Societies*, Cambridge: Cambridge University Press, 2010, pp. 236, 258 on issues of proprietorship.

45 A. D. Moses, "Conceptual Blockages"; A. D. Moses, "The United Nations, Humanitarianism and Human Rights: War Crimes/Genocide Trials for Pakistani Soldiers in Bangladesh, 1971–1974," in Stefan-Ludwig Hoffman, ed., *Human Rights in the Twentieth Century: A Critical History*, New York: Cambridge University Press, 2011, pp. 258–80; A. D. Moses, "Paranoia and Partisanship: Genocide Studies, Holocaust Historiography and the 'Apocalyptic Conjuncture,'" *Historical Journal* 54/2, 2011, pp. 553–83. On the Armenian case, see D. Bloxham, *The Great Game of Genocide*, esp. chs. 5–6; on Yugoslavia, P. Novick, *The Holocaust in American Life*, New York: Houghton Mifflin Company, 1999, pp. 245–55. On the tensions between commemoration and preventionism in British public life, and some suggested synergies, see D. Bloxham, "Britain's Holocaust Memorial Days: Reshaping the Past in the Service of the Present," *Immigrants and Minorities* 21/1, 2003, pp. 41–62.

46 D. Bloxham, "Britain's Holocaust Memorial Days." My opinions have not changed since writing that piece, and, indeed, have been reinforced on the basis of recent contacts with some of the trustees of the Holocaust Memorial Day Trust. In my view, any optimism about the day is largely related to the decentralization of so many of the local memorial activities.

47 M. Mazower, "After Lemkin: Genocide, the Holocaust and History," *Jewish Quarterly* 5, 1994, 5–8. M. Levene, *Genocide in the Age of the Nation State*, vol. 1, London: Tauris, 2005, pp. 26–7.

48 O. Bartov, "Genocide and the Holocaust," 23.

49 A selection: R. King and D. Stone, eds., *Hannah Arendt and the Uses of History: Imperialism, Nation, Race, and Genocide*, Oxford: Berghahn Books, 2007; J. Zimmerer, "The Birth of the Ostland Out of the Spirit of Colonialism: A Postcolonial Perspective on the Nazi Policy of Conquest and Extermination," *Patterns of Prejudice* 2/39, 2005, 202–24; J. Zimmerer, *Deutsche Herrschaft über Afrikaner: Staatlicher Machtanspruch und Wirklichkeit im kolonialen Namibia*, Münster/Hamburg: LIT Verlag, 2002; J. Zimmerer, "Colonialism and the Holocaust: Towards an Archaeology of Genocide," in A. Dirk Moses, ed., *Genocide and Settler Society*, New York: Berghahn Books, 2004, pp. 49–76; A. D. Moses, "Redemptive anti-Semitism and the Imperialist Imaginary," in Paul Betts and Christian Wiese, eds., *Years of Persecution, Years of Extermination: Saul Friedländer and the Future of Holocaust Studies*, London: Continuum Books, 2010, pp. 233–54; Moses, *Empire, Colony, Genocide*.

CHAPTER 5

Genocide and the Politics of Rape

Historical and psychological perspectives

Roger W. Smith

Rape is such a pervasive aspect of the history of genocide that it is surprising that until recently little attention has been paid to it.[1] On the other hand, there has been little recognition generally that victimization in genocide often follows lines of gender. Here I focus on sexual violence against women because it has historically been more common than that against men. And for women some of the consequences are quite different: pregnancy and the different possibilities that entails, including keeping the child, which will be seen as a badge of dishonor for both the woman and the ethnic community; the act of rape, and her likely rejection by her community, turning the pregnant woman into a killer herself, with children of rape being smothered at birth or abandoned in the fields. Males do suffer sexual violence too: rape, mutilation, continuing shame. It probably has been a facet of genocide for centuries, but one can certainly find examples of it in Bosnia, of mutilation in Rwanda, and of violation of male children, as well as adults, during the Armenian genocide. My guess is that the functions of rape and other forms of sexual violence against males and females overlap, but diverge in certain respects, and that culture will play a large role in the meaning of the violations and what they consist of, for both perpetrators and victims.

In an attempt to understand the systematic, sustained, and sanctioned rapes in Bosnia, and those that have occurred previously, and, unfortunately since, I shall focus on the politics of rape within the genocidal process, with attention to the meaning, functions, and consequences of such acts. A range of historical cases of rape within genocide will be used as illustrations. Psychological theory will be used to illuminate particular aspects of the politics of rape, such as rituals of degradation, especially noticeable in Bosnia, that endow the perpetrator with a sense of power and reduce the victim to a despised and powerless object. Other functions of rape, such as terror, revenge, reward for participation in genocide, demoralization of the victim group to the point that its will to resist genocide is impaired, and destruction of biological continuity within the victim group, through forced pregnancy, will also be discussed. The chapter concludes with reflections on the legal status of rape within the context of genocide. Throughout I shall emphasize that rape is part of a policy process rather than the result of "excesses" by individuals.

RAPE AND GENOCIDE: A HISTORICAL VIEW

Rape as an element in the genocidal process is probably as old as history, with an account from the twelfth century BCE making reference to it.[2] Similarly, it seems to be universal: it has been committed by, for example, ancient Hebrews, Greeks and Romans, Crusaders, Mongols, Spaniards in sixteenth-century America, Englishmen in nineteenth-century Tasmania and Australia, Americans in various instances dating back to the seventeenth century, Turks in twentieth-century Armenia, Pakistanis in Bangladesh in 1971, Serbs in Bosnia beginning in 1992, Hutus in Rwanda in 1994. And the list goes on, Darfur being prominent among them.

Ancient warfare was synonymous with genocide, with men being routinely killed and women and children enslaved. Further, the rape of women after victory was customary, a sign of triumph and a reward for those who had achieved victory. Women taken into slavery would then be subject to ongoing rape: their bodies were a form of booty, subject to ownership and use like other property taken as the spoils of war that regularly ended in the extermination of males.

In other situations, such as the long-term domination of indigenous peoples and their destruction by white Europeans, rape was more individual and spontaneous, but no less an expression of power and control over an inferior other. "To kill men and rape women: these are at once proof that a man wields power and his reward."[3] The words are from a study of the Spanish "conquest" of America, but they fit many other examples of the destruction of indigenous peoples over a long period of time. In Tasmania, for instance, many whites did not hesitate to kill the indigenous males and to seize young women, raping them, and then chaining them like animals until the male desire to use her again.[4]

Rape can also be something other than the routine or the individual expression of power; it can be a policy deliberately chosen to humiliate, intimidate, and demoralize a victim group, making resistance to genocide more difficult. In Bangladesh in 1971, for example, the Pakistani army engaged in a systematic policy of rape in an attempt to shame and humiliate the Bengali people, who were making strong demands for autonomy from Pakistan.[5] Women, both Muslim and Hindu, were taken from their homes, the fields, or the streets and subjected to individual and group rape. Many were taken to military brothels, where they were made to mimic the traditional roles of women as housekeepers and sexual objects. In desperation some of the women resisted by using their long braids to hang themselves; thereafter, the others were shorn and their saris replaced with shorts (and in some accounts, with nakedness).

The rape was widespread, with some 50,000 to 200,000 women being attacked, resulting in 25,000 pregnancies.[6] Rumors circulated that the rapes were an attempt to stifle Bengali nationalism by diluting the population with children fathered by Pakistanis; it was instead part of a policy of humiliation and domination. But we already see some of the functions of genocidal rape and why it might be adopted as policy: as an expression of power, as a reward to soldiers, as humiliation of the victims, as an attempt to demoralize and crush any will to resist.

Viewed historically, genocide almost always includes rape as a means of victimization. Nevertheless, there are two major examples in the twentieth century in which rape was relatively rare, each a consequence of the regime's racial or political ideology.

In the Nazi genocide of the Jews, some Jewish women were raped and some were forced into military and camp brothels, and a few were subjected to sexual abuse of a different sort — with breasts favorite targets for the whips of the more sadistic guards.[7] Far more common was the sexual humiliation that occurred through forced exposure of their naked bodies to the eyes of German males to the accompaniment of obscene comments and gestures. The Nazis thus committed acts of sexual abuse against Jewish women; they also created conditions in the camps that led a few women to prostitute themselves (to males or females) in order to gain extra food, exemption from exhausting labor, or in other ways to enhance the chance for survival. Humiliation of Jewish women was part of the Nazi policy of genocide, but, due to racial ideology, this was not achieved to any extent through rape.

What the Nazis demanded from Jewish women were their lives. With non-Jews, however, especially on the Eastern front, they did engage in rape on a large scale, offering the traditional reward to the soldier and signifying the defeat of the enemy.[8] Slavic women, although regarded as sub-human, were not seen as a source of racial defilement.

The other example of genocide occurring on a massive scale, with little sexual violation of those otherwise victimized, is the case of Cambodia under the Khmer Rouge regime.[9] Not only was rape punished by death, but ordinary human sexual relationships and love affairs were similarly punished: a dehumanized, functional view was taken of men and women — one's body and emotions belonged to the movement; sexual life was a prerogative of the regime. An extreme austerity, with a dehumanized view of persons and a disregard for their feelings was involved, but also the desire for total control. Indeed, the capacity to control sexuality is, as Orwell suggested in *1984*, perhaps the only way a regime can be sure that its control is total. But if for ideological reasons, the Khmer Rouge did not violate women through rape, for the same reasons they did not hesitate to take the lives of hundreds of thousands of Cambodian women in the genocidal pursuit of the "perfect" society.

RAPE AS GENOCIDAL POLICY

What, then, is the relationship between rape and genocide? More precisely, what is the source of rape (or less often, its relative absence) within the context of genocide? I am going to suggest that rape in such cases can best be understood in terms of the policy process. Other answers, however, have been put forward in the recent past; I shall begin by assessing their adequacy.

The first answer suggests that there is no particular relationship, that rape is simply incidental to genocide, as to war, and is the result of pent-up sexual desire. Rape, in this perspective, is a private act, with no connection to politics. But in ancient genocide, rape and enslavement of women was the rule, not the spontaneous actions of individuals. Moreover, the view of rape as the expression of individual desire cannot explain the rituals of degradation that often accompany rape, nor does it point to a central feature of such rape: the violation of women as celebration, and confirmation, of victory over males from the women's group. Nor, of course, does it tell us anything about the use of rape as a means of creating terror as part of a campaign of "ethnic cleansing."

A second view is that, although rape is incidental to genocide, as to war, it is the result of the male's desire to control women through fear. In one well-known formulation of this view, that of Susan Brownmiller, rape is said to be "nothing more or less than a conscious process of intimidation by which *all* men keep *all* women in a state of fear."[10] But, of course, in genocide, it is not all men keeping all women in fear, but rather men from one group attacking women from another group, and doing so, in some instances, precisely to produce terror, demoralization, and an inability to resist various genocidal acts directed at the group. Still, Brownmiller's perspective does involve a kind of politics, but it is a politics of males versus females, not of Serbs versus Muslims, or Turks against Armenians, or Hutu against Tutsi. Having assumed that male oppression and the threat of rape exist everywhere, there is, in this perspective, no need to explain any particular example of mass rape perpetrated by one group against another.

Brownmiller recognizes that mass rape has consequences such as intimidation and demoralization, but these are interpreted as by-products of private acts rather than the goal of any policy. Mass rape may contribute to "national terror and subjugation," but in Brownmiller's view, that is the result, not the origin of rape: "the original impulse to rape does not need a sophisticated political motivation beyond a general disregard for the bodily integrity of women."[11]

In this perspective, hostility to women replaces pent-up sexual desire as the source of rape within genocide. While such a view may help us to understand individual acts of rape, it tells us little about the motives of those who planned the genocide and set it into motion: Why did they select the particular group for victimization? Did they not foresee the consequences of mass rape, intend to utilize the "terror and subjugation" to help destroy a people, and thus turn rape, whatever its sources in individuals, into a policy? And if it was in fact a policy, what were the goals, either instrumental or expressive, that could only be achieved through the rape of women and, in many cases, their complete humiliation and degradation? Nor can the rape-as-hostility-to-women thesis explain why some genocides are relatively free from rape (Cambodia) and others (Bangladesh, Bosnia, Rwanda) seem inseparable from such violence and degradation.

Yet another view comes from the human rights organization Helsinki Watch, and is directed specifically at the mass rape in Bosnia. Here there is a clear recognition of a political dimension to rape:

> Whether a woman is raped by soldiers in her home or is held in a house with other women and raped over and over again, she is raped with a political purpose – to intimidate, humiliate, and degrade her and others affected by her suffering. The effect of rape is often to ensure that women and their families will flee and never return.[12]

This perspective represents a considerable advance over the previous two: it recognizes that there is a political dimension to rape, points to one of its goals – terrorizing members of the victim group into fleeing – and, in material I have not yet presented, takes note of the frequent attempt by the perpetrators to force pregnancy upon women of the group. Still, it leaves open the question of whether the mass rapes are the result of a deliberate policy sanctioned at the highest levels, or whether they are the result of a series of acts, basically independent of each other, committed at the local level. The question of a policy being deliberate is complicated by the fact that such sanctioning of mass rape may be either by *command* or by *permission*.

A command is usually explicit: thus, it has been claimed that the rape of tens of thousands of women and girls in Bangladesh resulted from orders that "came from the top military brass then ruling East Pakistan."[13] Whatever the accuracy of this claim, there probably are rapes based upon command, but this is hard to establish since the perpetrators are not likely to put such commands into writing. On the other hand, where there is a consistent pattern of rape, with mass rape either taking place simultaneously over a wide area, as in Bangladesh or Bosnia, or repeated in the same fashion over time, as in Burma, there is a strong likelihood that orders have in fact come down the chain of command.[14]

A command, however, need not always be explicit – it may be embedded in tradition and common expectation. In the ancient world and with the thirteenth-century Mongols, for example, genocide was synonymous with war, and the fate of women was understood to be that of rape and enslavement rather than death. The politics of genocidal rape was institutionalized; no explicit command was necessary. There were even standing rules about how the "booty" (a term that included the women from the defeated group) was to be distributed. Thus, the women (wives, daughters, and concubines) of the defeated ruler were reserved for service in the beds of the ruling house of the victors. The symbolism here is obvious, as is the consolidation of the victory.

Genocidal rape can be sanctioned, however, not only by command, but by authorization. Authorization in this instance means permission, which can involve encouragement of mass rape, approval of it, or simply non-interference with it. In such cases, the process of destroying a group in whole or in part is set in motion by the central authorities. They commit themselves to a policy of genocide, mobilize the men and materiel to carry it out, and issue general directives about such things as the need to "cleanse" the territory of the ethnic, racial, or religious group chosen for destruction. But the general directives have to be implemented and some of the implementation (including the decision to rape) will be left to local authorities.

Those who decide to commit genocide recognize that the manner in which the genocide is carried out – deporting, for example, unprotected women and children into remote areas – will lead to rapes and abductions along the way, or that the ethnic hatred they have stirred up and manipulated will likely lead to rape accompanied with great brutality. Or they foresee that commanders in the field will find ways of combining "ethnic cleansing" with toughening their soldiers for genocidal killing. Systematic rape is particularly suited for such purposes since it both causes members of the victim group to flee in terror and serves to desensitize the perpetrators, allowing them to commit increasingly brutal acts.

The leaders foresee mass rape as an outcome of the decision to commit genocide and they encourage it, approve of it, or do not interfere with it since rape helps to achieve the goal they have chosen (for whatever reason) of eliminating Armenians, Bosnian Muslims, Tutsi, or another targeted group. In fact, except where racial ideology is involved (the Nazis) or an ideology that insists upon total control of human action (the Khmer Rouge) there are *no incentives* for the authorities to prohibit mass rape within the context of genocide.

Where sanctioning takes the form of permission, the politics of rape combines central authority with the relatively independent acts and policies of local authorities and commanders. Beyond that, there may be spontaneous acts by individuals, but within the context of authorization granted to them through permission. Consequently, rape may not follow a single pattern. Thus, in Armenia, women were raped and killed, but others were abducted and incorporated into the perpetrators' society. Still, others were auctioned off in the marketplace to an unknown fate.[15] And, it is not always clear what constitutes a "pattern." Jeri Laber, for example, identified:

> several different patterns of rape in Bosnia: there are rapes that are intrinsic to the "cleansing" process; they occur during the initial stages of an invasion and are used to terrorize civilians into leaving their homes, and sometimes into signing papers that say they are doing so willingly. There are rapes that are committed in detention camps where guards have license to do as they please. And there are rapes that take place in temporarily commandeered houses, schools, or hotels where women are kept for many weeks, it seems, for the purpose.[16]

Has Laber identified three patterns of rape in Bosnia or rather shown the different facets of a single policy of rape as an instrument of genocide? In my view, she has shown the latter, but this does not resolve the issue of whether the policy came into being through command or through permission.

Of course, some observers may conclude that lacking a single pattern of mass rape, and one that is commanded by the top levels of authority, one can only speak of individual crimes, but not a *policy* of genocidal rape. But this is to mistake policy for that which originates on high. In many cases, the acts that become policy originate from the bottom and subsequently become policy by ratification. And if the patterns of rape are varied, still the authorities have both approved them and created the conditions under which genocidal rape can take place. If not command, then they provide permission.

This approach to policy is related to, but differs in an important respect from, the contrast in Holocaust studies between "intentionalists" (that the destruction of the Jews was intended in Nazi ideology from the very beginning of the movement) and "functionalists" (that the Holocaust arose from unforeseen circumstances and the attempts by various bureaucracies to implement general directives issued by the top leadership).[17] My approach to the question of rape as genocidal policy, however, is in terms of "command" and "permission," both of which are ways of providing sanctions for policy.

What I am suggesting, then, is that the policy of genocidal rape need not always rest upon command. There can be a decentralized and uneven use of rape to further rape, but when this is sanctioned by permission at the highest levels, it becomes a *policy* of genocidal rape. Moreover, whether such rape is by command or by permission, the leaders of the perpetrator group bear full legal and moral responsibility for it.[18] The idea of policy as sanctioned behavior can be illustrated further by a concrete example. The one I have chosen, but others would serve almost as well, is the mass rape in Bosnia by Serbs. One cannot be certain as to whether the rapes in Bosnia were commanded or permitted, but there can be no doubt that they were sanctioned by the Serbian leadership in both Bosnia and Serbia and, therefore, constitute a policy. That the rapes were official policy and not some sort of aberration or the result of private excess is clear: there were repeated episodes of mass rape in towns and villages across Bosnia, the rapes were often committed in public, there were detention centers in which multiple rapes took place. Yet, no one from the Serbian leadership condemned the rapes, punished anyone for them or removed offenders from positions of authority. Finally, following the modern practice by perpetrators of denying their genocidal acts, Serbian leaders maintained that, at the most, a few dozen rapes had occurred, all individual acts.

GENOCIDAL FORM: PATTERNS OF RAPE

Rape, as I have suggested, is typically part of the genocidal process, an expression of policy rather than an unintended form of "excess." But because rape is policy, its scale, purposes, and style (the extent to which it is systematic, for example, or accompanied by rituals of degradation) can vary considerably.[19] Where genocide is part of the routine of warfare, and slavery the form victimization takes for women, rape will be systematic and widespread. If retributive genocide is involved, the likelihood is either that women will be killed at the outset or raped and then killed; there will be no incorporation, as in slavery, of the women into the perpetrators' society. When utilitarian genocide takes place, typically in the conflict between indigenous peoples and settlers, rape occurs, but is more individualistic than systematic.

Genocides that arise out of ethnic or racial conflict and attempt to monopolize power in politics and society may or may not involve mass rape (Bangladesh and Rwanda did, Burundi apparently did not), but where it does, the object is primarily to create terror in an attempt to cause members of the group to flee or become so demoralized that they are unable to resist the genocide.

In some cases of ideological genocide, such as Nazi Germany and Cambodia, rape may not occur precisely because of the ideology. On the other hand, widespread and systematic rape accompanied by rituals of degradation is likely where the basis of the ideology is nationalism. Nationalism, more than most ideologies, seems to produce not only an extreme polarization, but one accompanied by hate. Fundamentalist religion is also capable of producing these effects, but whether the content of particular religions might restrain rape, while sanctioning genocide, is not clear. We know that the Crusaders committed rape as a means of harming the "infidels," but would the same be true of Muslim or Hindu fundamentalists? The potential is there, but at present there is little evidence on which to base a conclusion.

It is not sufficient, however, to look only at types of genocide and attempt to understand their relationships to different patterns of rape. One must also focus on the particular culture and goals of the political leaders involved in the genocide. Systematic rape, for example, derives from the policy process, which in turn reflects the ideology and goals of the leaders. The extensive use of rituals of degradation, or their relative absence, will similarly turn in large part on the extent to which the leaders dehumanize the victims. Finally, the culture itself may devalue the group subjected to genocide, but leaders heighten this to serve their own ends, such as holding onto, or expanding, their power, furthering an ideology, or mobilizing hate in the quest for say, a Greater Serbia.

In the details of how rape is carried out, as in the larger question of the type of genocide engaged in, we are thus brought back to the question of choice and political will – in short, to rape as part of a policy of genocide.

FUNCTIONS OF GENOCIDAL RAPE

The functions of genocidal rape are numerous but due to the policy process not all will be present in a particular case. Put differently, genocide is a calculated means to an end. The extent to which rape will be a part of the genocidal process, and the particular form it will take, depend heavily upon the goals of the perpetrators. In the ancient world, for example, women were seized in order to exploit their reproductive capacities, either replenishing a population diminished by war or disease, or expanding the population in order to augment power. Today, one of the functions that we have seen readily displayed in Bosnia and elsewhere is that of creating terror, the goal of which is, in large part, to cause members of the group to flee. Rape thus becomes a primary tactic in "ethnic cleansing" and in the attempt to weaken groups perceived to be politically dissident; for example in minority groups that seek equality of treatment by the state, or having failed in achieving that, greater autonomy.

Rape has traditionally been a reward to soldiers for services rendered, an opportunity for men to have their way with the women of the enemy. This type of rape takes place both during and at the conclusion of the genocide, and is often committed in the presence of the woman's family. In such situations, rape signifies the masculinity and the victory of the perpetrators and the weakness and impotence of the defeated males. "The body of a raped woman becomes a ceremonial battlefield ... The act that is played out upon her is a message passed between men – vivid proof of victory for one and loss and defeat for the other."[20]

Rape is also a means to desensitize those who engage in it. As social psychologists remind us, one learns by doing, and here one learns to devalue the victims further, to shut out any feelings of compassion, and to participate in ever increasing acts of brutality.[21]

In other ways, rape can directly facilitate genocide. For example, rape may be motivated by revenge (though this is often an excuse) to pay back the enemy for what it has, supposedly, done to the women of one's own group. Here rape is seen as justice, but it serves to further genocide in several ways: it creates terror, demoralizes the victim group making resistance more difficult, and where pregnancy results, weakens the biological links within the victim group.

Finally, rape when accompanied by rituals of degradation, is a form of torture, the object of which is not to extract information or to "punish." Rather it is to destroy the moral identity of the victims, reducing them, and, by extension, the group from which they come, to a powerless object.[22] Closely related to this is the attempt to force pregnancy on them in order to inflict continuing pain, humiliation, and shame on the women and their group. By killing the males and forcing pregnancy on the women, there is also the attempt to break the biological connections within the group. But these are large themes that will have to be addressed in more detail.

RITUALS OF DEGRADATION

The attempt of those who commit genocide is frequently not only to kill, but to humiliate and degrade the victims. Genocide, in other words, includes elements of both moral and physical destruction. The perpetrators typically try to destroy the victims' humanity by subjecting members of the group to various rituals of degradation. Thus rape, beyond its own trauma and humiliation, will be accompanied by brutalization (beatings, curses, threats of mutilation often carried out) and perverse acts of "sex":

> I was raped with a gun by one of those men, along with another woman and her daughter, while the others watched. Some of them spat on us; they did so many ugly things to us... There was no passion in this, it was only done to destroy us ... if they couldn't rape me, they would urinate on me.[23]

In Bosnia and elsewhere it was common practice to rape women in front of other men. When the men in question are those of the victim group (often including husband, father, or children), the point is to humiliate the men along with the women and to signify to the men their utter powerlessness. When it is committed before members of the perpetrators' group, the public rape is part of a bonding experience that, as was said in Bosnia, "is good for the Serbian fighters' morale."[24] It also serves to desensitize the perpetrators, making it easier for them to commit further acts of rape, graduate to brutality, including mutilation, and to commit murder against members of the rejected group with little compunction. In Bosnia, however, there was a further twist to this in that women were raped repeatedly, particularly in the detention camps set up by the Serbs, in front of other women. Here the object was to frighten those made to view the rapes, who know they were likely to be next, but above all to bring home to them their contemptible lack of power in a world where power is everything. The attempt through this means, and the many other rituals of degradation, is not only to inflict trauma on the women, but to destroy their very humanity. Closely related to this is the practice of forcing male members of the victim group to rape or sexually humiliate women of the group; in some instances, this has involved forcing sons to rape their own mothers. Such actions are intended to break down any sense of solidarity within the group, isolating both those raped and those forced to rape.[25]

Rituals of degradation enhance the perpetrator's sense of power, reduce the individual victim, and by extension her entire group, to an object without power or worth, allowing the perpetrators to revel in a kind of violation, even des-ecration, that borders on nihilism, where no human standards prevail, but rather power is all.

At their outer limits, such violations test and mock the possibility of any moral life, rejecting, as Leo Kuper notes, "the most deeply held human values, and the deepest sentiments of human attachment."[26] In some instances this involves forcing believers to desecrate holy places and to engage in sacrilege. Or, as previously men-tioned, it may involve forced mating between mother and son. But the example I want to focus on for a moment comes from Bosnia and involves representing the torture of women as an expression of "morality" and "love."

As the Muslim and Croatian women are gang-raped by Serbs, the soldiers "watch, laugh, encourage each other, and spew ethnic curses and epithets."[27] The rapists pretend that they are punishing the women for being "Ustasha whores," supporters of the World War II fascist regime in Croatia (which then included Bosnia-Herzegovina) that killed hundreds of thousands of Serbs, Jews, and Roma. They also pretend that they are teaching a lesson to those who would otherwise not listen to Greater Serbia's claims to the land. They also represent torture as normality as they turn the violation and brutalization of women into a parody of love. Or perhaps it is rather "sarcasm" that one should speak of: "a sharply mocking ... remark, typically utilizing statements or implications pointedly opposite or irrele-vant to the underlying purport," a term coming from the Greek word meaning "to tear flesh."[28]

The men who are gang-raping "laugh and chide each other 'for not satisfying her,' for not being able to 'force a smile out of her,' because she is not 'showing signs of love.' They beat her and ask if it is good for her."[29] There are similar accounts of this kind of behavior where the rapist acts apart from a gang: the violator pretends that he is the woman's husband as he rapes her before her husband's eyes; or he claims that he wants to marry her; or he crudely tattoos his name and the word "husband" on her thighs.[30]

Whether the "normalization" of genocidal rape as love has occurred in other cases, I am unsure, but it would seem to be an ever present possibility, serving as it does both to distance the violator from any remaining conscience and to add further hurt to women through mockery and sarcasm. The whole thing also has a universal quality to it in which young men tease and challenge each other in terms of sexual prowess.

The most common ritual of degradation is the subjection of women to multiple rape, in which typically anywhere from six to twenty men rape the victim, sometimes with rifles or other objects, as the others look on. Serbs used this ritual of degradation extensively in Bosnia, but examples can be found wherever a policy of genocidal rape is adopted, such as in Bangladesh in 1971, Burma in the 1990s, and Rwanda in 1994. In such cases, rape is a form of torture, deliberately inflicted upon women in order to destroy their moral identity and to create continuing hurt and shame. Such torture may, as in one report from Bosnia, involve being raped daily by six men over a five-week period.[31] Or it may involve continual rape over a four or five hour period:

> The number of men who came to rape us increased. First there were three, then four or five. I eventually counted twenty-eight different men who raped me that night, but I lost consciousness after that.[32]

CONTINUING HURT

Rituals of degradation, rather than being the expression of the sadistic inclinations of individual perpetrators, are part of a calculated policy. The goals of this policy, in addition to those already mentioned, are to intensify the victim's suffering, deepen her trauma, and produce continuing hurt. In this way, the victim's pain, violation, humiliation, and lack of power become permanent. By the same logic, the perpetrators' power remains long after the acts of violation and humiliation are committed. Women who are being raped and subjected to rituals of degradation are told again and again that they will "remember forever."[33] In other words, the perpetrators attempt to perpetuate their power (understood as the ability to inflict pain) through linking memory with pain, with the woman recalling for the rest of her life her violation and humiliation and, by extension, the shame brought upon her group.

The desire to inflict continuing pain is driven by hatred. "Hatred," the philosopher Leszek Kolakowski has written, "is more than a striving for destruction ... it includes a kind of infinity, that is insatiability. It does not simply strive for destruction, but for never-ending suffering."[34] But nihilism is similar – it too has an element of infinity, the never-ending exercise of power in a world void of moral possibility, a world where the only reliable test of power is the infliction of pain. Nihilism left to itself, however, is directionless, its victims are selected at random, and could simply be individuals, rather than members of a particular group. Nevertheless, nihilism does appear to be present in rituals of degradation where moral standards are not only violated, but mocked. It may be that this mocking results from the perpetrators' own *dehumanization* – loss of compassion, psychic numbing, detachment – through participation in brutality. But nihilism, once born, contributes a special vileness to genocidal acts.

Nowhere is the policy of producing continuing hurt more evident than in the perpetrators' attempt to impregnate women of the victim group. In part this is a matter of final conquest, the power of the perpetrator to make the women of the rejected group bear children who will in time stand in enmity toward her people. A good example of this comes from the pogroms against Armenians in Sumgait, Azerbaijan in 1988:

> While they were raping me they repeated quite frequently, "Let the Armenian women have babies for us, let them bear Azerbaijanis for the struggle against the Armenians." Then they said, "Those Muslims can carry on our holy cause. Heroes!" They repeated it very often.[35]

In some instances, the forced impregnation is presented as a chance for redemption. In Bosnia, a Muslim woman raped by Serbs reported: "They said I was a Ustasha and that I needed to give birth to a Serb – that I would then be different."[36]

There is in all of this a male pride in potency. There is also the intent to change the biological heritage of the victim group. The dominant goal, however, appears to be to humiliate and inflict continuing pain on the victim and her group. That the victims were aware of this can be illustrated by the comments of two women, the first Croatian, the second Muslim, raped by Serbs in Bosnia:

> It was their aim to make a baby. They wanted to humiliate us. They would say directly, looking into your eyes, that they wanted to make a baby. They seemed to be men without souls and hearts.[37]
>
> They wanted women to have children to stigmatize us forever. The child is the reminder of what happened.[38]

To make sure that the hurt will continue, and that the biological line will be altered, many women will also be held in detention camps in order to prevent them from terminating their pregnancies. Examples of this could be given from the genocidal rapes in Bangladesh in 1971, but as with the rituals of degradation, the clearest evidence comes from Bosnia. In November 1992 the US Department of State reported:

> At least 150 Muslim women and teen-age girls – some as young as 14 – who have crossed into Bosnian Government-held areas of Sarajevo in recent weeks are in advanced stages of pregnancy, reportedly after being raped by Serb nationalist fighters and being imprisoned for months afterwards in an attempt to keep them from terminating their pregnancies. "When we let you go home you'll have to give birth to a Chetnik" [a Serbian soldier], Serb fighters supposedly repeated to some of the women. "We won't let you go while you can have an abortion."[39]

▋ VIOLATION OF CHILDREN

Forced pregnancy is often an object of genocidal rape, but females unable to give birth are also attacked. Wherever genocidal rape occurs, its victims include many young children and also women in their eighties. Here I want to focus on why children are subjected to such violation, but later I shall comment also on the sexual violation of the elderly.

Examples of the genocidal rape of children abound. There are, for example, numerous accounts from the Armenian genocide of 1915 of rapes of young girls in their villages before deportation or along the march into the Syrian desert. One eyewitness reports: "It was a very common thing for them to rape our girls in our presence. Very often they violated eight or ten-year-old girls, and as a consequence many would be unable to walk, and were shot."[40] Another witness indicates that in her village every female over twelve (and some younger) was raped.[41]

From Bosnia comes further evidence of the violation of the young, with the youngest victim being three, many others seven or eight, and still others in their early teens. From Rwanda there are reports of the violation of babies as young as one month. In most cases, it is not known what percentage of rape victims are children or young teenagers, but in Bangladesh it appears that about 20 per cent of those raped (and many of whom became pregnant) were between the ages of twelve to sixteen.[42]

The problem, then, is not so much to document the rapes as to understand why they take place. Some of the reasons may be thought of as atypical in that they seem to explain the violation of the young in only a single type of genocide or in a particular situation. But for the perpetrators these reasons would have appeared to be the essential ones. Other reasons are implicated in a wider range of cases of genocide and are also more applicable to any explanation of genocidal rape in the contemporary world.

Two examples of what we would take to be atypical reasons for genocidal rape of the young can be given. The first is an expression of a type of genocide in which it was customary to kill the men and enslave the women, including the young, in large part to exploit women's reproductive capacity. The second is an expression of a particular conception of beauty. The two examples, otherwise so different, share the assumption that power entails access to the bodies of the young.

In one of the earliest accounts of genocide, the Israelites endured a drastic reduction in population due to plague. They then attacked the Midianite tribe, killing the males and the adult women (who supposedly had seduced some of the Israelite males into worshipping a false god). They seized the virgin girls, turning them into slaves and concubines, whose reproductive capacity, exploited over a period of years, would offset population losses due to war and disease.[43]

Reproduction, however, was not the object of the violation of the young in nineteenth-century Tasmania. Here white settlers and sailors viewed adult Tasmanian women as ugly and almost animal-like. After whites raped, it was usually girls in their early teens who were often so horrified by what they saw as the "ugliness" of the mixed offspring, that they killed their infants.[44]

Genocidal rape, however, typically includes female children and young girls among its victims for reasons other than reproduction or an idea about physical attractiveness.

In the first place, some of the violations may result from the personal predilections of the victimizers, which are allowed expression by those in charge. In this instance, the politics of genocide serves in part as a cover for sexual perversion. There is also a notion of "ruining" or "spoiling" the young by depriving them of their virginity. A good example is that of a Turkish official in 1915 who "openly boasted of having ruined eleven Christian girls, two of them under the age of seven."[45] Here one sees the power of the patriarchal assumption that females are a kind of property that loses its value if "damaged" through premarital intercourse (even if it takes the form of rape). The rape will have a permanent effect both in terms of personal trauma and of the child's prospects of eventually marrying. Moreover, the violation, the "ruining" of the female child or young girl is aimed simultaneously at the violated, her family, and her communal group.

In some societies, such as Bangladesh, the raped child will be rejected by her own family as a source of shame and as one who jeopardizes opportunities for other children in the family to arrange marriages. In fact, many of the Bengali victims saw themselves as having only two choices: to turn to prostitution in order to eke out a living or, out of shame, to commit suicide.[46] This infliction of hurt and continuing pain is an important goal of such genocidal rape.

The crucial element, however, is that the rape of a three-year-old child and a woman of eighty signifies that all members of the group are vulnerable, that the perpetrators will make no exceptions. The totality of such a vision is unmistakably genocidal, but from the perpetrators' point of view that is its strength. Whatever the sources of such a vision of rejection and hate, its purposes are to terrorize further the victim group, forcing them to flee, or through demoralization and despair to lose the will to resist, thus making their killers' job that much easier.

Finally, many of the children (and the elderly) will not only be raped, but killed. If the logic of atrocity to murder adults is to kill the present, to murder the children of the group is to kill the future. But whether such children live or are murdered is probably a matter of either the rapist's degree of hate or the whim of the moment. The perpetrator can be sure that whether he rapes, or rapes and kills, he will not be punished.

CONSEQUENCES

Genocidal rape has numerous and far-reaching consequences, some of which we have already encountered in the discussion of the functions of mass rape. In order to present a fuller picture of such rape, I now want to explore some of the consequences that have previously only been mentioned in brief. I shall also raise the question of what effects, if any, the rapes have on those who perpetrate them.

Let us begin with the forced incorporation into the perpetrators' society, illustrating this with both an ancient and a modern example. In ancient times, genocide resulted in the death of the men and the enslavement of women, that is, beings who lacked power, status, and honor, and who were seen simply as objects to be used and exploited. In practice, slavery was another name for recurrent rape, and since slaves had no rights to their bodies, they had no right to the children born as a result of sexual slavery. Slavery completed the genocide begun earlier by destroying whatever remained of the group biologically and socially.

Something similar happens, though not with the same degree of finality, when large numbers of women, as in the Armenian genocide, are abducted and incorporated into the perpetrators' society through force. Some abducted women and girls will literally become slaves and will even be branded to mark them as such; others will be "wives."[47] In either case the victim group is deprived of the women who can continue it biologically and socially. Further, the children of the forced unions will now retain only part of the biological heritage of the victim's group and, additionally, will be socialized into the ethnic and religious identities of the perpetrators.

Moreover, in the past, rape was usually an alternative to death, in large part because women were viewed as both non-threatening and valuable for their reproductive capacity. In the modern world, however, genocidal rape is frequently followed by death. One finds examples of it in the Turkish assault on the Armenians, which included both rape/murder and abduction/rape, in Bangladesh, Bosnia, and especially Rwanda. Much of the murder comes from perpetrators who kill the women, not to escape detection of the crime, but as an expression of a thoroughly dehumanized view of the "enemy." Such hatred no doubt has many sources, but nationalism and the cynical manipulation of it to dehumanize minority groups are a major part of it.

Yet if one looks at the eyewitness accounts of such rape/murders, one is struck by how casually the women were killed. In addition to the dehumanizing effects of nationalism, there may be a callousness that particular cultures encourage toward women, who are seen as objects to be used and then disposed. Such callousness in a "normal" society takes the form of seduction, pregnancy, and abandonment, but in a genocidal society is expressed in the form of rape, followed by murder.

Death may come from another direction: genocidal rape, and the threat of rape, has led many women to take their own lives. Some do so to avoid the humiliation and degradation of rape and multiple rape, others to escape the rape forced upon them daily in detention centers and military brothels, and still others at the shame of having been violated. Many Armenian women took their own lives to avoid rape by Turks and Kurds in 1915, and some jumped with their daughters into rivers to spare both themselves and their children. Numerous women in Bangladesh took their own lives, especially where pregnancy resulted from the rapes by Pakistani soldiers. Women also died unintentionally while trying to abort the forced pregnancy: in Bangladesh, for example, many deaths resulted from girls and women accidentally lacerating their wombs. When unwanted children were born, they were usually suffocated at birth.[48]

Another consequence of genocidal rape is that the trauma inflicted is both immediate and continuing. Many women report that they wish they were killed instead of being subjected to rape and humiliation. Some speak from their pain with a voice worthy of a tragic poet:

They raped me several times ... They made my husband watch. But he swore at them – terrible names that I did not know he knew. So they killed him with bayonets. When they left I took a rope and put it round my neck to kill myself. But I heard my children cry. I took them in our cart next morning and joined a great crowd of refugees like myself. I did not speak for a week.[49]

Others simply withdraw from the world. Still others end their lives.

Another consequence should be noted, even though for the victims it leaves open only a problematic future. Irving Louis Horowitz points out that "genocide is a fundamental mechanism for the unification of the nation state."[50] Today that unification can be described as "ethnic cleansing." In Burma in 1992 alone some 300,000 of the Muslim minority were forced to flee to Bangladesh; in Bosnia millions were displaced. But this is precisely the goal of genocidal attacks accompanied by mass rape: through terror, the stronger forces the victim group to flee, and kills those who remain. The survivors are turned into a people without a homeland or the means, except for international charity, to survive. How one recreates a civil society or becomes self-governing under these conditions is far from clear.

If the consequences of genocidal rape are devastating for the victims, what are the consequences, apart from the desensitization previously noted, for those who sanction or participate in it? Our sense of justice demands that they pay a price, legal or psychological, but there is little evidence that they do. For 2,000 years, those who kept female slaves captured during war were considered men of honor. The Crusaders saw themselves as men of righteousness. No one punished the rape of Armenian women in 1915, of Bengalis in 1971, and only a handful of those who raped some 20,000 Bosnian Muslim women in 1992 were brought to justice. Nor do those who sanctioned a policy of rape or carried it out, seem to suffer from a bad conscience or emotional conflicts. One does wonder if a man who has participated in numerous gang rapes and the brutalization of women becomes similarly brutal to his wife. But we do know that a man could kill at Auschwitz and then shed tears at the music of Puccini, could be brutal during the day and a kind father and loving husband at night. We know too that former members of the SS are among the most law-abiding citizens of Germany.[51]

Yet there can be exceptions, at least in terms of law. In addition to a few persons indicted for sexual violence in the former Yugoslavia, trials that involve indictment for rape continue in Rwanda. Moreover, the first conviction under international law was handed down by the ICTR in the *Akayesu* case, which found the accused guilty of, among other things, encouraging mass rape in his official capacity as a communal leader in Rwanda. Indeed, as we shall see, the court declared that rape, with the requisite intent, was genocide under the United Nations Convention on the Prevention and Punishment of the Crime of Genocide (UNCG, or Genocide Convention).[52] Also, Pauline Nyiramasuhuko, who had been the Hutu government's minister for family welfare and the advancement of women, was indicted in 1997 for genocide, in part for her role in encouraging the rape of Tutsi women: "Before you kill the women, you need to rape them."[53] In 2011 she was convicted of genocide for a variety of acts, but the charges against her of being responsible for instigating and authorizing rape were treated, unlike those against Akayesu, as crimes against humanity and war crimes.[54]

■ MASS RAPE AS AN ACT OF GENOCIDE

A question remains. Does sustained, mass rape, accompanied by signs of intent to destroy, at least in part, a national, ethnic, racial, or religious group, constitute an act of genocide and, if so, how? If it does not, then how are we to describe systematic rape directed at members of a particular group? The issue posed is not so much a question of finding a new basis for punishing such acts (they are already punishable under international and domestic law),[55] as of understanding more fully forms of victimization that follow gender lines.

Helsinki Watch describes rape as a war crime and a crime against humanity, calling particular attention to the prohibitions in international law against "torture or inhuman treatment" and "willfully causing great suffering or serious injury to body or health." But they also state that rape, which can be "one of the crimes used as a means of carrying out genocide ... does not by itself constitute genocide, even when committed on a mass basis." And although they take specific note of the use of rape to impregnate women of the victim group, they see such acts, or the intention to commit such acts, as "an abuse separate from the rape itself."[56] A strong argument, however, can be made that under international law mass rape and forced pregnancies are not only means of furthering genocide, but are themselves acts of genocide.

The Genocide Convention (Article II) defines genocide in terms of

any of the following acts committed with intent to destroy, in whole or in part, a national, ethnical, racial or religious group, as such:

(a) Killing members of the group;
(b) Causing serious bodily or mental harm to members of the group;
(c) Deliberately inflicting on the group conditions of life calculated to bring about its physical destruction in whole or in part;
(d) Imposing measures intended to prevent births within the group;
(e) Forcibly transferring children of the group to another group.[57]

In light of this definition, Helen Fein made a persuasive case in 1992 that mass rape and forced pregnancies, when used to destroy a group in whole or in part, fall within several of the five acts defined in the UNCG as genocide.[58]

Fein argued that mass rapes are acts of genocide in at least three ways: they involve a calculated and intentional causing of serious bodily and mental harm; they are attempts to inflict upon the group conditions that will bring about its physical destruction; and through forcible impregnation, and the killing of the males of the victim group, there is an attempt to interfere with births within the group. Her argument is developed specifically with regard to Bosnia, but is of wider applicability. Each of the acts that she calls attention to is in fact part of the definition of genocide found within the Genocide Convention. And she makes sense of the behavior that Helsinki Watch documents but fails to connect specifically with genocide. What is the point of the infliction of continuing pain on members of the group? What is the point of forcing Serbian babies on Muslim women? What is the point of creating terror through rape? Are not each of these acts, and even more so together, intended to destroy a group of people, defined in terms of their religion, ethnicity, nationality, or race? Are they not, in short, acts of genocide? What Helsinki Watch, and others, have forgotten, but Fein reminds us of, is that genocide has to do with the destruction of human groups, which can be done by means in addition to mass killing, particularly genocidal rape. In fact, only one of the five acts listed in the Genocide Convention as constituting genocide actually requires that deaths take place.

Within a few years, legal, political, and judicial support was given to the main argument, that rape, under certain conditions, could constitute genocide. For example, in its 1994 "Final Report" on whether there had been violations of international humanitarian law in the former Yugoslavia, the UN Security Council's Commission of Experts declared that:

> Under the Genocide Convention, sexual assault and rape are included within the meaning of Article II of the Convention, provided that the prohibited conduct is committed as part of an "intent to destroy, in whole or in part, a national, ethnical, racial or religious group."[59]

Further, in some cases, those who do not directly participate in rape or sexual violence, can be held responsible for the violence:

> Even though sexual assaults imply the commission of the crime by a given perpetrator, persons who do not perform the act but are indirectly involved in the commission of this crime, like decision-makers and superiors, are also responsible under the Genocide Convention (Art. III) and general norms of command responsibility ... [60]

Later the Security Council adopted resolution 1820 (2008) on Women and Peace and Security, and affirmed that "rape and other forms of sexual violence can constitute a war crime, a crime against humanity, or a constitutive act with respect to genocide."[61]

The report of the Commission of Experts and the Security Council resolution suggest there is now a consensus that, where there is the requisite intent, widespread and systematic rape can be considered a means of committing genocide, understood as the destruction in whole or in part of a group defined by race, religion, nationality, or ethnicity. However, the legal basis for this view was put forward in the verdict by the International Criminal Tribunal for Rwanda in the *Akayesu* case, rendered on September 2, 1998. Jean-Paul Akayesu was the *bourgmestre* of a commune in Rwanda in which some 2,000 Tutsi were killed, and many Tutsi women raped, with the permission, even encouragement of the defendant as the commune leader. In its verdict, the Chamber (court) declared that rape and sexual violence

> constitute genocide in the same way as any other act as long as they were committed with the specific intent to destroy, in whole or in part, a particular group, targeted as such. Indeed, rape and sexual violence certainly constitute infliction of serious bodily and mental harm to the victims and are even, according

to the Chamber, one of the worst ways to inflict harm on the victim as he or she suffers both bodily and mental harm ... Sexual violence was an integral part of the process of destruction, specifically targeting Tutsi women and specifically contributing to their destruction and to the destruction of the Tutsi group as a whole.

And the Chamber concludes: "Sexual violence was a step in a process of destruction of the Tutsi group – destruction of the spirit, of the will to live, and of life itself."[62]

The Tribunal, which early in its discussion put emphasis on interference with births within the group as the act that constituted genocide, later concluded that it was serious bodily and mental harm inflicted through sexual violence that best fit the facts in this case. But as we have seen, particularly in the case of Bosnia, rape has many functions within the context of the destruction of a group. As international case law develops, sexual violence when intended to destroy a group, will most likely be declared genocide on the basis of any of the five acts listed in Article II of the Convention: direct killing, inflicting serious bodily or mental harm to members of the group, inflicting on the group conditions of life calculated to bring about its physical destruction (and I would add, social destruction), prevention of births within the group, and forcibly transferring children of the group to another group.

CONCLUSION

The victimization of women, through enslavement, rape, abduction, and forced impregnation, is a major factor in genocide, but one that has until recently gone largely unnoticed. Bosnia is for us the painful reminder of what many women from many different groups have experienced throughout history. Yet, it also pointed toward the future in that only a few years separated the genocidal rape in Bosnia from that which took place in Rwanda.

In both cases, rituals of degradation were extreme, but there were also differences in the two cases. In Rwanda the rape went on for 90 days, in Bosnia for several years; yet, those who were raped in the Rwandan genocide were more likely to be killed than those attacked in Bosnia. Unlike Bosnia, the goal of the perpetrators in Rwanda was not so much to shame the women of the "enemy" group, as to exterminate members of the group. In Bosnia family members were often forced to engage in incest, something that apparently did not happen in Rwanda: there the desire was to rape, kill, and frequently (out of resentment of the supposed coldness of Tutsi women to Hutu men) to mutilate the sexual organs of the women.[63] Yet another difference was the lack of publicity about the rapes in Rwanda. It was nearly a year after the end of the genocide that the press reported anything about the extensive, systematic, and brutal violation of women in Rwanda. Perhaps this can be explained by the reluctance of those who survived to speak out, the mass exodus of refugees and the resulting chaos, and the focus of the media on the killings themselves. But it is hard not to believe that there was a perception among those in the media that rape is just something that happens in "tribal wars" in Africa.

Finally, there seems to have been another difference. In Bosnia, many have claimed, but without offering evidence, the rapes were frequently videotaped, allowing the rape and brutalization of the women captured on film to be shown again and again, a reminder to the perpetrators of the pleasures of power and an invitation to celebrate the "shame" of those raped.[64] On the other hand, sexual imagery and crude sexual cartoons against the Tutsi were common in Rwanda and circulated freely, encouraging rape and furthering incitement to genocide.

Despite the difference, there is also convergence. Genocide is as old as history, but it was left to the late twentieth century to turn rape and genocide into a pornography in which the brutal destruction of lives, physically and morally, is a form of entertainment as well as a record of accomplishment.

NOTES

1 The pioneering study by E. Sanasarian, "Gender Distinction in the Genocidal Process: A Preliminary Study of the Armenian Case," *Holocaust and Genocide Studies* 4/4,1989, 253–5, although limited to a single case, is an excellent example of the insights that can be gained by bringing together the history of women and the history of genocide. The most sophisticated discussion to date, although limited to three cases of genocide since 1990, is that of A. Reid-Cunningham, "Rape as a Weapon of Genocide," *Genocide Studies and Prevention* 3/3, 2008, 279–96. The volume edited by A. Stiglmayer, *Mass Rape: The War Against Women in Bosnia-Herzegovina*, Lincoln: University of Nebraska Press, 1994, contains many interesting essays. B. Allen, *Rape Warfare: The Hidden Genocide in Bosnia-Herzegovina and Croatia*, Minneapolis: University of Minnesota Press, 1996, has been widely cited and it certainly calls attention to genocidal rape in a specific case, but the study is both factually and conceptually flawed. The conceptual issue is that the author splinters the notion of genocidal rape, treating forced impregnation as "germ warfare," a crime that she argues should be included in a new convention against germ warfare rather than being treated as a form of genocide. The factual issue is that she states that while rape within genocide has a long history, the Serbs created a wholly new category: forced impregnation. But as I show later in this chapter, one can see the same thing in the case of Bangladesh in 1971. For an overview of rape in the Armenian Genocide, see M. Bjornlund, "'A Fate Worse than Dying': Sexual Violence during the Armenian Genocide," in Dagmar Herzog, ed., *Brutality and Desire: War and Sexuality in Europe's Twentieth Century*, New York: Palgrave Macmillan, 2011, pp. 16–58; for an in-depth study of women in the Armenian Genocide, see the excellent study by K. Derderian, "Common Fate, Different Experience: Gender-Specific Aspects of the Armenian Genocide, 1915–1917," *Holocaust and Genocide Studies* 19/1, 2005, 1–15. See also, L. Sharlach, "Rape as Genocide: Bangladesh, the former Yugoslavia, and Rwanda," *New Political Science* 22/1, 2000, 89–102.

There are two other studies of genocidal rape that deserve a wide audience. D. Bergoffen, *Contesting the Politics of Rape: Affirming the Dignity of the Vulnerable Body*, New York and London: Routledge, 2012; and the essay by E. Von Joeden-Forgey, "Gender and Genocide," in Donald Bloxham and A. Dirk Moses, eds., *The Oxford Handbook of Genocide Studies*, Oxford: Oxford University Press, 2010, pp. 61–80. Bergoffen describes the development of international law in recent years against the crime of rape, now seen as a crime, not against the "modesty of women," but as a crime against humanity. She also provides a philosophical account of the human right to sexual integrity. Joeden-Forgey's essay provides an excellent survey of the few studies that view genocide through a gender based approach. Her main contention is that "Gender can help us see that genocide is, in its most basic form, a crime against the generative power of a group and the institutions that support it, especially the family" (p. 78). Her focus, however, seems to be on physical reproduction; social reproduction is ignored.

Three valuable books on genocidal rape in Rwanda in 1994 are: Human Rights Watch, *Shattered Lives: Sexual Violence During the Rwandan Genocide and Its Aftermath*, New York: Human Rights Watch, 1996; Africa Rights, *Rwanda: Death, Despair and Defiance*, London: African Rights, 1995, ch. 7; and A. de Brouwer and S. Chu, *The Men Who Killed Me: Rwandan Survivors of Sexual Violence*, Vancouver, Canada: Douglas & McIntyre, 2009. An earlier version of my essay, now significantly revised and updated, was presented under its current title to the "Remembering for the Future" International Conference on the Holocaust and Genocide, Humboldt State University, Berlin, March 13–17, 1994.

Rape is also widely used as a means of social control and repression by governments as varied as India and Iraq. On India's use of rape to coerce and intimidate, see the report by Asia Watch and Physicians for Human Rights, *Rape in Kashmir: A Crime of War*, May 9, 1993. In Iraq, there were members of the bureaucracy whose *official* job description was "Violation of Women's Honor." See K. Makiya, *Cruelty and Silence: War, Tyranny, Uprising and the Arab World*, New York: W. W. Norton, 1993, p. 287.

2 Book of Numbers, *The Bible: Authorized King James Version*, Oxford: Oxford University Press, 1997, ch. 31.

3 T. Todorov, *The Conquest of America: The Question of the Other*, New York: Harper & Row, 1984, p. 246.

4 D. Davies, *The Last of the Tasmanians*, New York: Barnes & Noble, 1974, pp. 60–1, 69.

5 S. Brownmiller, *Against Our Will: Men, Women, and Rape*, New York: Fawcett Columbine, 1993, pp. 78–86.

6 *New York Times*, January 18, 1972, p. 7; March 5, 1972, p. 8; and May 12, 1972, p. 2.

7 G. Perl, *I Was a Doctor in Auschwitz*, New York: Arno, 1979, pp. 61–2.

8 The Nazis also attacked non-Jewish Polish and Ukrainian women as mothers, kidnapping their children when these were deemed to be of "good racial type" and incorporating the children into German society. Moreover, had their techniques for mass sterilization worked and Germany won the war, the Nazis would have launched another attack on woman as mother, using the healing arts of medicine to prevent births among the "sub-humans" except where this would have served the interests of the master race.

9 See R. Smith, " Women and Genocide: Notes on an Unwritten History," *Holocaust and Genocide Studies* 8/3, 1984, 315–34.

10 Brownmiller, *Against Our Will*, pp. 14–15.

11 Ibid., p. 37.

12 Helsinki Watch, *War Crimes in Bosnia-Hercegovina*, New York: Human Rights Watch, 1993, vol. 2, pp. 21–2.

13 K. Roy, "Feelings and Attitudes of Raped Women of Bangladesh Towards Military Personnel of Pakistan," in Israel Drapkin and Emilio Viano, eds., *Victimology: A New Focus, Vol. V, Exploiters and Exploited: The Dynamics of Victimization*, Lexington, MA: Lexington Books (D.C. Heath and Company), 1975, p. 65.

14 On the Rohingya, see E. Mirante, "Burma's Ethnic Minority Women: From Abuse to Resistance," in Cultural Survival, *State of the Peoples: A Global Human Rights Report on Societies in Danger*, Boston, MA: Beacon Press, 1993, ch. 7.

15 D. Miller and L. Miller, *Survivors: An Oral History of the Armenian Genocide*, Berkeley, CA: University of California Press, 1993, p. 110.

16 J. Laber, "Bosnia: Questions About Rape," *New York Review of Books* XL/6, 1993, p. 4.

17 For an overview of the debate between "intentionalists" and "functionalists," see M. Marrus, *The Holocaust in History*, Hanover, NH: University Press of New England, 1987, ch. 3. On destructiveness as social process, see N. Sanford and C. Comstock, eds., *Sanctions for Evil: Sources of Social Destructiveness*, San Francisco, CA: Jossey-Bass, 1971.

18 See, for example, the United Nations Security Council report by its Commission of Experts, May 27, 1994, S/1994/674, para. 104.

19 On the different types of genocide, see H. Fein, "Genocide: A Sociological Perspective," *Current Sociology* 38/1 1993, 28–31; and R. Smith, "Human Destructiveness and Politics: The Twentieth Century as an Age of Genocide," in Isidor Wallimann and Michael N. Dobkowski, eds., *Genocide and the Modern Age: Etiology and Case Studies of Mass Death*, Westport, CT: Greenwood Press, 1987, pp. 23–7.

   E. Wood, "Variation in Sexual Violence During War," *Politics and Society* 34/3, 2006, 307–41, does not deal with rape and genocide, but does document the wide variations in the frequency and form of sexual violations during war. In the end, she offers only a few "hypotheses" about why the variations occur, focusing on the armed unit, the small unit, and the individual. There is limited discussion of the policy process and how it affects sexual violence. And since genocide is not addressed, the author is unable to compare the functions and goals, as well as origins, of rape during genocide with those in war.

20 S. Brownmiller, *Against Our Will*, p. 38.

21 E. Staub, *The Roots of Evil: The Origins of Genocide and Other Mass Violence*, Cambridge: Cambridge University Press, 1989, pp. 17–18, 79–88; and E. Staub, "The Psychology and Culture of Torture and Torturers," in Peter Suedfeld, ed., *Psychology and Torture*, New York: Hemisphere Publishing Corporation, 1990, pp. 64–6.

22 See P. Suedfeld, "Torture: A Brief Overview," in P. Suedfeld, ed., *Psychology and Torture*, p. 4.

23 Report of "Fatima," a Bosnian Muslim, in Laber, "Bosnia, Questions About Rape," p. 3.

24 *New York Times*, March 31, 1993, p. A6.

25 The discussion of rape in Bosnia is based upon the reports in Helsinki Watch, *War Crimes in Bosnia-Hercegovina*, II, pp. 20–3, 163–86, 214–20, 228–34, 242–56, and 344–5; Amnesty International, *Bosnia-Herzegovina: Rape and Sexual Abuse by Armed Forces*, New York: Amnesty International, 1993; United States Department of State, *Dispatch* 3/46, November 16, 1992; A. Stiglmayer, ed., *Mass Rape: The War against Women in Bosnia-Hercegovina and Croatia*, Lincoln: University of Nebraska Press, 1994; and various accounts in the press, particularly the report in the *New York Times*, January 9, 1993, pp. 1, 4. It was Roy Gutman's article based on interviews with twenty rape victims in former Yugoslavia that brought the issue of genocidal rape before the public. See his report in *New York Newsday*, August 23, 1992, pp. 7, 39.

26 L. Kuper, *Genocide: Its Political Use in the Twentieth Century*, New Haven, CT: Yale University Press, 1982, p. 104.

27 C. Mackinnon, "Turning Rape into Pornography: Postmodern Genocide," *Ms.* IV/I, 1993, p. 27.

28 *American Heritage Dictionary of the English Language*, Boston: American Heritage Publishing Company and Houghton-Mifflin Company, 1969, p. 1152.

29 C. Mackinnon, "Turning Rape into Pornography," p. 29.

30 Helsinki Watch, *War Crimes in Bosnia-Hercegovina*, II, pp. 169, 253–5.

31 Ibid., pp. 214–15.

32 Ibid., p. 251.

33 Ibid., p. 218.

34 L. Kolakowski, *Modernity on Endless Trial*, Chicago: University of Chicago Press, 1990, p. 258.

35 Report of Lyudmila Grigirevna M. in S. Shahmuratian, ed., *The Sumgait Tragedy: Pogroms Against Armenians in Soviet Azerbaijan, vol. 1: Eyewitness Accounts*, New Rochelle, NY and Cambridge, MA: Aristide D. Caratzas and Zoryan Institute, 1989, p. 127.

36 Helsinki Watch, *War Crimes in Bosnia-Hercegovina*, II, p. 164.

37 Ibid., p. 215.

38 Ibid., p. 219.

39 United States Department of State, *Dispatch* 3/46, November 16, 1992, p. 830.

40 Bryce, Viscount, *The Treatment of the Armenians in the Ottoman Empire, 1915–16: Documents Presented to Viscount Grey of Fallodon, Secretary of State for Foreign Affairs by Viscount Bryce*, compiled by Arnold Toynbee, London: HMSO, 1916, document 24, p. 92.

41 Ibid., document 35, p. 161.

42 A. Roy, "Feelings and Attitudes of Raped Women of Bangladesh Towards Military Personnel of Pakistan," p. 66.

43 Numbers 31. This account cannot be accepted as accurate historical description, but it does indicate how genocide was imagined in the twelfth century BCE. See, R. Smith, "Women and Genocide," pp 316–19. On the dating of the account, see J. Milgrom, "Numbers, Book of," *The Anchor Bible Dictionary*, New York: Doubleday, 1992, vol. 4, p. 1149. Whether there was a prohibition against intercourse with a girl who had not reached puberty is unclear. Numbers 31 lays out in detail how the virgins are to be "distributed," but is silent on the question of intercourse with children.

44 Davies, *The Last of the Tasmanians*, pp. 26, 52, 60.

45 Bryce, *The Treatment of the Armenians in the Ottoman Empire, 1915–16*, document 35, p. 161.

46 *New York Times*, January 18, 1972, p. 7; March 8, 1972, p. 8; Roy, "Feelings and Attitudes of Raped Women of Bangladesh Towards Military Personnel of Pakistan," pp. 70–1.

47 Sanasarian, "Gender Distinction in the Genocidal Process: A Preliminary Study of the Armenian Case," pp. 253–5.

48 A. Roy, "Feelings and Attitudes of Raped Women of Bangladesh Towards Military Personnel of Pakistan," p. 71.

49 A. Menen, "The Rapes of Bangladesh," *New York Times Magazine*, July 23, 1972, p. 24.

50 I. Horowitz, *Taking Lives: Genocide and State Power*, 3rd edition, New Brunswick, NJ: Transaction Books, 1980, pp. 189–90.

51 J. Steiner, "The SS Yesterday and Today: A Sociopsychological View," in Joel E. Dimsdale, ed., *Survivors, Victims, and Perpetrators: Essays on the Nazi Holocaust*, New York: Hemisphere Publishing Corporation, 1980, p. 441.

52 International Criminal Tribunal for Rwanda, *Prosecutor* v. *Jean-Paul Akayesu*, case no. ICTR-96-T, September 1998.

53 P. Landesman, "The Minister of Rape," *New York Times Magazine*, September 15, 2002, pp. 82–9, 116, 125, 130–4; the quotation is on p. 84.

54 *New York Times*, June 25, 2011, A4.

55 For a discussion of rape and sexual violence as an element of genocide in the law, see the chapter by Sheri Rosenberg and Everita Silina in this volume.

56 Helsinki Watch, *War Crimes in Bosnia-Hercegovina*, II, pp. 20–2.

57 United Nations Convention on the Prevention and Punishment of Genocide. UN General Assembly resolution 260 (III) (December 9, 1948). Full text available at: www.un.org/ga/search/view_doc.asp?symbol=a/res/260(III). Accessed June 23, 2012.

58 Helen Fein, *The ISG Newsletter* 9, Fall 1992, p. 5; and *The ISG Newsletter* 10, Spring 1993, p. 8. A few years later and using reasoning similar to Fein's, Siobhan K. Fisher

made a strong case for considering forced impregnation, where the intent was to destroy a group in whole or in part, as genocide. See her study, S. Fisher, "Occupation of the Womb: Forced Impregnation as Genocide," *Duke Law Journal* 46/1, 1996, 91–133. Fisher's approach with regard to rape as genocide was narrow: her article never mentions the ways that rape, apart from forced impregnation, can also fit within a framework of genocide. Such exclusions have no basis in reason or experience; international law as it has developed in recent years does not make them.

59 Security Council, Final Report of the Commission of Experts Established Pursuant to Security Council resolution 780 (1992), May 27, 1994 S/1994/674, para. 107.

60 Ibid., para. 104.

61 Security Council resolution 1820 (2008), D/Res/1820 (2008), p. 3.

62 *Prosecutor* v. *Akayesu*, case no. ICTR-96-4-T, September 1998, paras 731 and 732.

63 D. Bergoffen, *Contesting the Politics of Rape: Affirming the Dignity of the Vulnerable Body*, pp. 52–8.

64 MacKinnon speaks of all this, but, surely errs in suggesting that the films were shown in public. The prosecutors at The Hague were never able to find any credible witnesses to such broadcasts. See C. MacKinnon, "Turning Rape into Pornography: Postmodern Genocide," pp. 27–30.

CHAPTER 6

Genocide by Attrition
Silent and efficient
Sheri P. Rosenberg and Everita Silina[*]

> He did not need bullets. He used other weapons: rapes, hunger, and fear. As efficient, but silent.
>
> (Luis Moreno-Ocampo, First Prosecutor of the International Criminal Court, regarding his application for a Warrant of Arrest of Sudanese President Omar Hassan al Bashir for the crime of genocide in Darfur)[1]

Definitions function to make the world and relations within it more ordered and predictable. The 1948 United Nations Convention on the Prevention and Punishment of the Crime of Genocide ("Genocide Convention") defines genocide as:

> Any of the following acts committed with intent to destroy, in whole or in part, a national, ethnical, racial or religious group, as such:
>
> (a) Killing members of the group;
> (b) Causing serious bodily or mental harm to members of the group;
> (c) Deliberately inflicting on the group conditions of life calculated to bring about its physical destruction in whole or in part;
> (d) Imposing measures intended to prevent births within the group;
> (e) Forcibly transferring children of the group to another group.[2]

The Genocide Convention defines genocide not only as immediate physical destruction but also as acts that create conditions that lead to physical destruction, including inflicting physical and mental harm, and measures intended to arrest procreation. Thus, attenuated and indirect methods of genocide are contemplated, acknowledging that genocide is a complex phenomenon that cannot be reduced to direct mass murder.

Nonetheless, many people conceive of genocide primarily as direct mass murder, with Auschwitz and stockpiles of machetes remaining the predominant images of genocide. There are a number of reasons for this perception. First, is the very success of the legal codification of "genocide".

The legal understanding of genocide subjects each scenario to a rigid test in order to maintain the integrity of the term and to determine the criminal nature of the event and individual culpability. In particular, a legal determination of genocide requires a high threshold of proof concerning a specific intent to commit the crime. Requiring proof of a deliberate plan and individual culpability imposes strict limits on cases that qualify as genocide, and by definition will require accumulation of such proof after the fact. Though the Convention calls upon member states to *prevent* and punish the crime, the strict legal analysis makes early identification impossible and prevention a moot point.

Second, as Martin Shaw notes, the Holocaust is often treated as the paradigmatic case determining the definition of what counts as genocide.[3] The resulting ad hoc comparisons between the Holocaust and any other case more often than not "tend to reproduce a narrow *exterminatory* conception" of genocide.[4] The interpretation of Nazi crimes as an unleashing of murderous violence that swiftly annihilated large numbers of victims has obscured the more complex and messy nature of the genocidal process that took place during the Holocaust. For example, approximately 13.7 percent of all Jewish Holocaust victims died as a result of disease and starvation due to their confinement in ghettoes, *prior* to their deportation to extermination camps.[5] The emphasis on strict legalism in genocide interpretation coupled with the conceptual linking of genocide with a particular understanding of the Holocaust have imposed a restrictive reading of the Genocide Convention. This perceived rigidity has led those witnessing developing crises and unfolding violence in today's complex international arena to search for a more flexible term that would nevertheless maintain the emotional and conceptual force of the genocide label. Thus, to capture what, according to some, is a genocidal process slowly unfolding in Darfur, Sudan, the term "genocide by attrition" has entered the lexicon of genocide discourse. Colloquially, the term refers to a slow-moving genocide. Though the term is bandied about with some frequency in the press and among policy makers and academics, there has been little attempt to provide it with a theoretical, legal, or conceptual foundation.

This chapter seeks to fill that gap by conceptualizing the term "genocide by attrition" in its legal and historical context and establishing its value as a descriptive tool for use in the prevention agenda. We argue that genocide by attrition refers to the slow process of annihilation that reflects the unfolding phenomenon of mass murder of a protected group, rather than the immediate unleashing of violence and death. The methods of genocide by attrition describe state and non-state policies and practices that deprive individuals of a specific set of human rights that do not cause immediate death, but rather lead to the slow and steady destruction of the group. These methods include, but are not limited to, forced displacement, denial of health and healthcare, denial of food, and sexual violence. Although the use of the term is relatively recent, we argue neither for a new typology or definition of genocide nor an expansion of the Genocide Convention. As will be explored further below, genocide by attrition is already contemplated in the Convention.

The chapter is an attempt to bridge an interdisciplinary divide between the legal community and political (and other social) sciences. The former are usually interested in establishing a clear legal definition because fundamental principles of law, and criminal law in particular, require that crimes be defined with precision as a matter of fairness to individuals who must be forewarned about the possible illegality of their actions. Political scientists view definitions and conceptual debates as useful tools for establishing some parameters for admissible cases and for elucidating the links between structures and agency. These in turn are crucial for building generalizable models that can explain the causal links between a set of variables and the observed phenomenon. This chapter attempts to strike a balance between the two sets of concerns: a fidelity to definitional precision balanced with the flexibility necessary to apprehend the fluid and chaotic reality of genocidal processes and the contexts within which they emerge.

The first section proposes a theoretical foundation and framework for the concept of genocide by attrition as a process, rather than as a discretely demarcated event of mass murder. The second section provides an overview of specific international human rights violations that often constitute the methods of genocide by attrition: forced displacement, the denial of health and healthcare, the denial of food (famine and malnutrition), and sexual violence. These methods are reviewed in the context of a series of historical case studies, which were selected because of the broad international consensus regarding their designation as genocide or politicide (the targeting of political groups for destruction): Ottoman Empire (May–August 1915), Cambodia (1975–9), Ukraine (1932–3), Warsaw Ghetto (1940–43), Bosnia-Herzegovina (1992–5), and Darfur, Sudan (2003–present).[6] In the final section we present a series of tentative recommendations to the humanitarian and policy communities for improving our ability to identify and prevent mass atrocity crimes.

IDENTIFYING GENOCIDE BY ATTRITION

Genocide is a complex process

Eric Reeves, who has closely monitored the situation in Darfur, Sudan, observed in 2005 that "[s]ometime in the Summer of 2004 (we will never know precisely when), genocidal destruction became more a matter of engineered disease and malnutrition than violent killing,"[7] as "there came a point … in which ongoing genocide was no longer primarily a result of direct slaughter, but of a cruel attrition."[8] He has been the most insistent supporter of the position that what we are witnessing in Darfur is a genocide by attrition[9] or what Nicholas D. Kristof and Gerard Prunier among others describe as "genocide in slow motion" or "killing by attrition."[10] Likewise, a number of news media outlets freely describe the situation in Darfur as genocide by attrition or genocide in slow motion.[11] Though rich in detail these accounts shy away from offering a definition or a conceptual map for what they are describing, leaving the term emotionally loaded but under-theorized. More importantly, they fail to draw the link between the many nuanced accounts of subtle shifts in methods and motivations and accumulating human rights abuses, and the complex nature of the genocidal process that is unfolding. It is this link between human rights violations and resulting mass deaths that elucidates the complex nature of the genocidal process. What we offer below is an articulation of the concept of genocide by attrition in its legal and historical context.

Many unfolding genocides have gone unrecognized because each death or massacre was treated as if it were a photograph, a snapshot, frozen in time, to be compared singularly to the definition of genocide. Emphasis on violent deaths and direct murder established genocide as a clearly demarcated and discrete event of mass killing.[12] Genocide by attrition is based on the premise that genocides are far more complex phenomena. The concept draws attention to the slow process of annihilation that reflects the unfolding of mass murder rather than the immediate unleashing of violence and death upon a targeted group. It is a long-term process that might take months or years.

Raphael Lemkin presented such a long-term view of the phenomenon:

> Generally speaking, genocide does not necessarily mean the immediate destruction of a nation, except when accomplished by mass killings of all members of a nation. It is intended rather to signify a coordinated plan of different actions aiming at the destruction of essential foundations of the life of national groups, with the aim of annihilating the groups themselves. The objectives of such a plan would be the disintegration of political and social institutions, of culture, language, national feelings, religion, and the economic existence of national groups, and the destruction of the personal security, liberty, health, dignity, and even the lives of the individuals belonging to such groups.[13]

Martin Shaw writes that this understanding of genocide as a process was captured in the Genocide Convention,[14] while Helen Fein originally coined "genocide by attrition" in order to describe the link between human rights violations and mass death that she observed in the historic cases of the Warsaw Ghetto, Cambodia and Sudan, in order to connect the denial of food, housing, or health maintenance with their final outcome – the dismissal of the right to life.[15] Understanding genocide as a process clarifies the relationship between the contextual factors, the various attributes of attrition and the resultant mass deaths. Throughout the process of genocide, the intent remains the same: to exterminate an unwanted group of people.

While many studies of twentieth-century genocide focus on the historical analysis of mass murder in specific cases, an increasing number of authors are taking the broader view of genocide as a process and exploring the causal contexts of genocides by analyzing structures of government, political systems, and relevant socio-economic, cultural, historical, and environmental factors, as well as general "stages" through which the genocidal process runs.[16]

Though these "stages" are broad enough to encompass most genocides, a single prototypical process of genocide does not exist. Genocide is a flexible concept that may not follow one particular developmental path. Rather, there are various types of processes of genocide that unfold based on their own particular internal logics. These differences across cases may include technological sophistication, various geographical conditions and concentration of victims, bureaucratic efficiency, and the threat of reciprocal violence by the victims. The linear models are based on discrete causal relationships that unfold into mass killings. With the notion of a complex process of attrition, one does not have to wait for the process to unfold to know that genocide is underway. Two factors foster this advantage: first, the model of the process of attrition is derived deductively from historical case studies; second, the mere presence of attributes indicates the *process* may be underway. Our model recognizes that there is no single attribute that moves through all the cases or "stages" of genocide, but rather there are a cluster of attributes that, after a tipping point, trigger an epic narrative of genocide.

Empirical evidence from the historical cases of genocide discussed herein points to a set of attributes suggesting several tentative conclusions about the genocidal process. First, indirect forms of mass killing play a much more important role in the genocidal process than is suggested by the linear models. Second, indirect methods of annihilation may occur at different points within the process and/or may reflect a coalescing, collapsing or rapid accumulation of "stages." The emergence of any one attribute should prompt investigation of the surrounding context. Although a situation may not have reached some kind of definitional milestone, it may still be dire. Most importantly, the view of genocide as a process of attrition rescues it from the restrictive demands imposed upon the term by the legal determinations of culpability, and recommends action long before the courts have been convened to establish if genocide has occurred.

It is crucial to emphasize that while the Genocide Convention provides a legal definition, it does not require or impose such a strict understanding of the concept. The Genocide Convention's definition can be given a more relaxed reading if we resist seeing it as specifying a legal determination of genocide and if we avoid focusing on separate elements and instead look at the Convention as a coherent whole. This strategy would require us to pay as much attention to the genocidal acts of causing *serious* bodily or mental *harm*, inflicting on the group *conditions of life* calculated to bring about its physical destruction, and *imposing measures* intended to prevent births, as we do to *killing*. If we focus on these aspects of the Convention (rather than only direct killing and deliberate intent) we can see an opening for a more nuanced and complex conception of genocide. Indeed, the drafters of the Convention had a much broader and complex understanding of genocide than what has been captured by the focus on mass executions. For example, Article 2(c) of the Genocide Convention was drafted, in part, *as a response* to the deplorable, deadly conditions to which the Jews were subjected in the Warsaw Ghetto.[17]

Interpreting genocide as a complex process of attrition draws attention to the link between direct and indirect means of annihilation and reveals the interdependence between the series of human rights violations that create conditions of life that bring about physical destruction and eventual mass deaths. This interdependence is already recognized in the international legal regime. Together, the Genocide

Convention, international human rights treaties, conventions, jurisprudence, and customary international law constitute a single overarching system of law.[18] The notion of genocide by attrition and the full meaning of the Genocide Convention itself are best understood in the context of similar or identical prohibitions found throughout international human rights law.

Identifying intent in an attrition scenario

The *sine qua non* of genocide is the perpetrator's intent to destroy the group. Without that intent, an extraordinary crime may be committed, but it is not the crime of genocide. The question for our purpose is whether – and if so, how – attritional elements of the crime of genocide can be established in advance of the culmination of the crime in order to aid in prevention (and prosecution).

Establishing the requisite level of intent is the central dilemma of genocide identification, prevention, and prosecution. The source of the conceptual complexity is manifold. It ranges from the diverging conceptions of the relevance and scope of intent by the drafters of the Convention, to the incomplete fit between national and international criminal law conceptions of intent, because in mass atrocities, the individual's culpability is assessed in the context of what is an essentially collective crime.[19] Two distinct approaches to the definition of the crime itself animated the debates among Convention drafters. Some state representatives argued that genocide should be limited to acts taken with the sole *purpose* of destroying the group. Others argued that the crime is committed if the individual acted with knowledge that her actions would lead to the destruction of the group, regardless of a specific purpose to bring about that destruction. With no clear resolution, the Convention itself does not set forth a particular approach, other than to require some level of intent. As the jurisprudence reveals, the tribunals seek to strike a balance, leaving the debate unresolved.

The concept of intent is based in criminal law where, in order to find an individual guilty of a crime, a prosecutor must establish both that an individual actually committed the criminal act of which he is accused (the *actus reus* – the material element of the crime) and that such an individual acted with the intent to commit the crime (the *mens rea* – the mental element).

The Genocide Convention requires that the *acts* of genocide enumerated in Article 2 (the *actus reus*) must be "committed with intent to destroy, in whole or in part, a national, ethnical, racial or religious group, as such" (the *mens rea*). In concrete terms, for any act to constitute genocide, it must have been committed against a member of a particular racial, religious, ethnic or national group, specifically *because* of their membership in that group, with the *intent to destroy* that group, in whole or in part. The International Criminal Tribunal for the Former Yugoslavia (ICTY) and the International Criminal Tribunal for Rwanda (ICTR) have interpreted the phrase "intent to destroy" as requiring the particular level of intent known as "special/specific intent," or *dolus specialis*,[20] in which the accused *deliberately* desired the prohibited act he committed to result in the destruction, in whole or in part, of a protected group.

The "specific intent" requirement has proved difficult to apply in the international criminal law context as a conceptual and evidentiary matter because of the inherently collective nature of the crime of genocide. Thus, it is a conceptual challenge to ascribe to individuals acting within the web of activities that comprise genocide, a specific mental desire to take an isolated action in pursuit of destroying a group, as such. Identifying personal animus to destroy a group in the web of interests that compel persons to act during genocide, including narrow opportunistic interests of personal gain, random rogue acts of cruelty, or personal acts of revenge, appears a fiction. Thus, in its quest to find individual specific intent, jurists have been forced to place in the background the "dynamic and diverse sources" of mass atrocity.[21]

Nonetheless, specific intent remains the key element of the crime of genocide. The conceptual and evidentiary burdens, however, are lessened with the tribunals' appeal to circumstantial evidence. International tribunals have concurred that genocidal intent is inferable from the general context in which an act of genocide was committed.[22] The tribunals' appeal to context utilizes an inherently retrospective lens, viewing individual acts through the prism of the past, including repetition of acts, gravity of acts and sense of an overarching plan.

Identifying the high level of *mens rea* required for a criminal prosecution is neither required nor possible pre-emptively due to the gradually unfolding nature of genocide. In particular, those actions that indirectly lead to the destruction of the group do not fit neatly into the criminal accountability paradigm. While the goals of prosecution and prevention differ, the legal appeal to *context* during prosecutions is similarly useful for prevention when we have a nuanced appreciation of the attritional elements of the genocidal process. In the prevention context, incoming information relating to the intent of the actors should be approached through an analysis of the process of genocide, rather than the outcome of the process; that is, through an analysis of the structures and agents that pursue genocidal plans rather than on individual actions that make up the legal crime. Gross human rights violations take time to develop and they leave behind a pattern of abuse or neglect that is sanctioned by human agency.[23] Conceptualizing the process of genocide as those policies and practices which deprive individuals of a specific set of human rights that do not cause the immediate death of an individual, but rather lead to the slow and steady destruction of a group, foregrounds and provides the context in which intention can be identified for the purpose of engagement at as early a stage as possible.

The focus on the indirect actions that comprise genocide engages the question of state agency (in its various capacities) from the start. This elucidates the obscured relationship between the victims, the perpetrators and the crime's enablers; that is, between the crime of genocide and the vague authority behind it.

The means employed to bring about mass deaths by forced displacement, or the denial of access to food, water, shelter, healthcare, medicine, or security, hint at government complicity and suggest a particular policy preference, but rarely provide a "smoking gun." Moreover, in the modern era of heightened international media attention to humanitarian crises, *genocidaires* have an incentive to use covert, indirect methods to conceal their intentions from international courts and the world at large.

Thus, to establish the intent to eliminate a group of people we have to weave together various discrete events and examine them against a specific context. For example, the forced displacement and confinement of Jews inside the Warsaw Ghetto was presented by the Nazi authorities as a salutary preventive measure, taken to protect the public health or prevent an outbreak of typhus among the population at large. The eliminatory intention of the Nazi leadership emerges after consideration of the contextual circumstances leading up to the Ghetto's creation and population, including the nature of Nazi antisemitism, Hitler's statements regarding his plans for the Jews, and most importantly to this chapter, the act of *confining* the ghetto Jews in a known-to-be deadly environment and refusing them exit. Such a conclusion can be drawn after a broad analysis of the scattered origins of a single event. Indeed a single death has exposed the consistency and predictability in the perpetrators' behavior and illuminated the patterns behind seemingly random or un-coordinated acts of brutality or confinement. It is from this pattern, this unfolding narrative, that the requisite level of intent in any genocide investigation may be inferred.

THE METHODS OF GENOCIDE BY ATTRITION

The attritional attributes of genocide have been deduced primarily from several historic cases that have been generally recognized as genocides. They are: the Ottoman Empire (May–August 1915), Cambodia (1975–9), Ukraine (1932–3), Warsaw Ghetto (1940–43), Bosnia-Herzegovina (1992–5), Rwanda (1994), and Darfur, Sudan (2003–present). The methods of attrition have long played a central role in facilitating mass murder and they have all been proscribed under international human rights law since the 1960s. In each case studied at least two or more elements presented themselves.

Forced displacement

Like other human rights violations, forced displacement can serve as either a warning sign of a potential genocide or as an element of genocide in progress. Forced displacements, sometimes begun under the cover of "non-deadly" national or social "restructuring," generally create an insecure environment in which other eliminatory acts flourish. The starvation in the Warsaw Ghetto, the dire conditions of Darfurian refugee camps, and the crimes of sexual violence that plagued Bosnia-Herzegovina only occurred once people were expelled from their towns and confined to situations of decreased resources and increased exposure to deadly conditions, whether human or natural. Indeed, in some cases all pretext is dispensed with and forced deportations and marches are utilized in and of themselves as instruments of murder. Even after the forced removals cease, their effects continue in what Adam Jones calls "a permanent post-genocide arrangement."[24] Those few who do survive are too traumatized by the brutality of the displacement process to ever consider returning to the territory from which they were expelled.

Forced displacement under international law

Internal displacement is not new in the catalogue of human sufferings. International law, however, has been slow to recognize the particularities of this type of human rights violation. Unlike refugees, who have by definition crossed a national border, internally displaced persons (IDPs) remain under the jurisdiction of the officials of the state who forced them from their homes in the first instance. As a result the risk of abuse to IDPs is particularly acute in generally insecure environments. Grounded in independent international law, the *Guiding Principles on Internal Displacement* ("the Principles") were introduced in 1998.[25] The Principles place a positive obligation upon states to "prevent and avoid conditions that might lead to displacement of persons"[26] and recognize that all internally displaced persons have a "compelling need for international human rights protection"[27] as they are at a high risk of being deprived of such basic rights as security, healthcare, food and work, and of being subjected to forced labor and sexual violence.[28] Principle 10 recognizes the role that forced displacement plays in a genocide and calls specifically for the protection of IDPs from genocide.[29]

More recently, the ICTR and the ICTY have recognized forced displacement as part of some genocidal processes. In *Prosecutor* v. *Krstic*, the ICTY noted that, inasmuch as forced displacement was "a means of advancing the genocidal plan," it fell within the category of culpable acts systematically directed against a group from which genocidal intent may be inferred.[30] While occurring prior to the establishment of the tribunals, the deportations of the Armenian population during the Ottoman Empire illustrate the use of forced displacement as a tool of mass annihilation.

When the Ottoman Empire entered World War I on the side of the Central Powers, its policy toward the Armenian minority veered from distrust to displacement and elimination. Echoing the policies and techniques of an earlier massacre in 1895, the 1915 displacement policy began with raids that destroyed homes, shops, and entire villages, leaving Armenians homeless and subject to arrest, torture, and political exile. Leading local town figures were accused of treason and then arrested, tortured, forced to sign confessions and executed. In April 1915 Ottoman authorities began the removal of some 2 million ethnic Armenians from Anatolia, the central region of the empire. "Under cover of darkness, on April 25, several hundred Armenian men – intellectuals, journalists, professionals, businessmen, clergymen – were taken from their homes and shot."[31] Those who were not killed *in situ* were forcibly expelled from their homes and cities of residence and deported to the Syrian desert in the south. On May 27, 1915, the government passed the "Temporary Law of Deportation," which authorized the deportation of "persons suspected of treason or sedition," namely, the vast majority of Ottoman Armenians.[32] The order gave women and children as little as three days in which to organize their effects and leave.[33] The men were forced to leave immediately and were shot outside of the towns.[34]

As deportations stretched over hundreds of miles, they became death marches, survived by only one-quarter of the deportees.[35] Hundreds of thousands died as a result of starvation, disease, exposure to the harsh Syrian desert and attacks by

Turkish soldiers and highway bandits. Between May and August 1915, approximately 1.2 million Armenians, almost a half of the pre-war Armenian population, "disappeared" from the Ottoman Empire in a gradual but coordinated process of attrition.[36]

The denial of health and healthcare

Though attritional acts of genocide are all essentially manufactured health crises, the *denial of the right to health* stands on its own as a distinct method of genocide. For the purpose of this study, the denial of the right to health and healthcare refers to a *denial* or *withdrawal* of *access* to healthcare and medicine, the introduction or fostering of viral pathogens, disease entities and biological agents to alter human health in order to bring about the destruction of a group of people, as well as the non-active, though intentional, "purposeful neglect" of dire public health situations.

International law of the right to healthcare

The right to health is firmly established in international law. Though international law does not require governments to provide universal healthcare, states must work toward realizing and fulfilling the enjoyment of the right and must ensure that the application of the right is non-discriminatory. Together the Universal Declaration of Human Rights (UDHR) and the International Covenant on Economic, Social and Cultural Rights (ICESCR) provide the baseline healthcare requirements in international law and a starting point from which to analyze critical human health crises. They also serve to pinpoint particular policies that may violate the obligations states have to provide universal *access* to medical and healthcare and also to *create the conditions* to provide for good health.

Particularly relevant to the concept of genocide by attrition, General Comment no. 14 to ICESCR Article 12(1) extends the right of timely and appropriate healthcare to include health-related requirements such as "access to safe and potable water and adequate sanitation, an adequate supply of safe food, nutrition and housing, healthy occupational and environmental conditions …"[37] These "underlying determinants" of good health must be available in sufficient quantity, and they must be accessible without discrimination, especially to the most vulnerable or marginalized sections of the population. Additionally, the ICTR has held that purposeful denial of available medicines or essential medical services, below the minimum requirements of survival, to a protected victim-group constitute acts of genocide under Article 2(c) of the Genocide Convention.[38]

When a state produces a healthcare crisis, it is particularly difficult to identify genocidal intent because the provision of healthcare varies widely from state to state and is highly resource dependent. But any inquiry into "genocidal intent" when a group is suffering a severe healthcare crisis can be simplified by the recognition that intent is inferable from the socio-historical context of a crisis as seen through the lens of all states' international human rights obligations. This precise point is illustrated by a review of Cambodia under the Khmer Rouge.

Starting in 1975 the Khmer Rouge undertook a systematic restructuring of Cambodian society. Drawing in part from Andre Gunder Frank's Marxist theory that "cities are parasitic on the countryside, that only labor value is true value, that cities extract surplus value from the rural areas,"[39] the Khmer Rouge expelled entire populations from Cambodia's cities, including the sick, crippled, and hospitalized. In Phnom Penh the entire population plus refugees, some 3 million people, were forcibly evacuated.[40] The mandatory evacuation policy took place with a lack of regard for food, health, or hygiene. Western observers reported witnessing a parade of hospital patients who were

> pushed along the road in their beds by relatives, the intravenous bottles still attached to the bed frames. In some hospitals, foreign doctors were ordered to abandon their patients in mid-operation [...] thousands died along the route, the wounded from loss of blood, the weak from exhaustion, and others by execution, usually because they had not been quick enough to obey a Khmer Rouge order.

Those who managed to survive the trek to the countryside were

> settled in villages and agricultural communes all around Cambodia and were put to work for frantic sixteen or seventeen hour days [...] Many died from dysentery or malaria, others from malnutrition, having been forced to survive on a condensed-milk can of rice every two days.[41]

In total, the Khmer Rouge claimed to have deported approximately 4,200,000 people. Most died as a result of the combination of forced labor and denial of healthcare.

Famine and malnutrition

Some of the twentieth-century's worst human rights disasters have been famines created or manipulated by governments.[42] Food and water are indispensable for human survival and, since they are easily controlled, withdrawn and selectively distributed, they become convenient tools for *genocidaires*.

The right to food under international law

The right to be free from hunger is a fundamental right implied in the right to life.[43] The UDHR and the ICESCR unequivocally establish the right to food. The ICESCR further establishes a positive obligation on the part of governments to maintain, "at the very least, minimum essential levels of each of the rights"[44] granted therein and to undertake all steps towards the "full realization" of such rights. In the context of the right to food, "a State party in which any significant number of individuals is deprived of essential foodstuffs [...] is *prima facie*, failing to discharge its obligations under the [ICESCR]."[45]

Stalin's rise to power in 1924 marked the end of the more permissive attitude toward the various nations of the Soviet Union, and the beginning of the brutal suppression of non-Soviet national identities. In 1928 the First Five Year Plan demanded "rapid industrialization" and "collectivization of agriculture,"[46] resulting in large-scale collectivization of farms throughout the Soviet Union which displaced the existing local ownership and caused "outrage and chaos in the countryside."[47] In the Ukraine, the hardships wrought by Stalin were not merely the growing pains of communism or modernization; rather they had a specific target and a deadly goal. The Kulaks were the Ukraine's "wealthier" peasants, seen as class enemies, dangerous to the collectivization of agriculture, and state socialism itself.

Stalin's first step was massive deportations. Robert Conquest estimated some 5 million people were deported to Siberia.[48] The deportations undermined any local power base from which opposition to collectivization might have arisen. The next step was to force collectivization on the population, and at the same time, increase demands for grain. In 1926, the Soviet central government collected 21 percent of the Ukrainian total grain harvest.[49] By 1930, the grain quota was increased to 33 percent of the harvest, and for 1931 the quota was 42 percent.[50] Despite fluctuating harvests, the quotas kept increasing to fantastic levels, such that the Ukraine could not possibly feed its peasantry.[51] James E. Mace estimates that, according to the official Soviet data, the 1932 grain harvest in the Ukraine was 14.4 million tons, reaching 53 percent of the demanded quota. That year the Soviet Union *exported* 1.54 million tons of grain, and another 1.77 million tons the following year.[52] Massive starvation ensued. Enforcement of the quotas was brutal and deadly. Watchtowers, guarded by armed secret police, protected the grain. Police were authorized under an August 1932 law to shoot anyone who attempted to steal "socialist property" from the collective farms.[53] A separate law promulgated in November 1932 prohibited collective farms from maintaining food reserves or distributing food until the central government's quotas were satisfied.[54] Finally, in December 1932 an order placed thirty-two administrative districts on a blacklist that forced local stores to close with their content confiscated, banned all farmers from trade, including trade in commodities like bread, halted the repayment of credit for food commodities, and purged all "foreign elements" or "saboteurs of the grain procurement" from the collective farms.[55] As a result of these laws, 25–30 percent of the Ukrainian agricultural middle management was arrested in 5 months in 1932.[56] Street-level enforcement was waged by "brigades" of thugs, who "beat people up"[57] with specially issued steel rods and killed domestic and wild animals to ensure that the starving peasants could not use them for food.[58]

While millions of people starved, the situation continued to deteriorate. On January 22, 1933 Stalin and Prime Minister Molotov issued secret instructions to blockade "Kuban and all of Ukraine," and utilized the secret police to prevent peasants from moving into neighboring areas in search of food.[59] State authorities were "ordered to take not only every last ounce of grain but anything that might be eaten or traded for food."[60]

The Ukrainian famine was carefully concealed by the Soviets, contributing to the difficulty in accurately assessing the death toll resulting from the man-made famine. In one conservative report, Russian demographer M. Maksudov estimates the death toll at 4.4 million.[61] Other estimates place the death toll between 3 and 4 million[62] and as high as 11 million.[63] In any event, the famine was, as David Marcus observed, "one of the most severe of the unprecedented European human rights disasters of the first half of the twentieth century [...] deliberately manufactured by the Soviet government to achieve a set of political and economic ends."[64] In the 1930s, famine was a convenient, low-tech tool for annihilating the Ukrainian nation.

Sexual violence and rape

Sexual violence has recently gained recognition as a tool of genocide, expanding from a concept describing an immediately violent act to one that takes account of the act's crippling long-term consequences. Entire groups may be placed at risk of destruction not just from the violence itself, but also from its residual effects. These include victims' depression and indifference, alienation from social groups, inability or lack of desire to procreate, and acquired sexually transmitted diseases.

Sexual violence, in the context of genocide, is both a psychological and a physical weapon of elimination. As the ICTR recognized in the *Akayesu* case, sexual violence "[i]s not limited to physical invasion of the human body and may include acts which do not involve penetration or even physical contact."[65] At its most fundamental, sexual violence "describes the deliberate use of sex as a weapon to demonstrate power over, and to inflict pain and humiliation upon, another human being."[66] In this regard, "sexual violence does not have to include direct physical contact between perpetrator and victim: threats, humiliation and intimidation may all be considered as sexually violent when they are used with the above purpose."[67]

Sexual violence in international law

The right to be free from sexual violence is well-established in international law. International humanitarian law extends the protection against sexual violence to internal armed conflicts, as both the Geneva Conventions and the Additional Protocols "implicitly and explicitly condemn rape and other forms of sexual violence as serious violations of humanitarian law."[68] More directly, General Comment no. 28 to the International Covenant on Civil and Political Rights (ICCPR) Article 3 recognizes that *women's* enjoyment of civil and political rights are extremely vulnerable in times of internal or international armed conflict and thus requires states parties to "inform the Committee of all measures taken during these situations to protect women from rape, abduction and other forms of gender-based violence."[69]

Since their founding, both the ICTR and the ICTY have held that sexual violence, particularly rape, can be a principal tool of genocide under Articles 2(b), 2(c), and 2(d) of the Genocide Convention, as well as a concurrent tool, utilized alongside other group-based armed conflicts. In *Akayesu*, the ICTR authoritatively affirmed "the intricate linkage of sexual violence to the genocide committed during the Rwanda conflict," and thus created "the most progressive case law on gender ever pronounced by an international judicial body."[70] The two tribunals have also recognized that transmission of HIV/AIDS as well as the measures taken to prevent birth are all relevant aspects of genocidal campaigns.

In Bosnia-Herzegovina, where the conflict was particularly protracted and brutal, rape was not merely incidental to the war, but served the strategic purpose of intimidation and degradation.[71] From the rape camps, such as Partizan Sports Hall and Buk Bijela, to direct attacks in victims' homes during their removal from Bosnian Serb held territories and in refugee transfer facilities, rape and other forms of sexual violence formed an important part of the "ethnic cleansing" campaign perpetrated by the Bosnian Serbs. Many rapes were committed in full view of other prisoners and "gang-rapes" were a common occurrence. The patterns of rape identified by the UN Commission of Experts reflected the obvious – that the rapes were not random occurrences, but rather were elements of a specific and organized method of brutality and elimination carried out via state encouragement.[72] One victim described her perpetrators as "a kind of military police [that] did nothing but rape. It was all organized; *they had a group for raping* and a group for killing."[73]

The sexual violence in Bosnia-Herzegovina had a drastic effect on victims' psychological and physical health, both resulting in death. Physically, the raped women experienced severe, permanent gynecological harm. Psychologically, the victims were traumatized, and often committed suicide.[74] Many of the female victims reported to the ICTY investigators that conquering Bosnian Serb forces often confessed to following rape orders, while raping. In total, approximately 20,000 to 50,000 women were raped by Bosnian Serb soldiers during the war.[75] It is necessary to keep in mind that sexual violence is usually an under-reported crime, as it carries with it a strong social stigma in most societies.

Rape has also been a "prominent feature" throughout the conflict in Darfur, taking place during attacks on the villages, and continuing both inside the IDP and refugee camps, and outside the camps, during women's daily foraging for food and water.[76] As Julie Flint and Alex de Waal observed, "rape was so ubiquitous that it appeared to be an instrument of policy to destroy the fabric of the targeted communities and perhaps even to create a new generation with 'Arab' paternity."[77]

Statistics bear out the horrors of the reports. Médecins Sans Frontières (MSF) reports that, "between October 2004 and the first half of February 2005 [...] they treated almost 500 rape victims in numerous locations in South and West Darfur."[78] MSF claims this number is a fraction of women who actually were raped. An October 2004 Physicians for Human Rights report located one Darfurian NGO that had documented at least 9,300 local rape cases.[79] Mass rapes are common and the same location is often attacked several times. In July 2003, an attack at Tawilah resulted in the mass rape of an alleged 120 women.[80] The same area was attacked again in February 2005, when 200 girls were raped, including 41 schoolgirls and teachers, some by up to 14 members of Janjaweed (government-supported militias).[81]

The nature and extent of rapes of ethnic African civilians was part of a purposeful strategy to terrorize and uproot Darfur's rural communities.[82] The vast majority of the rape victims are women and girls ranging in ages from 12 to 45 years old;[83]

many were gang-raped. Almost a third of the women interviewed by MSF reported that they were raped more than once, and in many cases, abducted and held in captivity as sex slaves to the Janjaweed and government forces.[84] In almost all accounts, rape is accompanied by additional violence and brutality. Women are severely beaten with sticks, whips, and axes and many girls report "the gouging of the leg with a knife in the manner used for branding animals and slaves."[85] That rape is being used as a genocidal tool is further suggested by reports that "during attacks, the *Janjaweed* often berated the women, calling them slaves, telling them that they would now bear a 'free' child, and asserting that they (the perpetrators) are wiping out the non-Arabs."[86]

Rape carries severe long-term physical and psychological ramifications. In Sudan, a strong social stigma attaches to rape victims; illegal pregnancy is a crime that carries a fine and a possible jail sentence. Husbands often disown wives who have been raped and unmarried victims may never marry, since they are perceived as "spoiled." Faced with the prospect of abandonment or incarceration, many women do not report the attacks. Societal stigma even prevents women from attempting to access life-saving medical care, since to do so could result in exclusion from their families or communities. All of these elements increase the prevalence of serious diseases and infections in the already unsanitary and poverty stricken environment in the camps. By destroying the individual existence of thousands of women and girls, rape compromises the health and survival of entire populations, and completely undermines the social cohesion of Darfurian society. Indirectly and subtly, rape and sexual violence exert a horrible hold over the lives of the victims, inflicting severe long-term pain, fear and suffering to individuals and entire communities, jeopardizing their ultimate survival.

PREVENTION THROUGH EARLY WARNING AND EARLY ACTION

Institutions addressing the after-effects of genocide, such as compensation committees, truth commissions, and international courts, hold *genocidaires* accountable for their actions and contribute to the re-establishment of justice and the rule of law in post-conflict countries. However, these punitive and fact-finding institutions cannot and do not prevent genocide, and in fact, reinforce a rigid and problematic conception of the crime of genocide. More often than not, genocide is conceived as a relatively fast moving, large-scale murderous event in which the intent is demonstrated by targeted mass killings. The model of genocide by attrition presented here highlights the indirect methods of genocide within the Genocide Convention that play a more significant role in genocide than is currently appreciated. Looking at genocide as a complex process of attrition does not require waiting until a country is already engaged in low-level conflict or worse yet standing by until large numbers of people have died. By drawing on reoccurring attributes and processes that have been observed in previous cases, genocide by attrition provides a framework for sorting information into meaningful patterns and sequences that reveal the familiar story of genocide. This reconceptualization is useful for genocide identification and prevention, not just prosecution.

Following the genocides in Rwanda and Bosnia-Herzegovina, attention has once again shifted to failures of the early warning models to anticipate mass atrocities. In response, scholars and policy specialists have proposed establishing an early warning system dedicated specifically to the prevention of genocide.[87] In particular, the challenge of genocide early warning is no longer a lack of data or that data are difficult to gather. To the contrary, with the advent of social networking and hand-held devices the communication of information around the globe through video and audio has risen exponentially in the past 5 years. One of the main challenges to early warning is now one of systematically compiling and interpreting the information coming in.

An effective early warning system must identify information that points to an escalatory development of situations that could potentially lead to genocide, and communicate that information to relevant actors in a timely manner. Similar to a criminal prosecution, there must be something about this information that indicates some level of intent to engage in genocide to justify intervention. However, while much ink has been spilled over the standard and nature of the proof required to prove intent in a criminal prosecution, less attention has been paid to identifying intent when prevention is at stake. Hence, the paradigm most frequently employed even in the prevention context is drawn from concepts of criminal law where legal fairness requires strict definitional parameters in order to ensure that an individual is aware of the scope of conduct that falls outside of the bounds of legality.

Increasingly, many early warning models focus on human rights violations to identify early markers of societies and groups in danger. However, emphasis on massive human rights abuses as warning signals has the potential of overwhelming the models with too much information. Early warning systems that simply survey for systematic violations that *may* become gross violations are too broad and inevitably imprecise. This creates the opposite problem to the overly rigid interpretation of genocide. The information overload makes it difficult to identify emerging patterns of genocidal violence from other deteriorating situations. The concept of genocide by attrition suggests a framework for use in an early warning system that can avoid both of these shortcomings.

Despite the complex nature of genocide and problems of prediction, Heikki Patomäki suggests that while there cannot be a law-like certainty about the causal factors when we are dealing with open systems, demi-regularities are pervasive throughout society. For her, "[a] demi-regularity ... is a partial event regularity which prima facie indicates the occasional actualization of geo-historical causal forces or mechanisms over a definite region of time-space."[88] The focus on attributes of attrition that have been observed in similar patterns across several cases presents just such a case of demi-regularity.

As such the model of genocide as a complex process of attrition improves upon other models that broadly identify the existence of human rights violations, by demanding a nuanced understanding of governments' human rights obligations, and forcing consideration of a specific spectrum of human rights violations as indicators. As international human rights evolves from encompassing "negative" restraints that require the state merely to leave individuals alone, to "positive" obligations that require the state to secure peoples' rights, human rights observers will be able to identify actionable violations earlier, raise the specter of genocide, and garner policy makers' attention.

Second, the model of genocide as a process of attrition provides a context for sorting multiple streams of data into meaningful patterns based on the attributes of historical case studies. Recognition of these patterns should trigger further inquiry and analysis of ongoing violations, their interaction with other acts of abuse and violence, and a structural inquiry into the socio-political context in which they are occurring.

Third, it is obvious that early warning does not guarantee successful prevention. But it is doomed to failure if it cannot at a minimum stimulate urgent, robust analysis of human rights violations that "fall short of genocide," but which may already be acts of genocide. Data useful to this task are already collected by many human rights non-governmental organizations for their "urgent appeals." If these "urgent appeals" were integrated into an early warning system, analysts could tally and analyze abuses against vulnerable groups, while searching for patterns that point to acts of genocide by attrition in situations where the identification of intent to eliminate can be established from the context in which the abuses are occurring.

The international community must embrace a more nuanced, complex and analytical conceptualization of genocide, and perhaps as well, a messier understanding of the real world. The rigid and sequenced conception of genocide that dominates policy circles all but ensures that recognition will come too late, after enormous numbers of people have died and the only tool for intervention left available is military action. As we have shown, "[t]he patterns of genocide are laid down months or even years before the actual killings begin."[89] By abandoning a restrictive, singular focus on direct killings and adopting a broader understanding about what constitutes the evidence of intent, scholars can identify individual human rights violations as possible methods and acts of genocidal attrition, before the bodies start piling up.

Finally, returning to a more elastic understanding of genocide will end the morally self-gratifying search for "safe" or narrow points of intervention that only satisfy a fragile sense of justice, and leave those most in need still waiting for help from the rest of humanity.

NOTES

* The authors would like to thank Mathew Miller for his valuable asistance on this chapter.

1 International Criminal Court, Office of the Prosecutor, "ICC Prosecutor Presents Case Against Sudanese President, Hassan Ahmad Al Bashir, for Genocide, Crimes Against Humanity and War Crimes in Darfur," news release, July 14, 2008.

2 Convention on the Prevention and Punishment of the Crime of Genocide, December 9, 1948, 78 U.N.T.S. 277, 102 Stat. 3045.

3 M. Shaw, *What Is Genocide?* Cambridge, UK: Polity, 2007.

4 Ibid., p. 45.

5 H. Fein, "Genocide by Attrition 1939–1993: The Warsaw Ghetto, Cambodia, and Sudan: Links between Human Rights, Health, and Mass Death," *Health and Human Rights* 2/2, 1997, 12.

6 All cases exemplify one or more elements of attrition.

7 E. Reeves, "The "Two Darfurs": Redefining a Crisis for Political Purposes," *Sudan Tribune*, May 20, 2005.

8 E. Reeves, "Genocide by Attrition: Agony in Darfur," *Dissent* 52/1, 2005, 21–5.

9 Ibid.

10 N. Kristof, "Genocide in Slow Motion," *The New York Review of Books* 53/2, 9 February 2006; G. Prunier, *Darfur: A 21st Century Genocide*, Ithaca, NY: Cornell University Press, 2008.

11 E. Reeves, "Whitewashing Darfur," *Guardian*, June 14, 2009; I. Cotler, "Genocide Starts With Incitement to Hate," *Africa News Service*, April 8, 2009; "Commentary Calls for Joint Efforts to Fight Against War Criminals in Sudan," *BBC Monitoring Middle East*, April 7, 2009.

12 See for example, F. Chalk and K. Jonassohn, *The History and Sociology of Genocide: Analyses and Case Studies*, New Haven, CT: Yale University Press, 1990, p. 23; B. Harff and T. Gurr, "Toward An Empirical Theory of Genocides and Politicides," *International Studies Quarterly* 32/3, 1988, 359–71.

13 R. Lemkin, *Axis Rule in Occupied Europe: Laws of Occupation, Analysis of Government, Proposals for Redress*, New York: Columbia University Press, 1981, p. 79.

14 Shaw, *What Is Genocide?* pp. 27–8.

15 Fein, "Genocide by Attrition," 10.

16 E. Weitz, *A Century of Genocide: Utopias of Race and Nation*, Princeton, NJ: Princeton University Press, 2003; G. Stanton, "How We Can Prevent Genocide: Building an International Campaign to End Genocide," *Genocide Watch*. Available HTTP: www.genocidewatch.org/howpreventgenocideic.html (accessed July 18, 2012); Fein, "Genocide by Attrition," 31.

17 UN ECOSOC, *Ad Hoc Committee on Genocide: Summary Record of the Fourth Meeting*, UN Doc. E/AC.25/SR.4, 14, April 15, 1948.

18 S. Craig, "The Interdependence and Permeability of Human Rights Norms: Toward a Partial Fusion of the International Covenants on Human Rights," *Osgoode Hall Law Journal* 27/53, 1989, 769, 787: "[i]nterdependence suggests a mutual reinforcement of rights, so that they are more valuable together, as a complete package, than a simple summation of individual rights would suggest [...]"

19 M. Drumbl, *Atrocity, Punishment, and International Law*, Cambridge: Cambridge University Press, 2007, p. 37.

20 See *The Prosecutor v. Clément Kayishema and Obed Ruzindana* (Trial Judgment), case no. ICTR-95-1-T, International Criminal Tribunal for Rwanda (ICTR), para. 91, May 21, 1999.

21 Drumbl, *Atrocity, Punishment, and International Law*, p. 37.

22 *Prosecutor v. Goran Jelisic* (Appeal Judgment), IT-95-10-A, International Criminal Tribunal for the former Yugoslavia (ICTY), para. 47, July 5, 2001; *The Prosecutor v. Jean-Paul Akayesu* (Trial Judgment), ICTR-96-4-T, International Criminal Tribunal for Rwanda (ICTR), para. 523, September 2, 1998.

23 F. Grünfeld and A. Huijboom, *The Failure to Prevent Genocide in Rwanda: The Role of Bystanders*, Leiden, Netherlands: Martinus Nijhoff Publishers, 2007, p. 8.

24 A. Jones, *Genocide: A Comprehensive Introduction*, New York: Routledge, 2006, p. 216.

25 "Guiding Principles on Internal Displacement," *Global Database*. Available HTTP: www.idpguidingprinciples.org (accessed July 15, 2012).

26 "Guiding Principles on Internal Displacement."

27 J. Fitzpatrick, ed., *Human Rights Protection for Refugees, Asylum-seekers, and Internally Displaced Persons: A Guide to International Mechanisms and Procedures*, Ardsley, NY: Transnational Publishers, 2002, p. 5.

28 Office of the United Nations High Commissioner for Human Rights, "Questions and Answers About IDPs," United Nations. Available HTTP: www.ohchr.org/EN/Issues/IDPersons/Pages/Issues.aspx (accessed July 18, 2012).

29 United Nations Commission on Human Rights, *Report of the Representative of the Secretary-General, Mr. Francis M. Deng, submitted pursuant to Commission resolution 1997/39 – Addendum: Guiding Principles on Internal Displacement*, Principle 10(1), February 11, 1998, E/CN.4/1998/53/Add.2.

30 *Prosecutor* v. *Radislav Krstić* (Appeal Judgment), IT-98-33-A, International Criminal Tribunal for the former Yugoslavia (ICTY), para. 33, April 19, 2004; see also *Prosecutor* v. *Radislav Krstić* (Trial Judgment), International Criminal Tribunal for the former Yugoslavia (ICTY), para. 595, August 2, 2001.

31 J. Winter, "Under Cover of War: The Armenian Genocide in the Context of Total War," in Robert Gellately and Ben Kiernan, eds., *The Specter of Genocide: Mass Murder in Historical Perspective*, New York: Cambridge University Press, 2003, p. 207.

32 R. Adalian, "The Armenian Genocide," in Samuel Totten, William S. Parsons and Israel W. Charny, eds., *Century of Genocide: Eyewitness Accounts and Critical Views*, New York: Garland Publishing, 1997, p. 43.

33 Adalian, "The Armenian Genocide," p. 43.

34 Ibid.

35 L. Einstein, "The Armenian Massacres," *Contemporary Review* 111, 1917, 490.

36 G. Chaliand and Y. Ternon, *The Armenians: From Genocide to Resistance*, Tony Berrett, trans., London: Zed Press, 1983, p. 15.

37 United Nations Economic and Social Council, "Substantive Issues Arising in the Implementation of the International Covenant on Economic, Social and Cultural Rights," General Comment no. 14 (2000), para. 11, 11 August 2000.

38 *The Prosecutor* v. *Georges Anderson Nderubumwe Rutaganda* (Judgment and Sentence), ICTR-96-3-T, International Criminal Tribunal for Rwanda (ICTR), para. 52, December 6, 1999; *The Prosecutor* v. *Alfred Musema* (Judgment and Sentence), ICTR-96-13-T, International Criminal Tribunal for Rwanda (ICTR), para. 157, January 27, 2000.

39 G. Stanton, "Blue Scarves and Yellow Stars: Classification and Symbolization in the Cambodian Genocide," *The Faulds Lecture*, Warren Wilson College, Swannanoa, North Carolina, March 1987.

40 D. Aikman, "The Situation in Cambodia," in Jack Nusan Porter, ed., *Genocide and Human Rights: A Global Anthology*, Lanham, MD: University Press of America, 1982, p. 252.

41 Aikman, "The Situation in Cambodia," pp. 252–3.

42 The majority of the information in this section is drawn from D. Marcus, "Famine Crimes in International Law," *American Journal of International Law* 97/2, 2003, 245–81.

43 Office of the United Nations High Commissioner for Human Rights, "General Comment no. 6: The Right to Life – Article 6." (Sixteenth Session, 1982), UN Doc. HRI\GEN\1\Rev.1 at 6 (1994).

44 United Nations Committee on Economic, Social and Cultural Rights, "General Comment no. 3: The Nature of States Parties' Obligations (Art. 2, Para. 1, of the Covenant)", E/1991/23, December 14, 1990.

45 Ibid.

46 J. Mace, "Soviet Man-Made Famine in Ukraine," in Samuel Totten and William S. Parsons, eds., *Century of Genocide: Critical Essays and Eyewitness Accounts*, 3rd edition, New York: Routledge, 2009, pp. 81, 85.

47 S. Fitzpatrick, *The Russian Revolution*, New York: Oxford University Press, 1994, p. 136.

48 Robert Conquest at the October 8, 1986 hearing of the US Commission on the Ukraine Famine. Text available at www.ukrweekly.com/old/archive/1986/448621.shtml

49 R. Conquest, *The Harvest of Sorrow: Soviet Collectivization and the Terror-famine*, New York: Oxford University Press, 1987, p. 221.

50 Ibid., p. 222.

51 Ibid., p. 223.

52 Mace, "Soviet Man-Made Famine in Ukraine."

53 Conquest, *The Harvest of Sorrow*, p. 223.

54 Mace, "Soviet Man-Made Famine in Ukraine."

55 Ibid.

56 Conquest, *The Harvest of Sorrow*, p. 229.

57 Marcus, "Famine Crimes in International Law," 253.

58 Conquest, *The Harvest of Sorrow*, pp., 224, 229.

59 Y. Bilinsky, "Was the Ukrainian Famine of 1932–1933 Genocide?" *Journal of Genocide Research* 1/2, 1999, 152.

60 Marcus, "Famine Crimes in International Law," 253.

61 Quoted in Conquest, *The Harvest of Sorrow*, p. 253.

62 Fitzpatrick, *The Russian Revolution*, p. 139.

63 W. A. Dando, "Man-made Famines: Some Geographical Insights from an Exploratory Study of a Millennium of Russian Famines," *Ecology of Food and Nutrition* 4/4, 1976, 219, 229.

64 Marcus, "Famine Crimes in International Law," 252.

65 *Prosecutor* v. *Akayesu*, para. 688.

66 P. Gordon and K. Crehan, *Dying of Sadness: Gender, Sexual Violence and the HIV Epidemic*, New York: HIV and Development Programme, United Nations Development Programme, 1999.

67 Ibid.

68 Human Rights Watch, *"We'll Kill You If You Cry": Sexual Violence in the Sierra Leone Conflict*, January 16, 2003, A1501.

69 United Nations Human Rights Committee, "General Comment no. 28: Article 3, The Equality of Rights Between Men and Women, CCPR/C/21/Rev.1/Add.10" (March 29, 2000).

70 K. D. Askin, "Sexual Violence in Decisions and Indictments of the Yugoslav and Rwanda Tribunals: Current Status," *The American Journal of International Law* 93/1, 1999, 100.

71 A. Stiglmayer, ed., *Mass Rape: The War against Women in Bosnia-Herzegovina*, Lincoln: University of Nebraska Press, 1994, p. 85.

72 United Nations Security Council, letter dated May 24, 1994 from the secretary-general to the president of the Security Council, S/1994/674 (May 27, 1994).

73 V. Clark, "Rape Thy Neighbour," *Observer* (London), February 21, 1993, quoted in Human Rights Watch, *Bosnia and Hercegovina: "A Closed, Dark Place" – Past and Present Human Rights Abuses in Foca*, 6 (Section D) ed., vol. 10, 1998 (emphasis added).

74 *The Prosecutor* v. *Gojko Janković , Janko Janjić, Zoran Vuković, Dragan Zelenović, Radovan Stanković*, IT-99-33-A, International Criminal Tribunal for the former Yugoslavia (ICTY), October 5, 1999.

75 *Frankfurter Rundschau*, March 3, 1993, quoted in R. Seifert, "War and Rape: A Preliminary Analysis," in Alexandra Stiglmayer, ed., *Mass Rape: The War against Women in Bosnia-Herzegovina*, Lincoln: University of Nebraska Press, 1994, p. 55.

76 "Darfur: Women Raped Even After Seeking Refuge," Human Rights Watch, online. Available HTTP: http://hrw.org/english/docs/2005/04/11/sudan10467.htm. (accessed July 14, 2012).

77 J. Flint and A. De Waal, *Darfur: A Short History of a Long War*, London: Zed Books, 2005, p. 108.

78 Médecins Sans Frontières, *The Crushing Burden of Rape: Sexual Violence in Darfur*, March 8, 2005.

79 T. Gingerich and J. Leaning, *The Use of Rape as a Weapon of War in Darfur, Sudan*, Prepared for US Agency for International Development/OTI, 2004, p. 16.

80 International Commission of Inquiry on Darfur, *Report of the International Commission of Inquiry on Darfur to the United Nations Secretary-General*, January 25, 2005, p. 60.

81 E. Reeves, "Children Within Darfur's Holocaust," Sudanreeves.org, December 23, 2005, online. Available HTTP: www.sudanreeves.org/2006/03/13/children-within-darfurs-holocaust-december-23-2005/

82 "Darfur: Women Raped Even After Seeking Refuge."

83 Médecins Sans Frontières, *The Crushing Burden of Rape*, p. 3.

84 Ibid., pp. 3–4.

85 Gingerich and Leaning, *The Use of Rape as a Weapon*, p. 20.

86 Ibid., p.15.

87 J. Davies and T. Gurr, *Preventive Measures: Building Risk Assessment and Crisis Early Warning Systems*, Lanham, MD: Rowman & Littlefield, 1998; W. Schabas, *Preventing Genocide and Mass Killing: The Challenge for the United Nations*, London: Minority Rights Group International, 2006. The United States government recently established an Atrocities Prevention Board with this aim in mind.

88 T. Lawson, *Economics and Reality*, London: Routledge, 1997, pp. 204–13, quoted in H. Patomäki, *The Political Economy of Global Security: War, Future Crises and Changes in Global Governance*, London: Routledge, 2008, p. 22.

89 A. Alvarez, *Governments, Citizens, and Genocide: A Comparative and Interdisciplinary Approach*, Bloomington: Indiana University Press, 2001, p. 133.

CHAPTER 7

Research and Teaching about Genocide

History, challenges and new directions

Joyce Apsel

Genocide studies has come of age. But, is "genocide studies" a subfield, concentration, or area of study? To what degree is the field dependent on the categorization of current cases of violence as genocide? Do new connections and directions point to the study of genocides being subsumed under larger frameworks, such as study of human rights and humanitarianism or postcolonial, development or globalization studies? What significant changes are there in the content of the literature and direction in research on genocide over the last decade and what impact does this have on the classroom?

BACKGROUND

The study of genocide and other mass violence represents a continuing rewriting of the curriculum that emerged most strongly from the 1970s on and continues with new directions and content today. The roots of this framework are part of a larger curriculum transformation that includes the voices of women, blacks, workers, indigenous peoples, and various ethnic and national groups whose histories were long silenced or marginalized.[1] The inclusion of previously marginalized cultural, social, political and other perspectives into contemporary historical accounts are also part of this transformation. Part of the processes of genocidal destruction entails cultural as well as physical elimination, the erasing of one people's history replaced by writing of history by the victors/perpetrators. Writing the history, culture, the story of peoples eliminated or targeted for annihilation goes beyond compensatory history and may be viewed as history as resistance to power and violence.

The study of genocides functions as an acknowledgment that the state-sponsored master narrative minimizes and often totally denies the state's role and that of other actors who sometimes act as proxies of the state in carrying out destruction against civilian groups. These tropes of disappeared peoples and homogenization often are part of the founding myths of states, and many of its citizens' identities may be tied to such distorted histories. The dynamic processes that are part of mass violence necessitate looking beyond static models of victim, perpetrator and bystander. Instead, it is crucial to explore the fluidity of human actions and relationships during societal and national crises. Psychological, economic and other factors contribute to a continuum of destruction that may begin with resentment and prejudice, and accelerate to heightened levels of support for and participation in the elimination of targeted groups.

Genocide is a recurrent phenomenon in world history. As Leo Kuper wrote in 1981 in *Genocide: Its Political Use in the Twentieth Century*: "The word is new, the crime is ancient."[2] The term "genocide" was coined by Raphael Lemkin in 1944 emphasizing the targeting of humans in groups, that is, the killing of a people, to emphasize the collective nature of the criminal act. The civilian deaths of World War II and in particular the targeting and destruction of Jews, and of Roma and Sinti, Poles, and other civilian groups, along with Lemkin's own Polish Jewish background, were crucial factors in his development of the term and further efforts to draft and lobby for an international convention on the prevention and punishment of genocide, which was adopted by the United Nations in 1948 and came into force in 1951. This background plays an important role in the direction of early research and courses in genocide; but broader aspects of Lemkin's writings have been taken up in new directions in recent genocide scholarship.

In thinking about why and how the field/subfield/area of study called genocide studies became a legitimate and distinct part of the scholarly lexicon and academic institutions (and why for example, there is no crimes against humanity studies), the pervasiveness of Holocaust research, courses and institutional structures was crucial. In fact, genocide studies continues to be relatively small in comparison with research and teaching about the Holocaust, and much less securely or permanently grounded in university structures. Interestingly, despite tensions and at times competing claims, genocide studies came into existence on the coat-tails of Holocaust studies (see Donald Bloxham's chapter in this volume on the interplay between Holocaust and genocide studies).

STAGES IN THE DEVELOPMENT OF GENOCIDE STUDIES

Initially, the Holocaust was the predominant model for identifying the characteristics of genocide and a yardstick of comparison with other genocidal events.

The current stage of genocide studies marks a shift away from the Holocaust as the model for what other genocides look like, and reflects an awareness that using the Holocaust as the blueprint means leaving out or ignoring different types of mass destruction. At the same time, within Holocaust research increasingly nuanced studies of the variations of human destructiveness within Nazi genocidal policies have also influenced genocide research. At present, a number of genocide scholars are moving beyond what Alexander Hinton refers to in this volume as the canon of established and studied cases, and creating a "critical genocide studies." As René Lemarchand points out in *Forgotten Genocides: Oblivion, Denial, Memory*, "many more genocides have been committed throughout history than is recorded in human memory."[3] And it is crucial "to drag out of the shadows a number of searing human dramas in Africa, Asia, Europe and the Middle East." As Lemarchand's early research in the neglected case of Burundi underlines, such selective memory raises questions "about how and why the past is so often ignored, manipulated, or denied."[4]

Indeed, in a number of respects, current approaches by some scholars to genocide studies are more radical than earlier ones in which genocide studies was established. The boundaries and parameters of genocide studies have become extended and at times blurred. There is more focus on the unfolding dynamics of violent processes, less setting genocide apart as a distinct entity in and of itself, and greater links with other events and processes such as war, colonialism, economic development, etc. Analyses include a range of themes (empire, environment, prevention, transitional justice, structural violence), a wider set of cases previously ignored or dismissed, direct and indirect methods of destruction (such as genocide by attrition described by Rosenberg and Silina in this volume) and events (displacement, famine, partition) that explore the pervasiveness and threat of different forms of violence that turns genocidal.[5]

Since the end of the Cold War, new scholarship continues to document the scale and variations of state directed killing against civilian groups in the former Soviet Union and Communist bloc countries. This rewriting of the range and scale of human destruction carried out before, during and after World War II will have important implications for future studies and perspectives. For example, Timothy Snyder's *Bloodlands: Europe Between Hitler and Stalin*, estimates 14 million people were "killed by purposeful policies of mass murder implemented by Nazi Germany and the Soviet Union"[6] and millions through starvation and displacement.

Holocaust education as the predominant model

These new subjects of analysis and research raise key questions: Why does teaching and research about the Holocaust continue to grow and predominate, and what is the impact on genocide studies? Part of the answer lies with the enormity and tragedy of the Holocaust, as well as the availability of related documents and funding for researchers. The extent and structures of institutionalization of Holocaust research and education are significant, including the presence of the US Holocaust Memorial Museum in Washington, DC and teacher training programs and events in over 100 Holocaust centers in the United States alone, as well as others in Canada and Europe. In Israel, particularly through the work of the Yad Vashem World Center for Holocaust Research, Education, Documentation and Commemoration, Holocaust programs in the last decades have been designed to train educators world-wide and emphasize Jewish victimization and the uniqueness of the Holocaust.[7]

The degree of private and public funding and state Holocaust mandates in the US all contributed to setting up a range of institutional structures. Given competition over which areas of study within institutions of higher education will get faculty and financial support, Holocaust study centers and programs have been among the most successful areas of growth over the last decades. These developments reflect the politics of education. While there is both faculty and student interest in the Holocaust, there also exists an outside constituency such as ongoing training of primary and secondary school teachers to fulfill state education mandates. Holocaust resource centers and established Jewish studies and Holocaust programs with endowed chairs, lecture series, travel tours, and other activities were created largely as permanent structures at the university level.

The Association of Holocaust Organizations (AHO) founded in 1985 serves as a network for university programs and resource centers as well as other types of educational/memorial organizations world-wide, from Australia to China and Japan to Europe (none are listed in Africa).[8] The largest numbers are in the United States; and New Jersey, which has a significant Holocaust survivor and Jewish population, provides an interesting example of the proliferation of Holocaust education. The New Jersey legislature passed a state mandate for Holocaust and genocide education at the pre-university level, established a commission for implementation and produced several curriculum guides for teachers. The majority of New Jersey (NJ) Holocaust centers focus on Holocaust related education, and to varying degrees may include sessions or resources about other genocides, and related issues. Some NJ Holocaust resource centers work with organizations like Facing History and Ourselves, which has developed a broad curriculum connecting the Holocaust with issues of racism, human rights and citizenship.[9]

Eleven of the eighteen AHO-listed New Jersey public and private educational sites provide courses primarily about the Holocaust for undergraduates, teacher training and other programs throughout the state, from Ramapo College in the north to Drew University to Richard Stockton College in the south. This small densely populated state is home to a series of privately funded resource centers (a number of them are located in the main university library) as well as endowed chairs in Holocaust studies (again in both public and private institutions), and there are two M.A. programs in Holocaust and Genocide Studies offered at two different New Jersey state universities (established at Richard Stockton College in 1998 and at Kean University in 2010).[10] In Massachusetts, the Strassler Center in Holocaust and Genocide Studies at Clark University offers a concentration for undergraduates and a teacher training program and is unique in offering a doctoral program with the History Department, and recently added a second Ph.D. offering in Psychology and Genocide.[11] Hence, in New Jersey, and in other states, each center and program may incorporate different aspects of genocide studies and human rights into its curriculum and programming, but courses and resources on the Holocaust generally predominate.

In 1998 the Task Force for International Cooperation on Holocaust Education, Remembrance and Research (ITF) was established with 31 country members as "an intergovernmental body whose purpose is to place political and social leaders' support behind the need for Holocaust education, remembrance, and research both nationally and internationally."[12] This initiative was in part a response to Holocaust denial and antisemitism. The ITF's Declaration of the Stockholm International Forum on the Holocaust states: "The Holocaust (Shoah) fundamentally challenged the foundations of civilization. The unprecedented character of the Holocaust will always hold universal meaning."[13] The ITF Declaration acknowledges the "horrors that engulfed the Jewish people. The terrible suffering of the many millions of other victims of the Nazis has left an indelible scar across Europe as well." The Declaration points out that humanity is "still scarred by genocide, ethnic cleansing, racism, anti-semitism and xenophobia," and is committed to fight those evils. "We share a commitment to encourage the study of the Holocaust in all its dimensions. We will promote education about the Holocaust in our schools and universities, in our communities and encourage it in other institutions."[14] It is noteworthy that there is no mention or link of education and research in genocide studies or human rights. Sociologist Martin Shaw observes that in the realm of public debate and high school education, "the Holocaust has assumed a position of overriding importance, universally commemorated and increasingly the dominant theme of the Second World War."[15]

In Holocaust centers at universities and community colleges, there are sometimes lectures, films and memorials about a number of genocides, including the Armenian, Cambodian, Rwandan and Darfur genocides and the current conflicts in places such as Congo. The extent to which university programs and centers allow for a more expansive subject matter and include, for example, issues related to present conflicts or social justice issues, varies considerably (such centers tend to privilege the Holocaust as exceptional or unique and past events over present day issues). Among the factors that contribute to resistance to moving toward a broader comparative genocide and human rights program are: the Holocaust-centered orientation of past and present donors (many are Holocaust survivors or family members), the training of directors and other personnel, and the restrictive by-laws written into the guidelines for Holocaust programs, academic chairs, and resource centers. Because there are so many programs that provide funding for training in Holocaust education (even where "and genocide" may be included in the heading, but such courses are not always offered), graduates of these programs look for employment in and are trained to continue Holocaust education. Despite the considerable pedagogical effectiveness of this education, the degree and content of Holocaust education has also been critiqued as a mechanism used by governments from the United States to Canada to Israel to ignore their own histories of discrimination and atrocity by emphasizing Holocaust education.[16]

On the other hand, awareness that there is increased student and public interest in a range of human rights issues from indigenous peoples to Rwanda and the Sudan has resulted in a number of Holocaust centers broadening their programs and other activities, and a few to add "and Genocide" to the names of the centers. In fact, realization that interest in focusing on the Holocaust has lessened among students (some argue because of saturation on the topic in the media; that it is 60 years since the end of World War II and students are more interested in current human rights issues; and finally, the uneven quality and extent of Holocaust education in pre-university curricula), has influenced some educators to argue that introducing new subjects at Holocaust centers may be an effective strategy to engage new audiences and reignite interest in aspects of the Holocaust. For example, ongoing issues of bullying and racism in the United States are subjects that are linked with Nazi antisemitism, racism and exterminatory policies. As a new generation of administrators and educators comes of age, in all likelihood Holocaust and genocide centers will expand their programs to include a range of human rights, prevention, and humanitarian programs; however, the degree to which they integrate a comparative genocide model remains an open question.

In the face of strains in European societies over immigration and citizenship, the last decade has witnessed an increase in the emphasis on World War II in states' curricula (each country providing its own perspective, often including resistance to Nazism), focus on the Holocaust, and visits by high school students to killing centers and concentration camps (see the Stockholm Declaration discussed earlier for example). However, the link between study of these subjects as effective tolerance and multicultural education has come under scrutiny. For example, the obligatory "white ambulance" tours in Norway for high school students to Nazi killing centers and camps in Poland (the trips originally were accompanied by Norwegian prisoners of war as tour guides) faced further criticism after the mass killings carried out by a young Norwegian ultra-nationalist in July 2011 and his manifesto attacking immigration and multiculturalism.

GENOCIDE STUDIES RESEARCH AND EDUCATION

The study of genocide began with a small number of teachers and scholars in anthropology, history, sociology, political science, psychology and sociology who connected ancient and modern atrocities and found links and comparisons between various violent events. As previously emphasized, some viewed the Holocaust as the model for comparison with other destructive events; for example, analyzing the Armenian genocide during World War I as a precursor to the Nazi genocides during World War II.[17] Initially, instructors teaching courses on more than one case of genocide had few resources or textbooks, and it was only from the late 1970s on that historians, sociologists and others began producing comparative works.

Raphael Lemkin's *Axis Rule in Occupied Europe: Laws of Occupation, Analysis of Government, Proposals for Redress* (1944) emphasizes how groups are controlled and targeted through legal state mechanisms. While study of the post-World War II trials and other legal issues continued, the increase in scholarship on genocide in international law accelerated from the 1990s on. Over 50 years after Lemkin's work, William Schabas' *Genocide in International Law: The Crime of Crimes*[18] presents an important analysis of genocide as an international crime; the literature on aspects of genocide and various cases and law has multiplied. Transitional justice issues such as the establishment and findings of tribunals and truth commissions, forensic findings, and issues of reparations, are among the growing areas of research, as Ernesto Verdeja points out in his chapter in this volume. There is a series of legal precedents expanding the interpretation of the UN definition of genocide to analysis of the "responsibility to protect" as an international norm. The growing discourse of genocide prevention is linked to earlier work such as the Minorities at Risk Project[19] as well as a series of new analyses and initiatives. In particular, the issues of just humanitarian intervention and the responsibility to protect have been taken up in academic and political circles. There is a new series of non-governmental organizations and academic centers such as the International Coalition for the Responsibility to Protect and the Auschwitz Institute for Peace and Reconciliation (AIPR), which conducts seminars on genocide prevention targeted at mid-level government officials, among others.[20] In April 2012, following a visit to the US Holocaust Memorial Museum, President Barack Obama announced the creation of the Atrocities Prevention Board to be headed by Samantha Power, a well-known writer and speaker on genocide and issues of intervention. These developments reflect the scholar–activist dynamic and tension that has characterized genocide studies throughout its history.

Within the university there is a new institutional positioning of genocide studies, with teaching and courses in programs such as Human Rights and Humanitarianism; Transitional Justice; Conflict, Security or Development Studies; Postcolonial Studies, and related areas. Studies of a range of atrocities and colonial settler societies are being pursued on their own and linked with later colonization and empire building practices and policies. This direction, initiated largely by scholars outside North America, emphasizes the impact of empire and other trans-national movements and factors from globalization to environmental degradation. There is also a critique of earlier limited case studies and historiographies of genocide studies,[21] with a new emphasis ranging from indigenous peoples to colonial and Soviet genocides. Scholarly journals such as the *Journal of Genocide Research* and *Genocide Studies and Prevention* reflect some of these debates and differences in emphasis.

Comparative and/or transnational history

While multi-disciplinarity is a feature of genocide studies, the discipline of history plays a crucial role in research and writing about genocide. The historian's lens is central to tracing and interpreting events. Historical methodology includes case studies, comparative and transnational histories, and sometimes combinations of these approaches.

The histories of genocides are not confined to bracketed dates or bounded. They are linked to a series of important events and processes such as war, empire and nation-building, colonialism and post-colonialism, state power, climate, development, and globalization, and the spillover effects of genocide and other mass violence that continue for generations afterward. Disentangling the deep and complicated roots and factors that contribute to mass atrocity, and uncovering and accessing sources from government records to oral testimonies, remains a central research task. Finally, genocide is part and parcel of world history, and patterns and characteristics of human destructiveness are found in different cultures, regions and historic periods.

The study of genocides links to a range of questions such as the methods, clarity and goals of both comparative and transnational historical analysis. Courses and texts in Western Civilization and more recently World History and Cultures and Global History are part of secondary and university curricula and include comparative analyses emphasizing similarities and differences between regions, traditions, and cultures. Nonetheless, "many professional historians remain skeptical of comparative history."[22] Proponents of "classical" or "traditional" history whose training and research focus on one country or theme emphasize that comparative and transnational perspectives lack historical detail, depth and mastery. Critics argue that the range of topics and civilizations precludes original research, specialization, mastery of languages, and depth of knowledge which they maintain are the hallmarks of the historian's craft.

Heinz-Gerhard Haupt and Jürgen Kocka emphasize that

> Comparative history deals with similarities and differences between historical units, e.g., regions, economies, cultures, and national states. It is the classical way of transcending the narrow boundaries of national history. Comparative history is analytically ambitious and empirically demanding. The last decades have witnessed the rise of comparative history, but its practitioners have remained a minority, and its critics have not been completely convinced.[23]

Some historical comparisons are primarily "contrasts, i.e., which are targeted at insights into the differences between individual comparative cases, and those which focus on insights into agreements, i.e. generalization and thus, the understanding of general patterns." Comparative historians generally "do both in different combinations."[24] The rationale behind doing comparative work influences both the "how" and the "what" that are compared. Popular assumptions and media representations of the causes of historic atrocity are often oversimplified, relying on discourses of age-old tribal conflicts and essentialism. "Comparison provides a counterfactual glimpse that illuminates a path not taken, or policies not pursued which serve to throw a wrench in over-determined historical narratives."[25]

Many historians and other scholars who study genocide begin with a focus on one phenomenon, event or country and to different degrees incorporate comparative and transnational frames. For example, historical sociologist Helen Fein's early work analyzes violence in India and includes analysis of antisemitism, and subsequently the bulk of her scholarship focuses on comparative analysis, from *Accounting for Genocide* (1979) to *Human Rights and Wrongs: Slavery, Terror and Genocide* (2007). Richard Hovannisian's multi-volume writings trace Armenian history from ancient times on, and include the history of the Armenian genocide. However, he also writes comparative essays and edits collections with the Armenian genocide as a continuing point of reference. Historian Ben Kiernan's initial focus was on the

Cambodian genocide and then extended to comparative and transnational analysis, most notably as co-editor with Robert Gellately of *The Specter of Genocide: Mass Murder in Historical Perspective*, and then his single-authored work, *Blood and Soil: A World History of Genocide and Extermination from Sparta to Darfur*.[26]

Eric Weitz's training is as a European historian focusing on Germany. His study of the interwar period and Nazism provides the background for his increasingly comparative work, such as a *Century of Genocide: Utopias of Race and Nation*,[27] and links to a range of human rights and humanitarian issues. The selection of works and the name of the Princeton book series Weitz edits, Human Rights and Crimes against Humanity, and the omission of the term "genocide" reflect a reframing of studying genocides along with other gross human rights violations. For example, this series includes: Emma Gilligan's *Terror in Chechnya: Russia and the Tragedy of Civilians in War*, and *Twilight of Empire: From Algiers to Baghdad* by Marnia Lazreg, as well as *Stalin's Genocides* by Norman M. Naimark and *If You Leave Us Here, We Will Die: How Genocide Was Stopped in East Timor* by Geoffrey Robinson.

A sample of historians of genocide trained primarily outside North America reflects the broadening and new directions of genocide studies, and their works first in Europe and Australia but increasingly in North America and elsewhere are increasingly influential in new scholarship. Mark Levene's early writings include analyses of antisemitism and massacres, and then of modernization and destruction in such cases as the Chittagong hill peoples. Most importantly, Levene's two published volumes in a planned four volume series entitled *Genocide in the Age of the Nation State*,[28] reflect the influence of Immanuel Wallerstein and provide a transnational model of analysis. Levene's work increasingly emphasizes the role of the state but also of a series of global processes, including the impact of the environment and scarcity on conflicts. Historians Levene and Donald Bloxham are the series editors for a forthcoming ten volume Oxford University Press monograph series entitled Zones of Violence.

European-trained historian Donald Bloxham's research interests focus on investigating "the perpetration, punishment and representation of genocide, war crimes and other mass atrocities" and "the history and practice of international law and humanitarian intervention."[29] Bloxham represents one of the new directions in the study of genocide, combining in-depth study of particular cases such as the Armenian genocide and the Holocaust with a broad international perspective that reframes analysis of genocidal events and processes, as in his book *The Final Solution: A Genocide*. His writings emphasize international and comparative historical analysis, for example his Institute for the Study of Genocide Lemkin Award winning work *The Great Game of Genocide: Imperialism, Nationalism, and the Destruction of the Ottoman Armenians*. Bloxham's writings include a series of edited collections and combine case study, comparative and transnational history.

Another example of the new directions in the historical study of genocide is the prolific work of historian A. Dirk Moses, who was educated in Australia, Scotland, Germany and the United States. Moses' writings include works on modern Germany such as *German Intellectuals and the Nazi Past*, and on a number of issues in comparative genocide. Moses emphasizes the need to write into history colonial and subaltern genocides including that of the aboriginal people in Australia.

Moses' edited collection *Empire, Colony, Genocide: Conquest, Occupation and Subaltern Resistance in World History* was important in placing such topics as part of the core rather than at the margins of genocide historiography. He has produced a series of single-authored and edited collections, including most recently a six-volume edited series called *Genocide* in the Routledge series Critical Concepts in Historical Studies.

Moses critiques what he sees as a number of trends and limitations in earlier genocide studies scholarship, underlining what he refers to as the limits of "the liberal theory of genocide" and exclusionary nature of what events were included in the lexicon of genocidal events. For example, in describing as valorization much of the writings and conferences about Raphael Lemkin, he writes, "To a great extent, 'genocide studies' has yet to break out of its self-imposed isolation."[30] In "Toward a Critical Theory of Genocide," after critiquing the methods of a number of particularly North American scholars, Moses asserts:

> It is time to consider the proposition that the missing variable in the equation is the *exogenous* pressure of the international state and economic system; and try to imagine the genocides of modernity as part of a single process rather than merely in comparative (and competitive) terms.

Moses' work expands the boundaries of research by looking at issues such as partition and its bloody results in India/Pakistan/Bangladesh, and other cases that have been on the sidelines of genocide research. While Moses' critique has a great deal of validity, his analyses find genocidal elements in a very broad range of historical phenomena.

While the above examples concentrate on a sample of historical writings, new directions appear in many other disciplines. The *Oxford Handbook of Genocide Studies*[31] coedited by Bloxham and Moses is a recent example of new frameworks and includes a section on interdisciplinary perspectives in law, sociology, political science, anthropology, social psychology and philosophy. Contributors such as William Schabas in law and Martin Shaw in sociology have played a significant role in the analysis of genocide research in their respective fields. In contrast to the two volume *Encyclopedia of Genocide* (1999) edited by Israel Charny[32] in which Holocaust-related entries predominate and the second largest number of entries are about aspects of the Armenian genocide, the *Handbook* includes a single chapter on each of these events and there are only five references indexed to the term "Holocaust" in the entire volume. Historian Christopher Browning's essay "Nazi Empire" emphasizes that

> ultimately the Nazi Revolution was to be a racial revolution that reconfigured the demographic make-up of the Nazi empire. The destruction of the Jews was the most comprehensive and far-reaching component of this racial revolution and has become the paradigmatic historical example of total genocide.[33]

This volume of essays by 31 international scholars reflects the broad range of subjects now linked with the study of genocide and incorporates important reframing going on both thematically and regionally in the field. Thematic essays look at concepts such as ethnic cleansing, the state, gender and memory, and others examine genocide in the premodern and early modern world, including colonialism in North America and Latin America. The longest section is on "Genocide in the Late Modern World", and what is significant is the shift away from genocides during World War I and World War II as archetypes; there are chapters by Hilmar Kaiser titled "Genocide at the Twilight of the Ottoman Empire" and Christopher Browning titled "The Nazi Empire." There is also an important essay by Daniel Feierstein looking at how the national security doctrine in Latin America and "the genocide question" are linked. The volume looks at Africa during the colonial period, and northeast Africa and Africa's Great Lakes region since independence. Essays analyze genocides in China, Indonesia and other parts of Asia, and the destructive policies in the late Russian Empire and during the Soviet period, including population displacement and genocide in post-communist Eastern Europe. The final section on the contemporary world includes essays on the Cold War and the UN, military intervention, the politics of prosecution and on prospects of avoidance. This volume provides the non-specialist reader with both an overview of new directions in the study of genocide in specific disciplines, and accessible scholarly work with bibliographies for beginning research on a range of concepts, issues and events. This work also reflects the continued predominance of European, Australian and North American training of scholars in the field. While Latin American scholarship is increasing, research by African and Asian scholars remains relatively small.

TEACHING GENOCIDE IN THE CLASSROOM

Most teaching about genocide began as an outgrowth of teaching about one historic atrocity linked with at least one other event. Initially, the Holocaust was a primary model and other events such as the Armenian genocide and later the Cambodian genocide were linked to it. Many of the themes in the study of the Holocaust were adopted in teaching about genocide, such as issues of memory, testimony, justice, representation, and restitution. Another method was to create a typology of genocides: utilitarian, retributive, ideological, and so forth, and fit different cases into each category. Since the field was so new, the classroom early on was a laboratory where various theories on causation or patterns were introduced. Over time some theories, such as linking genocide with totalitarian states,[34] became discredited or significantly revised; others such as the emphasis on modernity[35] and genocide have been modified or taken in new directions.

In the 1970s and 1980s, a number of courses focusing on comparative genocide generally analyzed one archetypal event, usually the Holocaust and sometimes the Armenian or the Cambodian genocides in comparison with other cases. Under this model, there was also often the categorization of "total" as distinct from "partial" genocide. It can be pedagogically very effective for students to learn in depth about one genocidal event and then use that case as a basis for understanding genocide as a phenomenon through comparison and contrast with other case studies; however, the archetype or paradigmatic frame is less widely used now and has undergone modification.

For the last ten summers the "Genocide and Human Rights University Program," held for ten days at the University of Toronto and sponsored by the Zoryan Institute, has been an interesting example of archetypal framing, with its underlying philosophy of the Armenian genocide as the paradigmatic model or archetype and linked with other case studies. When the seminar began, there were three days focused on the Armenian genocide; and this was reduced to one day due to time limitations and student feedback. References to the Armenian genocide are included throughout the course. Six to eight specialists each summer teach different cases and themes, and while originally the course was designed for undergraduates there has been a shift toward more doctoral and postdoctoral students. A number of graduates of the program have gone on to publish articles and books in genocide studies, and there is an unusual ongoing scholarly network between students, instructors and the Zoryan Institute.[36] Because of outreach efforts and scholarships, a disproportionate number of students are of Armenian and Turkish descent. One of the unanticipated outcomes is the degree to which the course provides an opportunity for young scholars of Armenian and Turkish background to meet face to face and to discuss issues about the Armenian genocide, the Turkish state's policy of denial, and reconciliation.

A number of other summer programs and workshops focused on genocide or issues related to genocide have multiplied in the last 15 years. For example, the nonprofit Auschwitz Institute for Peace and Reconciliation (AIPR) established in 2005 has genocide prevention as its mission. Its goal is to build "a worldwide network of leaders with the professional tools and the personal commitment to prevent genocide."[37]

The case model approach continues to be widely used, but which cases are included has changed both in response to world events and to new texts and emphases in research. For example, much more attention is now given to genocides against indigenous peoples and the links between colonialism and targeted destruction at the time of conquest and later. The initial static approach to genocidal occurrences as bounded in time and as circumscribed types of events has given way to a reconceptualization that views genocides as a more complex series of dynamic processes whose roots are deep and whose after-effects continue long after the height of violence ends. Indeed, from the concepts of intentionality and motives to links with a range of destructive policies and practices such as gendered violence, new frames for studying and analyzing comparative genocide have appeared in courses. While definitional debates still occur (largely over the UN Genocide Convention and those of various social scientists and historians), there is generally much less focus on this issue than earlier on. Also, scholars are exploring regional and international factors contributing to the processes taking place during genocide and the impact afterward regionally and globally. Hence, in various ways, a number of courses on genocide and related themes have integrated a more sophisticated and broader analysis than was previously the case.

Undergraduate course offerings on comparative genocide remain relatively small in number. They generally use the case study approach, are of one semester, and focus on the modern era. These courses may be offered in anthropology, history, law, philosophy, psychology, political science, sociology and other disciplines. Different lenses and emphases include US foreign policy and genocide, war and genocide, and post-genocidal societies. In the last two decades there have been a number of shifts in the methodology, content and framing of courses on genocide, particularly in graduate courses. One direction is linking the study of genocide with massacres, mass atrocities, ethnic cleansing and various other forms of violence including structural violence. Another perspective is emphasizing the international and global dimensions out of which genocides emerge. Looking forward, linking genocide curricula with development studies, and scarcity and environmental research will increase at the graduate level, but the more traditional case study approach will persist particularly in undergraduate offerings, in part due to institutional and funding structures that are in place (endowments for chairs, other funding by specific groups, and the like).

The trend continues to include genocide along with other life-integrity violations in multi-disciplinary courses on human rights, crimes against humanity, and related subjects. Since human rights and human wrongs are inextricably connected, there has been a shift toward looking at genocide within the larger frame of human rights and humanitarianism.

My own course titles reflect this shift: in the 1970s it was "Destruction of European Jewry" (including comparing Sinta and Roma and the Armenian genocide), then came "Comparative Genocide," and now recent courses are titled "Politics of Mass Hate and Genocide and Challenges of Humanitarianism"; "Cultures and Societies at Risk"; "Law, Genocide and Human Rights"; and "Languages and Literatures of Human Rights."

A number of new centers, programs, concentrations and degree programs largely follow the model of including genocide as one aspect within a larger framing. The Holocaust and Human Rights Program, now called the Holocaust, Genocide and Human Rights Program at Benjamin Cardozo School of Law, is directed by attorney Sheri Rosenberg and is multi-faceted, ranging from training students in international human rights law to writing briefs on cases ranging from discrimination in Serbia to Armenian genocide education in Massachusetts. It also sponsors a series of public forums and international conferences on the legacy of Nuremberg, free speech, Rwanda, and other topics linked to genocide and mass violence. In Europe, a consortium of four universities – Kingston University (Britain), Europa-Universität Viadrina Frankfurt (Oder), Universita degli Studi di Siena, and Collegium Civitas Warsaw – developed in 2004 an M.A. in Human Rights and Genocide. Requirements include a first semester study of human rights legal and institutional structures followed by the study of cases of genocide and other mass violence with a third semester internship in advocacy. The Center for the Study of Genocide, Conflict Resolution and Human Rights (the term Conflict Resolution was recently added to the name) established by Alexander Hinton in 2007 at Rutgers University–Newark, New Jersey, sponsors conferences and programs, a book series, and guest scholars. Beside undergraduate courses in genocide, human rights, conflict resolution and related topics, there is an M.S. in Global Affairs with a focus on genocide, political violence or human rights.

There is a range of certificate and degree granting programs in Human Rights (from a focus on NGOs to legal scholarship), Humanitarian Studies and

Development Studies that incorporate courses on genocide as part of their curriculum. Other programs are rooted in specific disciplines such as the master's program at the University of Sussex, England, in Anthropology of Conflict, Violence and Reconciliation linked to the university's Centre for the Study of Genocide and Mass Violence. Another model is the growth of a range of Public Policy programs (most at the master's level) and the study of genocide and human rights as a unit. New programs, some at universities and a number with government funding, have also been developed in Kigali, Sarajevo and other sites of mass violence. There are a number of new research centers such as the Center for Genocide Studies at Universidad Nacional de Tres de Febrero in Buenos Aires directed by Daniel Feierstein, as well as Jacques Sémelin's research projects including the *Online Encyclopedia of Mass Violence* at the Centre d'Etudes et de Recherches Internationales in Paris.[38] On the M.A. and Ph.D. level there has been an increase in the last 15 years in thesis research on genocide, including in post-genocidal societies from Guatemala to Cambodia, the Balkans and especially Rwanda. In fact, it is from this pool of young scholars trained in a traditional discipline who pursue research on a genocide-related topic that future genocide scholars are most likely to emerge.

Resources

In contrast to the early 1970s when teaching genocide began and there were few resources available for instructors (this was also the case for developing new courses about women and about indigenous peoples), there is now a range of resources on comparative study and on particular events, including a growing number of works on post-genocidal societies, memory, transitional justice, and other themes. There is also an expanding number of memoirs and novels as well as films for classroom use. The number of online resources continues to grow, including links with a textbook[39] to academic and research institutes to NGO and humanitarian sites, such as www.reliefweb.org. Careful evaluation and critiquing of resources (students seem particularly uncritical of web sources) is an important but all too often neglected part of research training.

Undergraduate courses in comparative genocide remain relatively small in number and are taught primarily by people who do research on genocide and other forms of violence. The textbooks *Genocide: A Comprehensive Introduction* and *Century of Genocide* are accessible single volume resources along with the earlier text *History and Sociology of Genocide*.[40] The publication of a range of single volume edited collections and texts on comparative analysis (by Alexander Hinton, Robert Gellately and Ben Kiernan, to name a few) and of single volumes on particular subjects from transitional justice to genocide prevention, encourages the "non-specialist" to offer courses in genocide, or what is more frequently the case, a section on genocide within a course on human rights, violence, or related subjects.

Choosing texts for general undergraduate courses focusing on genocide reflects a number of the same challenges that are written about concerning wider issues in higher education in the United States, especially that students are less well-prepared to read long and complicated volumes. Survey courses rely heavily on narrative and journalist accounts. For example, Philip Gourevitch's book *We wish to inform you that tomorrow we will be killed with our families*, and Paul Rusesabagina's *An Ordinary Man,* and the film *Hotel Rwanda* are the most widely used works introducing undergraduate students to the Rwandan genocide. This points to the interesting disconnect between the expansion and sophistication of the literature in genocide research and what undergraduates are actually reading. Another example is the widely read and accessible journalistic account by Samantha Power, *"A Problem from Hell": America and the Age of Genocide.*[41] Her focus on US power and influence reinforces many American students' belief in the omnipotence of American exceptionalism in world affairs. At the same time, Power's widely read volume and other popular works have promoted student interest in preventing genocide. There continues to be a growth of student interest in issues concerning human rights, genocide and humanitarianism, including careers (especially with non-governmental and intergovernmental organizations), which in turn provides impetus for a range of course offerings.

Teaching methods in the classroom

The following is a series of pedagogical issues, methods and challenges regarding the teaching of courses on genocide and other forms of mass violence at the undergraduate level. While based on experience of teaching for decades primarily in North America, it is hoped that they will be relevant to a broad audience.

Critiquing the syllabus

What is left in? What is left out? Why? The first day of class should be dedicated to going through the syllabus and discussing with students what is included and what is left out and why. Just as in world history courses, the enormity of the subject means that some events are left out and the instructor cannot be equally knowledgeable about all events. Indeed, like teaching a course in world history, the instructor for the most part relies on secondary sources. It is crucial to acknowledge that education is not a neutral undertaking, and to discuss the choice of readings and perspectives of assigned authors. For example, Adam Jones, in *Genocide: A Comprehensive Introduction* provides a discussion about how his perspective impacts the contents of his textbook. Looking at the politics of the text[42] and syllabus contributes to students' ongoing development of critical thinking skills.

Place, the state and genocide

Different cases of historical atrocities are discussed and emphasized depending on what country one is teaching in. For example, in the US students early on in my courses debate issues of whether destruction of the indigenous peoples in the Americas and slavery are genocides, as well as the US atomic bombings during World War II of Hiroshima and Nagasaki. Students generally do not know about the Cambodian genocide and I always include a section analyzing the "sideshow" and impact of US foreign policy and the Cold War. Violence is part and parcel of most people's history, and situating the history of the country one is teaching in *vis à vis* histories of violence (structural, political, colonial, etc.) provides an important beginning to distinguishing different levels and types of violence and their impact. Whether in Australia, Pakistan or Mexico, issues about the treatment of indigenous populations and slave and forced labor may provide a valuable way to educate about the local and global pervasiveness of human destructiveness.

Choosing texts

A range of books is available on particular events, as well as one-volume textbooks and collections. A good resource for beginning undergraduate and graduate research is the *Oxford Handbook of Genocide Studies*. Interestingly, at this point there are more and better resources available for graduate courses than for undergraduate programs. The challenge of choosing books for undergraduate students in North America for example, reflects larger issues in higher education about student reading skills and attention span, and many instructors are choosing shorter, more accessible texts as noted earlier.

One method is to begin with shorter essays that provide an overview or short pieces on topics and methods that will be referred to throughout the semester. Particularly helpful are essays in Alexander Hinton's edited collections *Genocide: An Anthropological Reader* and *Annihilating Difference: An Anthropology of Genocide*, and in Robert Gellately and Ben Kiernan's collection of essays *The Specter of Genocide*. Dirk Moses has edited six volumes of collected essays entitled *Genocide*, which provide a broad spectrum of topics from different disciplines.[43]

Locating the study of genocide

Since the term "genocide," like that of "human rights," is widespread and popularly referred to in covering a wide spectrum of events, it is helpful early on to discuss the term's meanings and definitions, including that of the UN Convention on the Prevention and Punishment of the Crime of Genocide. Creating a typology of different forms of violence provides a method for students to compare and contrast different forms of atrocity such as massacres, ethnic cleansing, colonization, etc., and also weighing the "cides" such as politicide, gendercide, ethnocide, and their effectiveness or not in understanding different types of destruction. Christian Gerlach's "extremely violent societies" provides a broad categorization that may be helpful for students locating different types of violence.[44]

How is genocide as a phenomenon described? What are its boundaries? Daniel Rothenberg writes:

> Few concepts carry the weight and power of the term genocide. The word's profound significance is bound to its unique role as a moral and legal marker of the very worst type of human behavior. Morally, genocide refers to acts of horrific violence such as mass murder, state terror and other strategies of brutal repression.[45]

Students benefit from critiquing early on the "iconic" status of genocide as the crime of crimes. It is interesting to note there is no "crimes against humanity studies" and despite the terrible crimes involved, it is unlikely there will be in the future. Why?

Student prejudices and viewpoints

Students enter the course with a range of preconceived ideas about genocide; many feel they "know" the Holocaust from education in middle and high school. The "great man" theory of evil and history – Hitler, Stalin, Pol Pot – is still widely taught and promoted in public culture. Part of the course's purpose is to introduce students to the complex nature of history and of historical destruction and to rethink how genocides are carried out. Essentialist concepts about certain peoples and continents, especially regarding Africa and Asia, and about genocide and other mass atrocities as the inevitable byproduct of age-old conflicts or tribalism are widespread. A key goal of the course is providing students with deeper and more nuanced understandings.

Dare to omit

After experimenting with teaching a world history of genocide, my conclusion is to choose a theme/s or series of cases and concentrate on studying them in more depth. Through research topics and group reports students may be introduced to additional events and topics. Hence, while I have used general textbooks such as Adam Jones' *Genocide: A Comprehensive Introduction* (and regularly assign selected chapters such as those on "Social Science Perspectives"), I prefer to select a series of more in-depth works on events and processes, including at least one memoir and novel, in comparative genocide courses.

Framing and patterns of genocide

The rationale behind, and utilitarian aspects of, states and groups carrying out targeted destruction is emphasized throughout my courses. Patterns of genocide emerge such as the use of war as a cover for civilian extermination, ideologies and propaganda of destruction, methods of destruction, etc. The impact of global movements, including empire building and post-colonialism as well as regional factors, is crucial in framing the escalation of conflict into genocide and other atrocities.

Incorporating at least one recent scholarly work each year

While this is helpful for students, for the instructor it provides an important way of rethinking issues given the new scholarship being produced. My experience is that, given the difficulty of the course's content, teaching new material helps me emotionally cope with presenting this difficult material. Often these works have an interesting methodology, add a new perspective, are based on new archival materials, or have a controversial thesis such as Alexander Hinton's *Why Not Kill Them All?* on Cambodia, Anna Politkovskaya's *A Small Corner of Hell: A Russian Reporter from Chechnya*, Mahmood Mamdani's *When Victims Become Killers* on Rwanda, or S. A. Barnes' *Death and Redemption: The Gulag and Building Soviet Society*.

Avoiding a hierarchy of suffering and competitive victimization

The difficulty of comparing and contrasting events has been discussed earlier in this chapter. In the classroom, the instructor may be specifically challenged by students who are insistent on "ranking" genocidal events based on their own background or education. For example, students sometimes refer to one event as "The Genocide" or "The Holocaust" and may assume everyone shares their understanding of these terms. Developing student's analytic abilities, including recognizing patterns, distinctions and differences among cases, is an ongoing goal throughout the course.

Denial of genocide

Over the years, there have been a handful of students who deny that specific events took place or are genocidal. What to do? Often, this is very disruptive and upsetting to other students and the instructor. I generally allow these students to talk and their classmates to effectively counter their arguments. Another method of addressing issues of denial is to have students go to websites and to analyze different official versions or omissions and connect to patterns of denial.

Avoiding the numbing effect and "just another genocide syndrome"

Sometimes students feel overwhelmed or numb after reading about so much human destruction and feel a sense of helplessness. This "just another genocide syndrome" may be lessened by using a broad lens, such as reconfiguring the course within a human rights and humanitarian framework. While there is a critical literature about "doing good" and various humanitarian practices, it is helpful for students to see what the possibilities for relieving suffering are. Linking with broader topics such as state building and issues of scarcity and conflict is also helpful for students in studying genocide and its prevention. Another method is to use film and literature as well as social scientific and historical analysis from, for example, trauma studies.

Moral education and teaching about genocide

Teaching genocide and human rights should be done as objectively as possible without preaching and proselytizing. As Veronica Boix-Mansilla points out in discussing the dangers of history as "values education," there is a tendency toward simplification and creating

> a collection of facile "myths" about one group or one person's "heritage," "identity" or "culture" ... Within this moral framework, the disciplinary skepticism that might lead one to legitimately question the validity of historical accounts is mistakenly perceived as an affront to the values that such an account is said to embody. Subordinating history to values education undermines deep historical understanding when it forces teachers and students alike to lose sight of the meticulous process by which understanding of the past is established and revised by historians, no matter how difficult and morally problematic the past may be.[46]

Another aspect of teaching history in general as values education is the goal of fostering empathy as a method to better understand events. Part of the underpinnings of teaching empathy is "the claim that one has to get into an informed appreciation of the predicaments and viewpoints of people in the past in order to gain real historical understanding (to see the past from its point of view)."[47] Keith Jenkins, in his classic work *Re-thinking History*, argues strongly on a number of philosophical and pedagogical grounds about the problems and limitations with focusing on getting into the minds of people in the past. He critiques teaching history as empathy and "the pedagogy of personal involvement" as often grounded in a liberal ideology that "values rationality and balance and tries to bring people in the past (who were so different from us) under our control ... to make them the same as us, propelled everywhere by rational calculation, liberal style."[48] Instead, Jenkins argues for an awareness that historians translate and interpret events (historians have their own orientation, situation no matter how "unbiased" they attempt to be), and promoting empathy tends to simplify history and detract from the elements of fluidity in peoples' lives and actions.

The tendency to teach the Holocaust, genocide and human rights as moral education promoting empathy and prevention is ongoing. In part, this may be a spillover from the exceptionalist and unique vocabularies within early Holocaust writings; that is, claims that this type of subject matter is unique, different and implicitly more important than others. Such pedagogical perspectives in many respects invite preaching more than educating, and are often seen for example in teaching human rights as advocacy. In fact, many students enter the class because they are concerned about past or current human rights violations such as those in Darfur, the Congo, Burma, Tibet, and elsewhere.

It seems to me crucial to teach about genocide and other atrocities *without* an advocacy/empathy overlay. Clearly, every teacher enters the classroom with his/her own interests and viewpoints, and part of going over the syllabus critically is to give students insight into the teacher's interests. However, students need to develop and refine their own philosophical perspectives and gain insights by engaging with the materials; teachers can facilitate this through class readings, lectures and assignments. For example, I sometimes ask students to keep a language "term" notebook over the course of the semester, including entries from readings and discussions. This assignment is a vehicle for allowing them to see how their ideas about the meaning and value of concepts such as "human rights" or "bystander" or "humanitarianism" have evolved, and the complicated, multi-layered histories and ideas they are grappling with. Such an assignment is in keeping with a pedagogy that believes students need to be able to absorb and evaluate materials for themselves rather than have teachers impose a moral framework.

The class is a learning environment for deepening analysis, providing content and refining critical thinking and other skills. Clearly, the material lends itself to students becoming morally engaged, and some of my students have gone on to teach or do advocacy work. However, they are far better served and prepared by learning how to critically analyze events and actors and to have a critical tool-kit to examine how and which events are and are not being written about, and the complex and contradictory ways that violent processes develop. Rather than the current popular discourse of the inevitable rise and inherent goodness of human rights, there now exists a more nuanced literature on the political and historical contextualization of the "strange triumph of human rights"[49] and its multiple functions for states and other civilian actors.[50] In other words, students learn about developing critical methods and understanding as they search out the complicated dynamics involved in understanding issues of genocide and human rights, just as they do in learning about other historic events.

CHALLENGES AHEAD

The rise in publications on genocide, as well as establishment of new scholarly organizations like the International Association of Genocide Scholars and the International Network of Genocide Scholars and field-specific academic journals, reflect a broad scholarly interest in keeping genocide as a distinct research area. However, it is unclear to what extent genocide studies will remain in its present institutionalized form. Certainly, the links as well as tensions between genocide and Holocaust education and research will continue. There are a number of important critiques and new directions in studying genocide, but a new "theory of genocide studies" and more refined analyses in comparative frameworks have yet to be articulated. The deepening of genocide research, as well as the creation of new connections with research areas like development studies, human rights and humanitarianism in all likelihood will continue. There seems to be an increasing number of "ands" in courses and research, such as genocide and war, genocide and the modern nation-state, human rights and genocide, development and genocide, and genocide and mass violence, which point to new links with other fields of inquiry. The study of and courses in genocide will certainly continue to grow, but more and more they are likely to be linked with, and at times subsumed under, other areas of academic research and programs.

■ NOTES

1 J. Apsel, "Education," in Dinah L. Shelton, ed., *Encyclopedia of Genocide and Crimes against Humanity*, Detroit, MI: Macmillan, 2005, pp. 276–8.

2 L. Kuper, *Genocide: Its Political Use in the Twentieth Century*, New Haven, CT: Yale University Press, 1983, p. 11.

3 R. Lemarchand, *Forgotten Genocides: Oblivion, Denial and Memory*, Philadelphia: University of Pennsylvania Press, 2011, p. viii.

4 Ibid., pp. 1–2.

5 For example, see A. Jones, "Genocide and Structural Violence: Charting the Terrain," in Adam Jones, ed., *New Directions in Genocide Research*, Abingdon, UK: Routledge, 2012, pp. 132–52.

6 T. Snyder, *Bloodlands: Europe between Hitler and Stalin*, New York: Basic Books, 2010.

7 For a recent article analyzing how the narrative of the new exhibition at Yad Vashem reflects Israeli politicization of representation of the Holocaust, see A. Goldberg, "The 'Jewish Narrative' in the Yad Vashem Global Holocaust Museum," *Journal of Genocide Research* 14/2, 2012, 187–213.

8 Available HTTP: www.ahoinfo.org/aboutaho.html The website lists AHO members and affiliates and has a yearly conference, traveling exhibits and serves as a network for a range of Holocaust education organizations.

9 See NJ Commission on Holocaust Education, HTTP: www.state.nj.us./education/holocaust, for teacher education programs, publications, and activities in the US. For Europe and other locations see the Facing History and Ourselves website, www.facinghistory.org

10 Available HTTP: www.stockton.edu/grad. Stockton College of New Jersey has around 8,000 full and part time students. The college offers a minor for undergraduates and an M.A. in Holocaust and Genocide Studies. It has two endowed chairs in Holocaust Studies. The Ida E. King Distinguished Visiting Professorship of Holocaust Studies began in 1990 (and in spring 2009 I taught in the program as holder of the King chair). The Sara and Sam Schoffer Holocaust Resource Center is housed in the college library and its director Gail Rosenthal has been the crucial figure in fund raising, teaching and coordinating the $1 million-plus renovation completed in 2009 (www.stockton.edu/holocausthrc.htm). The academic programs and resource center work together and offer lectures, film series, publish Holocaust survivor memoirs, and educational tours; they work with Facing History and Ourselves, Yad Vashem and other organizations, and sponsor talks on a range of human rights topics. Another M.A. program in Holocaust and Genocide Studies at Keen University (http:grad.kean.edu/mahgs) was approved by the New Jersey state educational authorities in 2010. Stockton and Kean are located about 144 miles apart, and the educational goals on each website appear similar in most respects.

11 Available HTTP: www.clarku.edu/departments/holocaust. "The Strassler Center for Holocaust and Genocide Studies trains students, educators, and activists to develop a sophisticated understanding of genocide." Under its director and Rose Professor of Holocaust History, Deborah Dwork, the program has a series of outstanding scholars such as Thomas Kuehne and Taner Akçam, and faculty from eight departments offer courses. There are endowed professorships (including in Armenian history and genocide) and scholarships, and internships for doctoral candidates; the center sponsors scholarly conferences, teacher training programs, etc. According to the center's website annual reports, the small number of doctoral graduates have found jobs primarily in Holocaust community and education programs.

12 The International Task Force on the Holocaust (ITF) was initiated by Swedish Prime Minister Goran Persson. See available HTTP: www.holocausttaskforce.org/

13 www.holocausttaskforce.org/about-the-itf/stockholm-declaration.html

14 Ibid.

15 M. Shaw, *What Is Genocide?* Cambridge: Polity Press, 2007, p. 38.

16 See P. Novick, *The Holocaust in American Life*, New York: Houghton-Mifflin, 1999.

17 See for example, R. F. Melson, *Revolution and Genocide: On the Origins of the Armenian Genocide and the Holocaust*, Chicago: University of Chicago Press, 1992.

18 W. A. Schabas, *Genocide in International Law*, Cambridge: Cambridge University Press, 2000.

19 Minorities at Risk Project; www.cidcm.umd.edu/mar/

20 http:www.auschwitzinstitute.org

21 See D. Stone, ed., *The Historiography of Genocide*, London: Palgrave Macmillan, 2007; A. D. Moses (2008) "Toward a Theory of Critical Genocide Studies," *Online Encyclopedia of Mass Violence*, Available HTTP: www.massviolence.org; D. Bloxham and A. D. Moses, eds., *The Oxford Handbook of Genocide Studies*, Oxford: Oxford University Press, 2010.

22 M. Weiner-Hanks, *Historical Comparisons*, Teaching to Think Historically series, Washington, DC: American Historical Association, 2007.

23 H. G. Haupt and J. Kocka, eds., *Comparative and Transnational History: Central European Approaches and New Perspectives*, New York: Berghahn Books, 2009, p. vii.

24 Ibid., pp. 1–30.

25 D. Cohen, "Comparative History: Buyer Beware," in Deborah Cohen and Maura O'Connor, eds., *Comparison and History*, New York: Routledge, 2004.

26 R. Gellately and B. Kiernan, eds., *The Specter of Genocide: Mass Murder in Historical Perspective*, Cambridge: Cambridge University Press, 2003. B. Kiernan, *Blood and Soil: A World History of Genocide and Extermination from Sparta to Darfur*, New Haven, CT: Yale University Press, 2007.

27 E. D. Weitz, *A Century of Genocide: Utopias of Race and Nation*, Princeton, NJ: Princeton University Press, 2003.

28 M. Levene, *Genocide in the Age of the Nation-State*, vol. 1: *The Meaning of Genocide* and vol. 2: *The Rise of the West and the Coming of Genocide*, London: I. B. Tauris, 2005.

29 See his professional biography at www.shc.ed.ac.ukhistory/staff/

30 A. D. Moses (2008) "Toward a Critical Theory of Genocide Studies," *Online Encyclopedia of Mass Violence*. Available HTTP: http://massviolence.org

31 D. Bloxham and A. D. Moses, eds., *Oxford Handbook of Genocide Studies*, Oxford: Oxford University Press, 2010.

32 I. Charny, ed., *Encyclopedia of Genocide*, 2 vols, Santa Barbara, CA: ABC-Clio, 1999.

33 C. Browning, "Nazi Empire," in Donald Bloxham and A. Dirk Moses, eds., *Oxford Handbook of Genocide Studies*, pp. 407–25.

34 R. J. Rummel, *Death by Government*, New Brunswick, NJ: Transaction Publishers, 1997.

35 For example, see Z. Bauman, *Modernity and the Holocaust*, Ithaca, NY: Cornell University Press, 1989.

36 J. Apsel, "Educating a New Generation: The Model of the Genocide and Human Rights University Program," *Human Rights Review* 12/4, 2011, 465–86. Joyce Apsel has taught in the program since 2004 and is current course Director.

37 www.auschwitzinstiute.org/who-we-are.html

38 The online encyclopedia is available at www.massviolence.org

39 A. Jones, *Genocide: A Comprehensive Introduction*, 2nd edition, New York: Routledge, 2010.

40 A. Jones, *Genocide: A Comprehensive Introduction* is the most comprehensive text available and includes photos, bibliography and web-related materials. S. Totten and W. Parsons, eds., *Century of Genocide*, 3rd edition, New York: Routledge, 2004 includes a series of eyewitness testimonies and histories of selected cases. F. Chalk and K. Jonassohn, *The History and Sociology of Genocide: Analyses and Case Studies*, New Haven, CT: Yale University Press, 1990 spans ancient to modern times.

41 S. Power, *"A Problem from Hell": America and the Age of Genocide*, New York: Basic Books, 2002.

42 See M. Apple and L. K. Christian-Smith, eds., *The Politics of the Textbook*, London: Taylor & Francis, 1991.

43 A. D. Moses, ed., *Genocide*, 6 vols, Concepts in Historical Studies Series, New York: Routledge, 2010.

44 C. Gerlach, *Extremely Violent Societies: Mass Violence in the Twentieth Century World*, Cambridge: Cambridge University Press, 2010.

45 D. Rothenberg, "Genocide," in Dinah L. Shelton, ed., *Encyclopedia of Genocide and Crimes against Humanity*, vol. 1, Detroit, MI: Macmillan Reference, 2005, pp. 395–7.

46 V. Boix-Mansilla, "Historical Understanding Beyond the Past and Into the Present," in P. N. Stearns, P. Seixas and S. Wineburg, eds., *Knowing Teaching and Learning History*, New York: New York University Press, 2000, p. 391.

47 K. Jenkins, *Re-thinking History*, New York: Routledge, 1991, p. 47.

48 Ibid., pp. 52–4.

49 M. Mazower, "Strange Triumph of Human Rights 1922–1950," *Historical Journal* 47, 2004, 379–98.

50 S. L. Hoffman, ed., *Human Rights in the Twentieth Century*, Cambridge: Cambridge University Press, 2011.

CHAPTER 8

Humanitarian Military Intervention After the "Responsibility to Protect"

Obstacles and prospects

Paul D. Williams

INTRODUCTION

If genocide studies is to contribute to stopping episodes of mass atrocities rather than just studying their consequences, it needs to think more systematically about the practical and theoretical questions related to military intervention and the use of force. This is especially important in light of the evolving "responsibility to protect" (R2P) principle and recent episodes of mass atrocities in Libya, Côte d'Ivoire, Sudan, Syria, Yemen, Bahrain and elsewhere. Indeed, during 2011 debates about humanitarian military intervention entered a significant new phase. On March 17, United Nations (UN) Security Council resolution 1973 authorized member states to invade Libya to stop Muammar Gaddafi's regime slaughtering its own people.[1] This was the first time the Security Council had authorized the use of military force for human protection purposes against the wishes of a functioning, *de jure* regime. Also in early 2011, the Security Council authorized UN peacekeepers and French troops to use military force to protect civilians and oust the incumbent (but illegitimate) regime of Laurent Gbagbo. It did so on the basis that Gbagbo's government was no longer the *de jure* authority because it had rigged the country's election results, its forces had attacked and killed UN peacekeepers, and because it carried out atrocity crimes against local civilians.[2] And yet while mass atrocities in Libya and Côte d'Ivoire triggered a military response from the UN Security Council, similar types of violence used by the regimes in Syria, Sudan, Yemen, Bahrain, and elsewhere did not. Part of the reason is that humanitarian military intervention remains a deeply controversial idea within contemporary international society for a combination of moral, political, and practical reasons. Nevertheless, as long as international society continues to denounce genocide and mass atrocities but fails to stop them, thinking about the theory and practice of such intervention must continue.

In this chapter, humanitarian military intervention refers to the use of military force without host state consent aimed at preventing or ending widespread and grave violations of human rights such as genocide, ethnic cleansing, or crimes against humanity. Put bluntly, it is about invading a country and waging war, but that war is carried out in the name of humanity and to protect foreigners rather than citizens. For some, the idea of "humanitarian war" is simply a dangerous oxymoron. For others, it is a realistic way of thinking about how to stop genocide and mass atrocity crimes and thereby open up political space for conflict resolution initiatives.

At the outset, it is important to distinguish humanitarian military intervention from the related concept of "civilian protection" as it has been discussed and practiced in peacekeeping operations conducted by the UN and a variety of other international organizations, principally the African Union (AU) and European Union (EU). This is the key distinction between what happened in Libya and Côte d'Ivoire. The protection of civilians (PoC) agenda, which has been codified within the UN system since the late 1990s through Security Council resolutions and statements as well as various reports, refers to attempts by peacekeepers *already on the ground with the consent of the host authorities* to protect populations under imminent threat from direct physical violence.[3] None of these peace operations, whether carried out by the UN, AU or EU, have been conducted against the will of the official, *de jure* host government and hence none of them count as humanitarian military interventions. This is what took place in Côte d'Ivoire in early 2011: a peacekeeping operation authorized to use force to protect its own personnel and civilians. There is, of course, considerable overlap in the substance of these agendas, especially at the operational and tactical levels, but at the strategic level the PoC agenda has generated a degree of international consensus that has been completely lacking in the debate about humanitarian military intervention, which is what occurred in Libya between March and October 2011.

In order to address these issues, the first section of this chapter analyzes five clusters of obstacles to the theory and practice of humanitarian military intervention: legal challenges, legitimacy challenges, political challenges, strategic challenges, and prudential challenges. The second section then assesses the extent to which the UN's endorsement of R2P has overcome these hurdles and altered the prospects for saving strangers during the world's worst cases of genocide and mass killing. The overall argument is that the emergence and codification of the R2P principle is slowly enhancing the prospects for saving strangers in several respects.

Ironically, however, given the controversy surrounding the Libyan intervention, advocates of R2P are likely to shift the focus of responding to mass atrocities away from questions of military action and into the realms of prevention and early warning.

OBSTACLES TO HUMANITARIAN MILITARY INTERVENTION

Debates about humanitarian military intervention have generated a large and growing literature. This can be crudely divided into works discussing when it might be permissible to conduct such interventions;[4] studies that analyze which strategies of intervention are likely to be most successful;[5] and publications that debate which agents are most appropriate for conducting such interventions.[6] For this chapter, the key question is why there have been so few examples of humanitarian military intervention despite (a) the increasing number of governments that regularly espouse "never again" rhetoric, i.e. that claim to be committed to preventing and/or stopping genocide; and (b) the simultaneous persistence of numerous episodes of mass atrocities against civilian populations (see Figure 8.1). Assuming that at least some of these "never again" claims are sincere, part of the explanation for this puzzle requires an examination of the major obstacles to such interventions. For analytical purposes, I discuss these under five headings: legal challenges, legitimacy challenges, political challenges, strategic challenges, and prudential challenges.

Legal challenges

The first challenge revolves around whether international law permits a right of humanitarian military intervention. Adam Roberts accurately summed up the

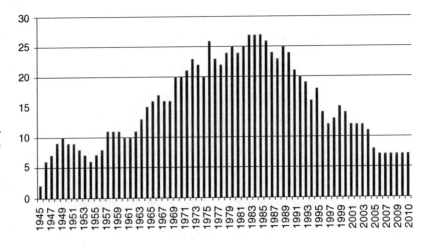

Figure 8.1 Ongoing episodes of mass killing involving more than 5,000 intentional civilian fatalities, 1945–2010

Source: Updated from the appendix in Bellamy and Williams (2012).

situation in the early twenty-first century when he wrote: "there is not at present a one-word general answer to this seemingly clear question. Nor is there any chance of such an answer emerging in the near future."[7]

While it is widely acknowledged that the UN Security Council has the right to authorize a humanitarian military intervention, the dispute centers on whether actors other than the Security Council could conduct such an intervention legally.[8] The challenge for advocates of humanitarian intervention is that although the Council retains the right to authorize the use of force to protect populations in danger, it was not until March 2011 and Security Council resolution 1973 on Libya that it had done so against the will of a sovereign government. Before that, the closest it had come was in December 1992 when after noting the UN secretary-general's view that there was no government in Somalia "that could request and allow such use of force,"[9] Security Council resolution 794 determined that "the magnitude of the human tragedy caused by the conflict in Somalia" constituted a "threat to international peace and security" and authorized the deployment of the US-led Unified Task Force. The Security Council's track record thus suggests that it is highly unlikely to consistently authorize humanitarian military intervention as a response to genocide and mass atrocities.

The central legal issue in the case of other, non-UN actors conducting a humanitarian intervention is the indeterminacy of international law. Even on such fundamental questions as the use of military force, this indeterminacy stems not only from different sources of international law placing different emphasis on human rights as opposed to state's rights, but also from the varied interpretations of state practice and *opinio juris* offered by international lawyers and other legal experts. Thus while a small handful of international legal experts have argued that it is permissible for actors other than the Security Council to authorize humanitarian military intervention – largely on the basis of an interpretation of customary international law and a reading of specific treaties and sources of international humanitarian law – the majority view remains that such interventions are illegal.[10] As a consequence, any potential humanitarian military intervention not authorized by the UN Security Council would have to be carried out without a strong basis in international law, while likely being perceived as clearly illegal by most states within international society. In such a political climate, probably the best that the agents conducting the intervention could hope for is to acknowledge the general perception that their action stretched the limits of international legality and to make a plea in mitigation in light of the current, exceptional circumstances.[11]

Legitimacy challenges

In addition to its precarious status in international law, the legitimacy of humanitarian military intervention has also been challenged on the explicitly normative grounds that its frequent application would be detrimental to international peace and security. Despite some notable efforts to make the moral case for humanitarian intervention, including by former UN Secretary-General Kofi Annan, a majority of the UN's member states have repeatedly demonstrated their opposition to a norm sanctioning such interventions without prior authorization from the Security Council. The various challenges to the legitimacy of humanitarian military intervention have come in three principal forms related to its potential to encourage *instability*, *abuse*, and *selectivity*.

One argument suggests that endorsing a norm of humanitarian intervention within a society of states whose members rarely agree on what counts as just conduct is a recipe for undermining the normative basis of the contemporary international order and provoking instability which will lead to greater levels of human suffering in the long run.[12] From this perspective, other norms, such as the principles of non-intervention and self-determination, are equally, if not more important than the idea of humanitarian intervention. Indeed, both of these norms have attracted more persistent support within international society as a better basis on which to build a stable international order.[13] Moreover, the concept of humanitarian intervention has been regularly and explicitly rejected by significant numbers of states as an unacceptable breach of sovereignty, which, after all, is the last line of defense against imperialism for the world's small states.[14]

A second objection is that whatever altruistic motivations may lie behind the desire to codify a norm of humanitarian military intervention, its practical application in contemporary world politics will always be open to abuse by powerful governments. As the recent cases of the US-led invasion of Iraq (2003) and Russian military action in South Ossetia and Georgia (2008) illustrate, powerful states are still willing to use humanitarian rhetoric as a fig leaf for the pursuit of narrow political interests. Indeed, it was notable that key members of the coalition of states which claimed to be enforcing resolution 1973 in Libya quickly overstepped the terms of the UN mandate to protect civilians by demanding regime change and by recognizing the rebel Transitional National Council as the legitimate Libyan authority and then supplying it with arms. From this perspective, it is no coincidence that US military power has led the way in almost all of the most controversial cases of intervention in the post-Cold War period, including northern Iraq (1991), Somalia (1992), Haiti (1994), Kosovo (1999) and Libya (2011).

A third challenge stems from the related argument that the moral legitimacy of humanitarian intervention would be greatly strengthened if it were applied in a consistent manner. In practice, however, various reasons have been put forward by powerful governments to justify why the suffering of certain groups of humans should be considered more important than others. Thus, during the 1990s, NATO forces were called on to act in response to the indiscriminate killing of civilians in Bosnia and Herzegovina and Kosovo but not those in, for example, Chechnya, Turkey, or Palestine. During 2011 this debate revolved around why there was no equivalent imposition of the no-fly zone over Libya in Syria, Yemen, or Bahrain despite plausible evidence of mass atrocities against civilians in these countries.

Of course, despite all these concerns, the society of states has been reluctant to completely de-legitimize the idea of humanitarian military intervention in truly dire circumstances, such as the genocide which occurred in Rwanda during 1994 and the slaughter which was thought highly likely to occur in Benghazi, Libya in 2011. Nevertheless, the majority of states prefer to see humanitarian intervention as a generally *illegitimate* practice which represents a dangerous exception to the usual rules of international politics.

Political challenges

If the legal and legitimacy obstacles were not enough, advocates of humanitarian military intervention also have to overcome a range of tough political challenges. First and foremost, "saving strangers" (read "foreigners") is rarely a priority for any state's foreign policy. As a consequence, despite the broad support for the principle that saving human lives represents a worthy cause, in real and potential cases of genocide and mass atrocities states can usually point to a range of more important political priorities to justify non-intervention. For example, in the recent debates about the possibility of humanitarian intervention in Darfur, Western governments were able to point to a range of arguably more pressing policy issues, including the ongoing wars in Iraq and Afghanistan as well as issues related to nuclear containment strategies regarding Iran and North Korea. Another layer of obstacles was raised by the fact that key bilateral relationships for these Western powers with China, India, Russia, Brazil, etc., might have been strained by pushing for an intervention which was unpopular with the ruling regimes within these states.[15]

In essence, the root of many of these political obstacles stem from the fact that the appeal of humanitarian intervention is largely based upon cosmopolitan political theories and ideals of global justice.[16] Thus humanitarian intervention makes perfect sense if one subscribes to these starting points and assumptions. The central political problem is that the most prevalent sentiments held by domestic publics about foreign policy are currently more nationalistic and communitarian than cosmopolitan. Even in liberal democratic states, most politicians do not see a vote-winning opportunity in sending their soldiers into harm's way and getting caught up in somebody else's complicated war in the name of common humanity. As the cases of Kosovo (1999) and Libya (2011) have demonstrated, while such leaders might prove willing to commit their air forces, the deployment of ground troops is a much more controversial issue. There is, of course, no reason why this state of affairs should continue indefinitely. But it is clear that the center of political gravity in most domestic debates about intervention see politicians' primary responsibilities lying with the protection of their citizens rather than foreigners. For example, in the aftermath of the Black Hawk Down incident in Somalia in October 1993, 60 percent of Americans polled agreed with the statement that "nothing the U.S. could accomplish in Somalia is worth the death of even one more soldier."[17] As a consequence, risking "our" soldiers to save "their" people usually requires politicians to make a set of arguments which run against the political grain of opinion within their electorates.

Other political obstacles derive from this basic disconnect. Two of the most commonly asserted relate to financial costs and political capital. In the former case, it is a truism that military interventions will inevitably be a costly drain on the state's financial resources, so once again politicians have to make the case for why intervention is worth the money. In addition, it has also been pointed out that if one is interested in saving strangers' lives, then the military invasion of another country is never likely to be a cost-effective method of going about it. Since literally millions of people around the world die each year from preventable diseases, it makes sense that investing in better international public health programs would save many more lives at a fraction of the cost (it would also probably "not require killing anyone or violating any international laws").[18] Moreover, even when leaders muster the necessary political capital to embark on an intervention and build support for it, they will be acutely aware that it is a risky venture which is unlikely to go completely smoothly and much more prone to face various complications along the way which will jeopardize their invested capital. This appears to have weighed heavily on George H. W. Bush's decision to begin Operation Restore Hope in Somalia just prior to handing over the White House to Bill Clinton's team, and in Clinton's desire to quickly hand over control of the mission's difficult and dangerous disarmament and stabilization agenda to the UN.

Beyond the costs in finance and the risks to political capital, advocates of humanitarian intervention are also sometimes depicted as turning complex political situations into simple caricatures of "good guys versus bad guys." In relation to Sudan, for example, this was a criticism leveled at the various faces of the Save Darfur movement on a regular basis.[19] Similarly, in relation to the Libyan intervention, critics raised a range of concerns about the motives and commitments of the Transitional National Council and its potential links with Islamist extremists. The central problem here is that although the desire to intervene is stimulated by evidence of "perpetrators" massacring "victims," it is also clear from the history of warfare that these are shifting categories which can change over time. Warfare, genocidal violence and mass killing tend to be messy and advocates of humanitarian intervention must expect to have answers which support action despite the messiness.

Strategic challenges

Assuming that the various legal, legitimacy and political challenges can be overcome, advocates of humanitarian intervention also face charges that it deals only with the symptoms and not the causes of genocide and mass killing. As the UN secretary-general's Special Adviser on the Responsibility to Protect, Edward Luck, has argued:

> The problem with the concept of humanitarian intervention was not just that it was decidedly unpopular with many Member States but, more fundamentally, that it was a poor basis for policy or strategy. As the [UN] Secretary-General has asked, would it be morally acceptable to limit oneself to responding after the slaughter is underway? How many thousands would have to die before the international community would consider getting involved? How many effective policy options, and at what costs and risks, would remain at that point?[20]

Viewed from this perspective, if the problem to which humanitarian intervention is responding is indeed genocide and mass killing, then it makes no sense, logically or morally, to work with a policy that deals only with the symptoms rather than the underlying conditions which make such episodes more likely. As a result, calls for humanitarian intervention risk taking attention away from what happens before and after episodes of genocide and mass killing. As Luck went on to note, "Good policy starts with anticipation and prevention, early engagement, and keeping as many reasonable options open as possible."[21] In other words, as traditionally conceived, the policy response of humanitarian intervention tackles only part of the mass killing equation. At best, therefore, it represents one potentially useful instrument in a larger toolbox of policy options aimed at prevention as well as response.

Prudential challenges

The final set of challenges discussed here appears most acutely once humanitarian intervention has been recognized as a legitimate policy option. They are the variety of prudential considerations that go into determining whether, on balance, a practical intervention is likely to do more harm than good. In essence, they are usually framed as calls to engage with the issues raised by the problems of genocide and mass killing but couched in a broader argument that the use of military force will always be a blunt tool for dealing with inherently political problems.[22]

There is a wide range of prudential considerations related to humanitarian intervention. Examples include: What combination of air, sea, and/or land forces should be deployed? What is the likelihood that the injection of foreign military forces will make things worse in the short term, and/or harder to resolve in the longer term? Will military action in this particular case jeopardize other important foreign policy goals such as cooperation among the Permanent Five members of the Security Council? How long should the intervention last and what is the exit strategy or political endgame? To what extent should foreign forces engage with and/or transform local political structures?

There is also the problem of a lack of clear and tested military doctrine in relevant states and international organizations on how to perform the core tasks of humanitarian intervention and civilian protection.[23] As one recent analysis put it, at the strategic level there has been a lack of systematic "thinking about *how* military forces might respond" to situations of mass killing.[24] Stated another way, asking soldiers trained to defeat enemies and capture territory may sometimes be appropriate for responding to episodes of genocide and mass killing, but not always.

For all these reasons, and probably some others as well, humanitarian military intervention remains hugely challenging both in theory and practice. Taken together, it is hardly surprising that there have been so few historical examples. And yet while the civilian bodies keep piling up the issues raised in these debates will not go away. This stubborn fact spurred the advocacy that shifted the debate away from the question of whether actors had a right to intervene to stop atrocities and instead focused on the responsibilities that all states have to protect populations in danger. The purpose of the next section is therefore to examine the extent to which the R2P principle has altered the prospects for overcoming these challenges.

HUMANITARIAN MILITARY INTERVENTION AND THE RESPONSIBILITY TO PROTECT

After a long advocacy campaign during which the "responsibility to protect" phrase was coined, in October 2005 the UN's member states unanimously endorsed the R2P principle in three paragraphs of the World Summit Outcome Document (WSOD).[25] This principle affirmed that each state had "the responsibility to protect its populations from genocide, war crimes, ethnic cleansing and crimes against humanity" as well as "their incitement" (paragraph 138).[26] Moreover, should any state be found to be "manifestly failing to protect their populations" from these four crimes, the world's governments committed themselves "to take collective action, in a timely and decisive manner, through the Security Council, in accordance with the Charter" (paragraph 139).

Since then, the R2P principle has been endorsed in a variety of international venues including in Security Council resolutions related to peacekeeping and the protection of civilians – notably resolutions 1674 (2006), 1706 (2006) and 1894 (2009) – and in a UN General Assembly resolution which appeared after a long series of debates.[27] As noted above, it has also now been invoked in resolutions on the situations in Libya and Côte d'Ivoire in 2011.

Within the UN Secretariat, the secretary-general, Ban Ki-moon, and his special adviser, Edward Luck, have led an effort to translate the R2P principle from "words to deeds."[28] This included the publication of an important report of the secretary-general in January 2009, *Implementing the Responsibility to Protect*.[29] This argued that the strategy for implementing the R2P should be seen as resting on three equally important and non-sequential pillars. The first pillar is the responsibility of each state to use appropriate and necessary means to protect its own population from the four crimes as well as from their incitement. The second pillar refers to the commitment that UN member states will help each other exercise this responsibility. This includes specific commitments to help states build the capacity to protect their populations from the four crimes and to assist those under stress before crises and conflicts erupt. The third pillar refers to international society's collective responsibility to respond through the UN in a timely and decisive manner, using Chapters VI, VII and VIII of the UN Charter as appropriate, when national authorities are manifestly failing to protect their populations from the four crimes listed above.

Defined in this manner, the R2P is both a principle that applies in all states at all times and an ambitious policy agenda in urgent need of implementation.[30] Although it has attracted many supporters, the policy agenda has not yet been clearly worked out and has drawn a range of critics. Some advocates of humanitarian military intervention argue that the R2P principle adopted by the UN was watered down in the pursuit of international consensus and changed little with regard to the international use of force. Others complain that R2P is a mere slogan that encourages actors to overestimate what can be achieved by military peacekeepers. Still others contend that it is too vague to be a functional legal norm; some see it as a thinly veiled cloak for the West's neo-imperial ambitions; and some argue that far from protecting populations from mass atrocities, R2P actually causes genocidal violence that would not otherwise occur.[31]

The question for this section is therefore to assess how far the development of R2P has altered the prospects for saving strangers from genocide and episodes of mass killing. To do so, it examines the evidence using the same five categories of challenges that were used to structure the previous section.

Legitimacy responses

Has the development of the R2P principle helped to overcome some of the legitimacy obstacles placed in the way of humanitarian military intervention? The short answer is that in comparison to the concept of humanitarian intervention, R2P has made major strides in winning acceptance within contemporary international society. However, the main reason for this is that R2P's principal advocates within the UN system – the UN secretary-general and his special adviser, Edward Luck – have been keen to distance the principle from the idea of humanitarian military intervention. Thus, nowhere in any of the documentation setting out the details of the UN's R2P agenda is reference made to any potential use of military force without prior Security Council authorization.

This approach has clearly paid political dividends since it has helped to consolidate support for R2P among the UN's member states, and it has played a role in the Security Council authorizing its first ever humanitarian military intervention in Libya (albeit with ten votes in favor and five abstentions). Before the Libyan intervention, arguably the most public test of R2P's popularity came in the General Assembly debate in the summer of 2009. Despite a prepared attack on the idea of R2P organized by the president of the General Assembly, Fr. Miguel d'Escoto Brockmann from Nicaragua, the vast majority of the UN's members explicitly defended the concept and argued that the organization's previous commitments on R2P should not be unpicked.[32] Of course, concerns were raised but these related primarily to the selectivity of international responses to atrocity crimes, the Security Council's previous failures to halt mass atrocities, and worries about the possibility of unilateral action rather than criticisms of the R2P principle specifically. Since then, there has also been a favorable response to R2P in the 2010 dialogue in the General Assembly.

Over the course of international debates since the WSOD in 2005, advocates of R2P have generally helped to clear up some of the myths surrounding the principle and its implementation, all of which have helped to ease some of the legitimacy challenges which bedeviled humanitarian military intervention. On the one hand, R2P has put the focus of the debate firmly on the responsibilities of sovereigns and the rights of the victims of genocide and mass atrocities rather than the interests and positions of the external actors who may or may not intervene. It has also helped to recall the historical fact that the notion of sovereignty has never been synonymous with a license to slaughter innocent civilians free from external interference. Rather, sovereign power has always rested on some obligations to protect – or at least refrain from slaughtering – one's civilian population.[33] R2P's novelty lay in singling out the four core crimes and clarifying when, where and how international society had a responsibility to protect foreigners when the sovereign state in question failed to live up to these responsibilities.

The R2P discourse has also gained further acceptance within international society by enunciating various gradations of responsibility for preventing the four core crimes. Clearly, host governments have the primary responsibility in these matters but the interesting debate has revolved around which actors are responsible for assisting governments to live up to their responsibilities, and who has the secondary and/or tertiary responsibility to act when host governments fail. In the WSOD version of the R2P principle, secondary responsibility clearly lies with the UN Security Council in general and its five permanent members in particular. However, one of the lingering problems is that the R2P framework has not managed to resolve the issue of indeterminacy in practical cases – that is, what should be done if the UN Security Council cannot agree that R2P crimes have been committed, or are likely to be committed imminently; and whose responsibility it is to act if the Security Council agrees such crimes have been committed but fails to agree on a course of action in response. This does not make for clear and easy politics but then again, R2P is no different from many other norms that tend to be specific about the kind of behavior that is prohibited but much less clear about what kind of response is required in particular cases.[34]

Legal developments

As discussed above, humanitarian military intervention is widely considered to be illegal without UN Security Council authorization and highly unlikely to occur with Security Council authorization. Consequently, would-be interveners would be acting in, at best, a precarious legal position. Although R2P is principally a political principle and not a legal rule, it is directly relevant for certain dimensions of international law and, far more so than humanitarian intervention, is embedded within a wide range of existing legal obligations which UN member states have previously accepted. In this sense, while R2P may change the international legal terrain slightly, it is primarily a political concept which calls upon legally recognized actors to respect already existing obligations under international law, especially those related to international humanitarian law/the laws of war. As the UN secretary-general recently clarified:

> It should be underscored that the provisions of paragraphs 138 and 139 of the Summit Outcome are firmly anchored in well-established principles of international law. Under conventional and customary international law, States have obligations to prevent and punish genocide, war crimes and crimes against humanity. Ethnic cleansing is not a crime in its own right under international law, but acts of ethnic cleansing may constitute one of the other three crimes. ... In that regard, the responsibility to protect does not alter, indeed it reinforces,

the legal obligations of Member States to refrain from the use of force except in conformity with the Charter.[35]

Nevertheless, R2P has not been completely devoid of a legal impact. For one thing, it has certainly reinvigorated debates about the precise nature of the legal obligations – deriving from international humanitarian law, human rights law, and the laws of occupation – that peacekeepers have to civilians in their theaters of operation.[36]

It has also had some discernible impact on wider debates about international law and questions of international peace and security. As Michael Doyle recently concluded, R2P may be on the way to having at least three identifiable effects. First,

> From the standpoint of international law, the doctrine and practice of RtoP was not legislative – not equivalent to either a Charter amendment of Chapter VII or an international treaty. But it was part of an ongoing process bending the meaning of "international threats to the peace" as defined by the Council under Chapter VII.[37]

Second, it may also be in the process of encouraging a record of general practice which might affect "the sense of obligation that builds customary international law." And, third, "although the R2P does not quite qualify as *opinio juris vel necessitatis* – acting on the basis of legal obligation – the use of 'responsibility' language is approaching that normative strength."[38]

In sum, it seems reasonable to conclude that, to date, R2P has played a significant part in clarifying existing legal obligations related to its four core crimes, and has also started to affect the way states interpret their legal obligations in this area. But R2P has not succeeded in entrenching new legal obligations in how states should respond to atrocity crimes beyond their borders.[39]

Strategic responses

Unlike the debates over humanitarian military intervention, the R2P demands a much wider range of policy tools including diplomacy, early warning, and prevention as well as coercion – this is partly because the WSOD formulation explicitly called upon states to prevent the *incitement* as well as perpetration of these crimes. This should be a welcome development for policymakers who benefit from a broader range of options which might give them a reasonable degree of flexibility to respond to the unique challenges raised by particular cases.

Of all the possible policy tools, preventive mechanisms are the most fundamental part of the R2P agenda since the ultimate objective must be to prevent these crimes and violations from happening in the first place. Ultimately, therefore, R2P will stand or fall depending on how well it facilitates the prevention of genocide and mass atrocities.[40] This was made abundantly clear in the UN secretary-general's 2009 report, *Implementing the Responsibility to Protect*, which argued that "Prevention ... is a key ingredient for a successful strategy for the responsibility to protect."[41] And yet, he also noted that "The United Nations and its Member States remain underprepared to meet their most fundamental prevention and protection responsibilities."[42]

Under pillar one, the secretary-general suggested that relevant preventive actions which states might undertake include "effective management, even encouragement, of diversity through the principle of non-discrimination and the equal enjoyment of rights"; joining relevant international treaties, including the Rome Statute of the International Criminal Court; participating in "State-to-State learning processes" as well as "training, learning and education programmes" about human rights, and creating networks of survivors.[43]

Under pillar two, states might engage in "confidential or public suasion, education, training and/or assistance," tell potential perpetrators of the costs of committing mass atrocities and the benefits of pursuing peaceful resolution instead, develop the civilian capacities of regional organizations,[44] invite the deployment of an "international military presence," provide development assistance that is "sensitive" to armed conflicts and mass atrocities, build indigenous mediation and dispute resolution capacity, support "impartial and disciplined" security sectors, and foster the "capacity to replicate capacity."[45] Naturally, there is much less clarity on what might be done under pillar three, when the opportunity for prevention has already been lost.

One of the difficulties for any preventive agenda is that the core crimes at the heart of the R2P can occur in contexts of armed conflict as well as during peace time. While not all armed conflicts produce mass atrocities, most cases of mass atrocities occur within the context of armed conflict. According to Alex Bellamy,

> of 103 episodes of mass killing (defined as a minimum of 5,000 civilians killed intentionally) observed since 1945, 69 cases (67%) occurred within, and 34 cases (33%) occurred outside, a context of armed conflict. All except five of the peacetime cases commenced prior to 1980 and since then only 15% of new episodes occurred outside of armed conflict. Of these, four were in countries that had recent experience of armed conflict in which mass atrocities were committed (Burundi [twice], Democratic Republic of the Congo [DRC], and Myanmar).[46]

Outside of a context of armed conflict, Bellamy identifies three principal forms of "peacetime atrocities": state-directed oppression, communal violence, and post-war retribution.[47] The variety of contexts in which mass atrocities might occur raises the question: Should R2P generate a distinct prevention agenda or be subsumed within the more traditional prevention of an armed conflict agenda (or vice versa)?[48] According to the UN secretary-general's report on early warning and the R2P, these agendas (preventing armed conflict and preventing mass atrocities) need to be kept distinct.[49]

This would be a mistake, however. In fact, to prevent the crimes and violations at the heart of R2P, we need a bit of both agendas. As Bellamy has argued, "what is required is an "atrocity prevention lens" which informs and, where appropriate, leads policy development and decision making across the full spectrum of prevention-related activities."[50] Using such a lens, Lawrence Woocher has identified three distinct but complementary approaches to operationalizing R2P-inspired prevention: (1) direct prevention of R2P crimes/violations via strategies to dissuade potential perpetrators and/or diminish their capabilities to carry out these crimes; (2) structural prevention focusing on preventing violent conflicts; and (3) structural prevention focusing on preventing human rights abuses from escalating in the absence of armed conflict.[51] The next practical steps for this multidimensional and interrelated agenda must revolve around building political support for such initiatives and finding the resources necessary to undertake them.

Prudential developments

While advances on the preventive dimensions of the R2P agenda are fundamental, the evidence from Libya, Syria, Yemen, Bahrain, Côte d'Ivoire, and Sudan in 2011 alone show that mass atrocities will continue to occur. This is partly because prevention is difficult to put into practice, but also because the current period of global financial contraction has made it more difficult for preventive mechanisms to attract the additional resources they so badly require.[52] As a consequence, more reactive mechanisms such as military force should not be totally ignored by supporters of R2P.

As discussed above, it is perfectly understandable why many R2P advocates wish to distance themselves from discussions of military operations given the sensitive and controversial nature of the topic among UN member states, but they need to remain in the background, if not the foreground, as part of the debate. Indeed, demonstrating the existence of effective military instruments to stop mass atrocities might have some deterrent effect by making would-be perpetrators think twice before committing such crimes. Thus, while it is clearly correct that those wishing to prevent mass atrocities must have more than just military intervention in their practical toolbox, a toolbox which does not contain any military instruments is unlikely to succeed, not least because it is unlikely to generate the necessary deterrence and/or coercive effects. This is particularly important given that recent studies which have examined how genocidal violence comes to an end have concluded that (1) responses short of military force did little to de-escalate or end mass killing, and (2) with few exceptions, genocides ended because the perpetrators chose to stop or were defeated militarily by local opponents. Interestingly for advocates of R2P, they also concluded that external humanitarian military intervention was among the rarest ways such episodes are brought to an end.[53]

The good news is that the development of R2P has been part of the inspiration for more pragmatic thinking about how military power and the use of military force can help put an end to mass atrocities. This type of thinking has come in two main strands. The first is what, as noted above, has become known as the protection of civilians (PoC) agenda within contemporary peace operations. This has influenced documents setting out guidelines, principles and to some extent doctrine within the UN, AU, and EU in particular. The principal scenario for these efforts is when peace operations are deployed with the official consent of the host government but operate within environments where a plethora of threats to civilians remain, usually from insurgents, predatory government soldiers and/or criminal gangs.[54]

The second strand has emerged from attempts to develop new doctrine for the US armed forces that might help them function effectively in situations of mass atrocities.[55] Arguably the most useful example of this type of approach has been the Mass Atrocity Response Operations (MARO) military planning handbook, a collaborative effort between the Carr Center for Human Rights Policy at the Harvard Kennedy School of Government and the US Army's Peacekeeping and Stability Operations Institute. The central objective of the handbook is to persuade the US government to enshrine the MARO concept in its military doctrine. A MARO "describes a contingency operation to halt widespread and systematic use of violence by state or non-state armed groups against non-combatants" which is distinguished in military terms by its "primary objective of stopping the killing of civilians."[56] MAROs take place in contexts characterized by multiparty dynamics between victims, perpetrators and bystanders rather than traditional contexts between enemy and friendly forces; where the intervening force will inevitably be seen as siding with the victims against the perpetrators; and where there is a tendency for the mass killings to rapidly escalate once begun.

The handbook significantly advances the wider international debate on how to protect civilians through its discussion of seven approaches to direct military intervention: the saturation, "oil spot," separation, safe areas, partner enabling, containment, and defeat perpetrators approaches (Table 8.1 summarizes the six substantive approaches, "partner enabling" not being a separate approach). Sarah Sewall and her co-authors claim their handbook "does not advocate for a military intervention or response in a given situation" – instead it seeks only "to prepare states operationally for that possibility."[57] Strictly speaking this is correct but it belies the whole purpose of the project which is precisely to make sure that future responses to genocide do not replicate the past.

The MARO has already had some influence with senior officials in the Obama administration and was apparently debated in the context of the Libyan operations.[58] However, it has also been criticized on several grounds. The main objections have been that its analysis of genocidal dynamics is too crude and dangerously simplistic; the explanation for non-intervention in cases of genocide is a lack of political will not a lack of relevant military doctrine; the publication of the handbook will itself produce greater emphasis on military reactions at the expense of preventive efforts to promote human rights; it is based on abstract analysis rather than learning lessons from detailed historical case studies, especially previous US failures; it assumes US motives are altruistic and ignores the double standards that occur when mass atrocities are committed by regimes friendly with the US; it has an overly optimistic view of what US military power can achieve in such circumstances; and it ignores the potential for MAROs to increase the total level of violence against civilians.[59]

Political developments

Arguably the central political question for advocates of R2P is, as Edward Luck queried, "Have the costs of committing R2P crimes or of failing to act in the face

Table 8.1 Six military approaches to civilian protection

Approach	Description	Considerations
Saturation	Establish control and provide security over a large region with dispersed units on the ground.	• Requires adequate forces, extensive logistics and weak adversary • Suitable when victim population is widely dispersed • Extensive stability operations necessary
Oil spot	Focus on control of selected key locations and gradually expand to other areas.	• Fewer forces required than Saturation • Suitable with strong perpetrators and concentrated victim populations • Cedes territory to perpetrators • Extended commitment
Separation	Establish a buffer zone between victims and perpetrators.	• Limited forces required • Suitable when perpetrators and victims are separated • Cedes territory to perpetrators • Forces may be caught between belligerent groups • Potential long-term division
Safe areas	Secure internally displaced persons (IDP) camps and other areas with high densities of vulnerable populations.	• Limited forces required • Suitable when victims are concentrated • Cedes territory to perpetrators • Large humanitarian assistance burden • May "reward" perpetrators
Containment	Strike perpetrators or isolate them with blockades and no-fly zones.	• Requires effective air, sea, logistics capacity, etc. • Limited in-country presence • Does not provide direct protection to victims • Risk of collateral damage • Precursor to other approaches
Defeat perpetrators	Attack perpetrators' leadership and forces to eliminate their capability to commit mass atrocities.	• Large force required • May be required for long-term resolution • Extensive reconstruction and stabilization effort required • High casualties and collateral damage

Source: Paraphrased from Sewell et al. (2010: 63–78).

of such mass atrocities risen since 2005?"[60] Luck answered his own question by writing that by late 2010,

> the responsibility to protect could expect no mark other than an incomplete. It has yet to prove it can make a deep and sustained difference in terms of either preventing genocide and other atrocity crimes and their incitement or offering or spurring a modicum of protection to vulnerable populations.[61]

In the United States at least, some positive, partly R2P-inspired, developments have been occurring which might tilt future administrations to favor tougher action to prevent and stop genocide and mass atrocities. Within civil society a variety of activists have been spurred on by dire events in Rwanda (1994) and Darfur (2004) to try to build an anti-genocide constituency within American domestic politics. Two of the more prominent examples are the ENOUGH project and the Genocide Intervention Network.[62] While ENOUGH was established by former senior members of the Clinton administration who had moved into the advocacy world, the latter emerged from student activism in relation to Darfur which subsequently broadened its focus. The rationale behind both of these organizations is that tough action by the US government to prevent/stop mass atrocities is more likely if there is a permanent anti-genocide constituency which can mobilize domestic voters. If such a constituency existed, politicians who did not act to prevent/stop genocide might lose votes whereas those who acted decisively may attract new supporters. Naturally, the longer-term aim of such activists is to develop these organizations into transnational movements and build similar constituencies abroad. Their existence and continued growth will provide a concrete test case in the realm of genocide prevention for Luck's conclusion that "Political will is not a given or static quantity. It can be built or destroyed by actions over time."[63]

Within the government sector there have also been notable developments. Following the recommendations set out in the Genocide Prevention Task Force report chaired by Madeleine Albright and William Cohen, the Obama administration gave the prevention of genocide a new and elevated status within its conception of US national security. In its National Security Strategy, for instance, the administration stated:

> The United States is committed to working with our allies, and to strengthening our own internal capabilities, in order to ensure that the United States and the international community are proactively engaged in a strategic effort to prevent mass atrocities and genocide. In the event that prevention fails, the United States will work both multilaterally and bilaterally to mobilize diplomatic, humanitarian, financial, and – in certain instances – military means to prevent and respond to genocide and mass atrocities.[64]

In addition, President Obama established a new position on the National Security Staff with responsibility for coordinating and supporting the administration's policies on preventing, identifying, and responding to mass atrocities and genocide. As a result, David Pressman served as the National Security Staff's first director for war crimes, atrocities, and civilian protection. This was followed in August 2011 with the announcement of Presidential Study Directive (no.10) on Mass Atrocities, which established an Interagency Atrocities Prevention Board "to coordinate a whole government approach to preventing mass atrocities and genocide." This Board met for the first time in April 2012.[65]

These developments do not guarantee that the US government will take action to stop all cases of genocide and mass atrocities. Nor do they guarantee that if the government acts it will do so wisely. But the emergence of anti-genocide constituents does raise the stakes for administration officials and political leaders who ignore these issues, while the development of these new government structures should hard-wire anti-genocide thinking into the government's policy deliberations.

CONCLUSION

Humanitarian military intervention continues to face a range of theoretical challenges and practical obstacles. As such it remains a deeply controversial concept within international society. And yet while civilians continue to be slaughtered, sometimes by their own governments, the debates about the use of military force will persist. During 2011, this was clearly demonstrated by the debates about how to respond to mass atrocities in Libya, Côte d'Ivoire, Sudan, Syria, Yemen, Bahrain and elsewhere.

Compared to humanitarian military intervention, the R2P principle has attracted a much greater degree of support from the world's governments. This is largely because its principal advocates at the UN have tried to disassociate it from any use of military force not authorized by the UN Security Council. Although it is early days for judging R2P, it has made significant progress in terms of generating political support and overcoming several of the obstacles that stymied earlier debates about humanitarian military intervention. Now that support needs to be translated into positive results on the ground.

In the near term, R2P will probably be judged most on how it shapes international reaction to crises and mass atrocities such as those in the countries listed above. In the longer term however, R2P should be judged on how it can bolster preventive efforts to reduce the number of such crises occurring in the future. This will, rightly, take the focus off debates about humanitarian military intervention. The world's governments and international organizations must then give prevention a chance by investing more significant resources. But it is unlikely that talk of the military dimension of protection will disappear completely; nor should it.

NOTES

1 See P. D. Williams, "Briefing: The Road to Humanitarian War in Libya," *Global Responsibility to Protect* 3/2, 2011, 248–59; and P. D. Williams and A. J. Bellamy, "Principles, Politics and Prudence: Libya, the Responsibility to Protect and the Use of Force," *Global Governance* 18/3, 2012, 273–97.

2 See A. J. Bellamy and P. D. Williams, "The New Politics of Protection? Côte d'Ivoire, Libya and the Responsibility to Protect," *International Affairs* 87/4, 2011, 825–50.

3 The best overview is V. Holt and G. Taylor with M. Kelly, *Protecting Civilians in the Context of UN Peacekeeping Operations*, New York: UN DPKO/OCHA, 2009.

4 For example, N. J. Wheeler, *Saving Strangers: Humanitarian Intervention in International Society*, Oxford: Oxford University Press, 2000; International Commission on Intervention and State Sovereignty (ICISS), *The Responsibility to Protect*, Ottawa: IDRC, 2001; A. Roberts, "The So-called Right of Humanitarian Intervention," *Yearbook of International Humanitarian Law* 3, 2001, 3–51; J. L. Holzgrefe and R. O. Keohane, eds., *Humanitarian Intervention*, Cambridge: Cambridge University Press, 2003; J. M. Welsh, ed., *Humanitarian Intervention and International Relations*, Oxford: Oxford University Press, 2004.

5 For example, V. K. Holt and T. C. Berkman, *The Impossible Mandate? Military Preparedness, the Responsibility to Protect and Modern Peace Operations*, Washington, DC: Henry L. Stimson Center, 2006; T. B. Seybolt, *Humanitarian Military Intervention: The Conditions for Success and Failure*, Oxford: Oxford University Press, 2007; S. Sewall, D. Raymond and S. Chin, *Mass Atrocity Response Operations: A Military Planning Handbook*, Cambridge, MA: Harvard Kennedy School and PKSOI, 2010.

6 For example, J. Pattison, *Humanitarian Intervention and the Responsibility to Protect*, Oxford: Oxford University Press, 2010; K. E. Smith, *Genocide and the Europeans*, Cambridge: Cambridge University Press, 2010.

7 Roberts, "The So-called Right of Humanitarian Intervention," 1.

8 See, for example, J. I. Levitt, "The Peace and Security Council of the African Union: The Known Unknowns," *Transnational Law and Contemporary Problems* 13, 2003, 126–32.

9 UN doc. S/24868, November 30, 1992, p. 3.

10 The legal issues are well discussed in the symposium on NATO's intervention in Kosovo in *International and Comparative Law Quarterly* 49/4, 2000, 876–943. See also, S. Chesterman, *Just War or Just Peace?* Oxford: Oxford University Press, 2001.

11 See M. Byers and S. Chesterman, "Changing the Rules about Rules? Unilateral Humanitarian Intervention and the Future of International Law," in J. L. Holzgrefe and Robert Keohane, eds., *Humanitarian Intervention*, Cambridge: Cambridge University Press, pp. 199–200.

12 See R. Jackson, *The Global Covenant*, Oxford: Oxford University Press, 2000.

13 See M. Finnemore, "Paradoxes in Humanitarian Intervention," in Richard Price, ed., *Moral Limit and Possibility in World Politics*, Cambridge: Cambridge University Press, 2008, pp. 197–224.

14 See, for example, the UN General Assembly Declaration on the Inadmissibility of Intervention in the Domestic Affairs of States (December 1965); Declaration on Principles of International Law concerning Friendly Relations and Co-operation among States in Accordance with the Charter of the United Nations (October 1970); and Declaration on the Inadmissibility of Intervention and Interference in the Internal Affairs of States (1981).

15 For an overview see D. R. Black and P. D. Williams, eds., *The International Politics of Mass Atrocities: The Case of Darfur*, London: Routledge, 2010.

16 See, for example, Mary Kaldor's notion of "cosmopolitan law enforcement" in *New and Old Wars*, Oxford: Polity, 1999 and Simon Caney's cosmopolitan theory of global justice in *Justice Beyond Borders*, Oxford: Oxford University Press, 2005.

17 Cited in B. Valentino, "The Perils of Limited Humanitarian Intervention: Lessons from the 1990s," *Wisconsin International Law Journal* 24/3, 2006, 731.

18 Ibid., pp. 734ff.

19 See, for example, M. Mamdani, *Saviors and Survivors: Darfur, Politics and the War on Terror*, New York: Pantheon, 2009.

20 E. Luck, "A Response," *Global Responsibility to Protect* 2/1–2, 2010, 181.

21 Ibid.

22 For the general case and Bosnia in particular see, for example, K. Booth, "Military Intervention: Duty and Prudence," in L. Freedman, ed., *Military Intervention in European Conflicts*, Oxford: Blackwell, 1994, pp. 56–75. For a practical example related to Syria, see M. Lynch, *Pressure Not War: A Pragmatic and Principled Policy Towards Syria*, Washington, DC: Center for a New American Security, 2012.

23 See, for example, Holt and Berkman, *The Impossible Mandate?*

24 Sewall et al., *Mass Atrocity Response Operations*, p. 5. One thing that has become clear, however, is that the use of air power alone is a badly suboptimal approach for civilian protection.

25 *2005 World Summit Outcome* (UN doc. A/60/L.1, October 24, 2005), paras 138–40. The advocacy campaign was spearheaded by those people associated with the International Commission on Intervention and State Sovereignty and its subsequent report, *The Responsibility to Protect* (Ottawa: IDRC, 2001). A common problem in much of the relevant literature is the basic confusion between the version of R2P that was set out in the ICISS report which gave rise to the R2P label, and the version that was actually adopted by the UN General Assembly which represents the R2P norm/principle adopted by international society.

26 This version of R2P thus set out a hierarchy of harm in world politics whereby these four core crimes were deserving of special attention compared to other forms of human suffering such as starvation, disease, natural disaster, etc. In the latter category, presumably more traditional, Westphalian notions of sovereignty still hold sway.

27 *The Responsibility to Protect* (UN doc. A/RES/63/308, October 7, 2009).

28 Ban Ki-moon, "On Responsible Sovereignty: International Cooperation for a Changed World," Berlin, SG/SM11701, July 15, 2008.

29 Report of the UN secretary-general, *Implementing the Responsibility to Protect* (A/63/677, January 12, 2009).

30 See, for example, G. Evans, *The Responsibility to Protect*, Washington, DC: Brookings Institution Press, 2008; A. J. Bellamy, *Responsibility to Protect*, Cambridge: Polity, 2009; A. J. Bellamy, "The Responsibility to Protect: Five Years On," *Ethics and International Affairs* 24/2, 2010, 143–69; and A. J. Bellamy, *Global Politics and the Responsibility to Protect*, London: Routledge, 2011.

31 See, respectively, T. G. Weiss, *Humanitarian Intervention*, Cambridge: Polity, 2007, p. 117; A. de Waal, "Darfur and the Failure of the Responsibility to Protect," *International Affairs* 83/6, 2008, 1039–54; J. E. Alvarez, "The Schizophrenias of R2P," in P. Alston and E. MacDonald, eds., *Human Rights, Intervention and the Use of Force*, Oxford: Oxford University Press, 2008, pp. 275–94; D. Chandler, "*The Responsibility to Protect*: Imposing the Liberal Peace," *International Peacekeeping* 11/1, 2004, 59–82; and A. J. Kuperman, "Rethinking the Responsibility to Protect," *Whitehead Journal of Diplomacy and International Relations*, 2009, 33–43. For a variety of critical perspectives see P. Cunliffe, ed., *Critical Perspectives on the Responsibility to Protect*, London: Routledge, 2011.

32 See *The 2009 General Assembly Debate: An Assessment*, New York: Global Center for the Responsibility to Protect Report, August 2009, Available HTTP: http://globalr2p.org/media/pdf/GCR2P_General_Assembly_Debate_Assessment.pdf

33 For relevant discussions see C. Reus-Smit, "Human Rights and the Social Construction of Sovereignty," *Review of International Studies* 27/4, 2001, 519–38; L. Glanville, "The Antecedents of 'Sovereignty as Responsibility'," *European Journal of International Relations* 17/2, 2011, 233–55.

34 E. C. Luck, "The Responsibility to Protect: Growing Pains or Early Promise?" *Ethics and International Affairs* 24/4, 2010, 362.

35 UN secretary-general, *Implementing the Responsibility to Protect*, para. 3.

36 See, for example, S. Wills, *Protecting Civilians: The obligations of Peacekeepers*, Oxford, UK: Oxford University Press, 2009.

37 M. W. Doyle, "International Ethics and the Responsibility to Protect," *International Studies Review* 13/1, 2011, 82.

38 Ibid., 83.

39 This is my summary of the conclusions drawn by the six articles on "The Responsibility to Protect and International Law," in *Global Responsibility to Protect* 2/3, 2010, 191–306.

40 The importance of prevention had also been emphasized in the ICISS report, *The Responsibility to Protect*. However, the ICISS did not flesh out in any detail what this might entail in practice.

41 UN Secretary-General, *Implementing the Responsibility to Protect*, para. 11b.

42 Ibid., para. 6.

43 Ibid., paras 14, 17, 22, 24, 27.

44 There is, of course, a need to do more than this. Edward Luck has identified three areas where relations between the UN and regional arrangements might be productively strengthened: (1) two-way provision of R2P relevant information and assessment; (2) cooperation in responding to imminent emergencies; (3) facilitating cooperation between the regional arrangement and the UN in supporting operations authorized by the UN Security Council. Cited in A. J. Bellamy, *Mass Atrocities and Armed Conflict* (Stanley Foundation Policy Analysis Brief, February 2011), p. 15. At www.stanleyfoundation.org/publications/pab/BellamyPAB22011.pdf

45 UN Secretary-General, *Implementing the Responsibility to Protect*, paras 30, 32, 38, 42, 43, 48, 45.

46 Bellamy, *Mass Atrocities and Armed Conflict*, p. 2.

47 Ibid., p. 3.

48 Ibid.

49 Report of the Secretary-General, *Early Warning, Assessment and the Responsibility to Protect* (UN doc. A/64/864, July 14, 2010), p. 4.

50 Bellamy, *Mass Atrocities and Armed Conflict*, p. 2.

51 L. Woocher, "The Responsibility to Prevent: Towards a Strategy," in F. Egerton and A. Knight, eds., *The Routledge Handbook of the Responsibility to Protect*, Abingdon, UK: Routledge, 2012.

52 One exception is the British government's recent emphasis on investing in "upstream prevention." See *Building Stability Overseas Strategy*, London: DFID-FCO-MOD, 2011.

53 A. de Waal and B. Conley-Zilkic, "Reflections on How Genocidal Killings are Brought to an End," *Social Science Research Council*, December 22, 2006, Available HTTP: http://howgenocidesend.ssrc.org/de_Waal/; A. J. Bellamy, "Military Intervention," in D. Bloxham and A. Dirk Moses, eds., *The Oxford Handbook of Genocide Studies*, Oxford: Oxford University Press, 2010, pp. 599–601.

54 For discussions see Holt et al., *Protecting Civilians in the Context of UN Peacekeeping Operations*; Wills, *Protecting Civilians*; A. Giffen, *Addressing the Doctrinal Deficit: Developing Guidance to Prevent and Respond to Widespread or Systematic Attacks Against Civilians*, Henry L. Stimson Center, workshop report, spring 2010; and P. D. Williams, *Enhancing Civilian Protection in Peace Operations: Insights from Africa*, Washington, DC: National Defense University, ACSS research paper no.1, September 2010.

55 Genocide Prevention Task Force (GPTF), *Preventing Genocide: A Blueprint for US Policymakers*, Washington, DC: US Institute for Peace, 2008; Sewall et al., *Mass Atrocity Response Operations*.

56 Sewall et al., *Mass Atrocity Response Operations*, p. 21.

57 Ibid., p. 11.

58 Author's communications with several US government officials, Washington, DC, April–June 2011.

59 This is my summary of the principal criticisms raised in the "Symposium on MARO," *Genocide Studies and Prevention* 6/1, 2011, 1–80.

60 Luck, "The Responsibility to Protect," 354.

61 Ibid., 363.

62 See www.enoughproject.org/ and R. Hamilton, *Fighting for Darfur*, New York: Palgrave, 2011.

63 Luck, "The Responsibility to Protect," 359.

64 *National Security Strategy of the United States*, Washington, DC: The White House, May 2010, p. 48.

65 See http://m.whitehouse.gov/the-press-office/2012/04/23/fact-sheet-comprehensive-strategy-and-new-tools-prevent-and-respond-atro

CHAPTER 9

Transitional Justice and Genocide

Ernesto Verdeja

Human suffering on a massive scale is not new. History is littered with accounts of killings, displacement, genocide and other atrocities. However, what are new and noteworthy are efforts to respond to mass atrocities that take seriously the imperative to reckon with the past in some morally satisfactory way. Following a range of mass killings of civilians, including the Holocaust and other genocidal atrocities, along with the transitions from authoritarianism and violent social conflicts in the late twentieth century, new voices and movements emerged demanding that the legacies of large-scale human rights violations be addressed appropriately and thoroughly. The justifications given for these demands are complex; some rest on ethical claims about the importance of human dignity while others argue in more consequentialist terms that unaddressed histories of violence may feed future conflict.

This broad area of research known as "transitional justice" is concerned with the strategies, practices, and theories of social repair and transformation for societies dealing with a recent history of authoritarianism, civil war or massive human rights violations, including genocide. The International Center for Transitional Justice, a leading non-governmental organization (NGO) in this area, defines transitional justice as

> a response to systematic or widespread violations of human rights. It seeks recognition for the victims and to promote possibilities for peace, reconciliation and democracy. Transitional Justice is not a special kind of justice but justice adapted to societies transforming themselves after a period of pervasive human

rights abuse. In some cases, these transformations happen suddenly, in others they may take place over decades.[1]

The transitional justice literature has grown enormously over the past three decades, and today constitutes its own interdisciplinary field of research. Scholars from across the humanities, social sciences and law (and even occasionally from the natural sciences and engineering) work on transitional issues in a number of settings, and numerous conferences, journals, books, encyclopedias, and scholarly organizations have developed. There has also been a proliferation of human rights research institutes, non-governmental organizations and national and international organizations devoted to transitional justice.[2] Indeed, some scholars have called this an "industry" composed of its own cadre of consultants, experts, vocabularies, and occasionally problematic reliance on entrenched sources of political and financial power.[3]

Genocide studies scholars have studied post-genocide developments in specific cases, such as the use of international tribunals in former Yugoslavia or Rwanda, but there has been relatively little systematic engagement with the general findings of transitional justice literature.[4] Donald Bloxham and Dirk Moses' important survey of the field, *The Oxford Handbook of Genocide Studies*, provides only a limited assessment of post-genocide reconstruction.[5] Adam Jones' valuable *New Directions in Genocide Research* canvasses a number of topics across cases related to genocide studies, but addresses post-violence justice mechanisms and programs in only one country, Rwanda.[6] However, focusing on limited cases raises certain theoretical problems. By examining the transitional justice challenges of only a subset of cases (those that experienced genocides) rather than systematically analyzing the broader findings of transitional justice research, genocide scholars risk drawing erroneous conclusions about the utility, limitations and interactions of various transitional justice mechanisms. In other words, if genocide scholarship focuses only on one or two post-genocides to understand how transitional justice mechanisms may succeed or fail, it may miss the general patterns that have emerged from research on a much wider range of cases. For instance, genocide studies scholars have shown that Rwanda's *gacaca* courts ("traditional justice" venues) have had limited success in promoting reconciliation, one of the government's stated objectives. The reasons given for these failures varied considerably, but scholars rarely asked: compared to what? Are there other traditional justice mechanisms for mass atrocities that have worked? Are there certain institutional, procedural, cultural or other factors that may give traditional mechanisms greater public resonance? One way of answering these questions would be to compare a set of traditional justice mechanisms and see whether there are general factors – or interactions of factors – that provide insights into their success or failure. Luc Huyse and Mark Salter have done precisely this, comparing traditional justice policies in Rwanda, Mozambique, Uganda, Sierra Leone, and Burundi, with remarkable findings.[7] However, this kind of inclusive comparative work has been missing in genocide studies discussions on post-genocidal societies. Likewise, discussions in the field about the value of trials normally focus on post-genocides (Rwanda, Bosnia, the Holocaust), not on the use of trials during a wider set of transitions in which countries have grappled with equally systematic experiences of mass violence (in Latin America, Africa, Asia, etc.).

This chapter reconstructs and critiques some of the developments and current research advances in the transitional justice field. The chapter is motivated by the concern that much of the best research in transitional justice and genocide studies remains largely unconnected and "silo-ed" from one another. With a few exceptions – such as Alexander Hinton and Kevin Lewis O'Neill's work – scholarship advances in one area have gone unnoticed in the other.[8] In some respects, this is not a problem: genocide scholars tend to focus on the specific issue of genocides and mass atrocities, while transitional justice scholars are concerned with how to address the aftermath of different types of mass violence. Naturally, different research communities develop around shared interests and have only partial overlap. However, as genocide studies scholars further investigate the challenges of post-conflict settings and engage in advocacy for the prevention and punishment of genocide, it is crucial to have some understanding of the transitional justice literature. By mapping this literature, this chapter hopes to contribute to furthering useful links and cross-fertilization between the two fields.

This chapter proceeds in several steps. The first section focuses on retributive theories and practices for punishing perpetrators, establishing the rule of law, and reforming the security apparatus. This area of transitional justice has the oldest roots, and is deeply tied to the institutionalization of punishment in the Nuremberg and Tokyo tribunals following World War II and later the United Nations courts in the 1990s. Most recently, the retributive approach has expanded to include so-called "hybrid" tribunals, part international and part domestic prosecution efforts, as well as a variety of novel domestic strategies to address violations. The second section looks at the more recent restorative approach to transitional justice, which underplays the role of punishment in favor of victim-centered strategies and social reconstruction. Restorative approaches emphasize the importance of truth-telling and collective memory, the moral and public acknowledgement of victims and survivors, forgiveness, and reconciliation. State-sanctioned truth commissions are prominent institutional examples of restorative justice, and they often cultivate relations with civil society networks promoting truth and victim recognition. The third section looks at contemporary efforts to connect restorative concerns – especially reparations – with economic development and social justice, as well as addressing the root causes of overt and structural violence. The fourth section highlights a set of empirical constraints that shape the opportunities available for transitional justice.

RETRIBUTIVE JUSTICE

Modern transitional justice has its roots in prosecution efforts following World War I, when the victorious Western powers sought to hold accountable the leaders of Germany, Austria-Hungary, and the Ottoman Empire. These first attempts were largely failures. The defeated nations were unwilling to confront their crimes, and the victors had little interest in committing the necessary resources and attention required to ensure that the trials were successful. The Nuremberg tribunal after World War II represents the first 'successful' modern international prosecution of major war criminals, and was followed by a series of trials across Europe. Nevertheless, the Nuremberg example of internationally constituted trials based on international human rights and humanitarian law failed to take hold in the years after World War II. The retributive impulse gained strength in domestic trials, first during the 1970s in Southern Europe, continuing through the Latin American transitions of the 1970s and 1980s, and moving into the 1990s in Eastern and Central Europe after the fall of communism. In virtually all of these cases, trials were seen as state responses to domestic challenges of impunity for human rights violations, and Nuremberg-style prosecutions were considered unfeasible or otherwise inappropriate. Because many of these demo-cratic transitions were the result of negotiations with outgoing elites, amnesties were often important features of the post-transitional landscape. Trials were frequently limited in scope or reach, and it was not uncommon for prosecutions to start and stop fitfully.

The end of the Cold War and genocides in Rwanda and Bosnia and Herzegovina changed much of the landscape. In the 1990s, the United Nations established two international tribunals, the International Criminal Tribunal for the Former Yugoslavia (ICTY) and the International Criminal Tribunal for Rwanda (ICTR). These new courts were partly chastened responses by the West to its inaction during the genocides, and the courts had limited temporal and territorial jurisdiction. Nevertheless, they represent an important step in placing the law at the center of responses to mass atrocities. Both tribunals have made significant contributions to international law, including the definition of genocide, war crimes, crimes against humanity and violations of the 1949 Geneva Conventions, as well as furthered greater understanding of the concept of intentionality at the heart of genocide. Since their establishment, international human rights law has flourished and moved in several parallel directions.

The clearest example of an international retributive institution is the International Criminal Court (ICC), the first permanent tribunal with near universal jurisdiction to prosecute war crimes, crimes against humanity and genocide (and, eventually, crimes of aggression). The ICC has yet to make major contributions to interna-tional law, but given its centrality in the human rights firmament it will likely do so in the near future. We have also witnessed the creation of "hybrid" tribunals that combine, to various degrees, domestic and international jurisprudence and national and international judges. These hybrid institutions include the Special Court for Sierra Leone, the Serious Crimes Panels of the District Court of Dili in East Timor, the War Crimes Chamber in the State Courts of Bosnia and Herzegovina, Regulation 64 Panels in the Courts of Kosovo, the Special Tribunal for Lebanon, and the Extraordinary Chambers in the Courts of Cambodia. Hybrid courts are candidates for contexts where there is little domestic institutional capacity to prosecute major crimes, including legal, forensic, and technical expertise for fair prosecutions, though their records have been mixed.[9] Finally, national courts have drawn on international law as part of an effort to incorporate international norms into domestic settings. In Belgium, Argentina, and Spain, among other places, national courts and investigative judges have employed principles of universal jurisdiction or expanded conceptions of national jurisdiction (through passive and active personality principles) to prosecute human rights violators.

These tribunals are significantly different from one another, but all are based on the principle of retributive justice, which centers on holding perpetrators accountable for their actions. The retributive approach attempts to distance itself from vengeance by emphasizing the importance of proportionality and procedural and substantive requirements that constrain the actions of the court and provide protections for the accused. For its supporters, retribution distinguishes itself by its basis in the rule of law. This requires a commitment to redress past abuses using generalized, codified and pre-existing standards; the use of formal institutions characterized by impartiality and transparency with a host of due process protections; a commitment to prosecute individuals only for specific crimes for which there is valid evidence; and the power to impose a binding sentence on the defendant that is more than public censure without coercive force.[10]

Over the past decade, a number of countries, mostly in Africa, sought to create alternative mechanisms of punishment that rely, to differing degrees, on "traditional" sources of accountability. Concerned that international courts are too remote, expensive and often irrelevant to the needs of victims and survivors, Burundi, Mozambique, Rwanda, Sierra Leone, and Uganda established a variety of judicial and semi-judicial institutions to address accountability at the local level.[11] Presumably, local efforts are superior to international justice because the former allow local residents a greater stake in the outcome. State officials and local leaders have encouraged these traditional practices as a way of reintegrating former combatants and rebuilding social relations, drawing on complex rituals with extensive community participation. There is enormous variation in these practices and systematic comparative work is still in progress, making definitive conclusions on "what works" difficult. Many of these institutions are often considered forms of "restorative justice" since they may include public confessions and reconciliation practices and focus on social regeneration. Nevertheless, in some cases they also include significant punitive elements as well. Rwanda's *gacaca* system is perhaps the best-known retributive example of this phenomenon. The *gacaca* are part of a system of local justice with roots in traditional forms of conflict resolution. However, the final version was implemented nationally in 2005 and is a highly structured, "top-down" system meant to address the large population of perpetrators who could not be processed by national and international courts. The goal here is to secure greater legitimacy for punishment by grounding retributive practices in cultural norms and mores that resonate with indigenous populations. The results of the *gacaca* experiment are mixed: they have been criticized for politicization, patriarchal values, weak training for local judges, minimal due process protections, inadequate psychological support for victims who testify, and relatively lenient sentences.[12] Nevertheless, given the challenges that post-conflict societies face, some analysts consider the "indigenous turn in justice" a moderate success.[13]

Justifications and limitations

Supporters of retributive justice offer numerous justifications for trials, of which I will identify only the most salient here.[14] The most common justification is *deontological*: there is a duty that violators be held responsible for their actions – that they receive their "just deserts" – regardless of other possible social benefits of prosecutions.[15] This is a "backward-looking" justification, since the principle is meant to hold regardless of the consequences of punishment and in its strongest formulation allows for little flexibility. Trials also help *individualize* the responsibility of key actors and institutions and thus mitigate the tendency to blame entire ethnic or national groups for harms, and may *curtail demands for vengeance* by redirecting popular calls for accountability into institutionalized, fair proceedings and thus respond to concerns over continued impunity. This is best captured in Nuremberg Chief Prosecutor Robert Jackson's famous statement that courts help "stay the hand of vengeance."[16] Trials also generate a *public record* of crimes by collecting and interrogating evidence, thus helping establish some factual baseline of events and crimes. The Nuremberg tribunal amassed millions of pages of evidence of Nazi atrocities that formed the basis of much subsequent historical work on the Holocaust, and the ICTY has generated crucial information on the patterns of violence in Yugoslavia. Lastly, the strongest supporters argue that retributive justice through trials can *deter* future dictators, signaling to them what may happen if they violate the rights of their citizens, and thus promote the rule of law – and in certain instances, reconciliation – in the long term. In contrast to the deontological justification, this is the most explicitly consequentialist and forward-looking argument for trials, and given the relatively few international prosecutions, unsurprisingly the one with least empirical support.[17]

The retributive model receives its strongest support from the international legal community, especially high profile international non-governmental organizations that equate prosecutions, institutional reform and the rule of law with successful transitions and moral reckoning.[18] Trials have also dominated much of the media and popular discourse on transitions, and often take a central role in scholarly discussions on how to deal with massive crimes, particularly in the genocide studies community. Nevertheless, trials face a number of limitations that should give pause before advocating their role as central elements in transitional justice.

Trials have been criticized on several grounds, including their cost, their adversarial structure, their lack of resonance with victims and the broader public, and – for international tribunals – their remoteness from the communities that suffered. These are powerful critiques, but perhaps the strongest criticism is the contention that trials create a misleading portrait of responsibility and guilt. Based on a liberal–legalist framework that individualizes human rights violations and creates stark distinctions between perpetrators and victims, trials reinforce a historical account of rational, autonomous individuals whose behavior and motives are clearly open to legal scrutiny. The complexity of collaboration, bystander responsibility, and broader political and social–psychological dynamics are discarded in favor of legally neat distinctions between violator and victim. For prosecution skeptics, the result is not so much an incomplete as a distorted account of the history, one where responsibility can be assigned to a relatively small group of perpetrators and broader social and structural issues of complicity are held at bay.[19] Moral scrutiny ends with the final court decision.

The reductive nature of liberal tribunals is manifested in a number of ways. For instance, tribunals provide a limited scope of prosecutions, given that only a certain number of violators can be put on the dock. In confronting massive violations like genocide, this is obviously problematic, since significant coordination and logistical planning may be required for large-scale and systematic killings. In response, international tribunals mostly focus on high-level "intellectual authors" of crimes, such as political and military leaders, rather than subordinate violators. Nevertheless, even with sophisticated legal doctrines like command responsibility and joint criminal enterprise that seek to account for purposeful collective violations, tribunals can at best prosecute only a handful of offenders.[20] Similarly, the demands of procedural due process require that prosecutors focus only on evidence connecting perpetrators to specific crimes, which risks artificially separating events from one another and broader historical patterns of violence. Some observers have gone further, arguing that evidentiary constraints mean that only certain types of "truth" are considered admissible: specifically, those that are directly quantifiable or pass a standard of forensic "objectivity." This may distort witness testimony, as victim witnesses do not always provide information that can easily be assessed using a "true/false dichotomy."[21] Some major trials have allowed extensive victim testimony of suffering that go beyond a defendant's direct responsibility, as in the trial of Adolf Eichmann, but these have been criticized for loose evidentiary and procedural standards. The ICC permits greater victim participation at trial sessions but it still seems to represent an exception to the trend and its results remain unclear. In contemporary trials, witnesses are rarely permitted extensive unstructured accounts of their experiences.

The greatest danger to the use of prosecutions is the risk of their political manipulation. Trials are ritual events insofar as they communicate that certain acts are so terrible that they rise to a level requiring strong moral and legal condemnation. Prosecutions focusing on the most abhorrent violations signal that in the future these acts will not be tolerated and that the state is committed to new norms of human rights. This didactic element is a constitutive part of mass atrocity prosecutions: they teach the nation the wrongness of certain behavior in a theatrical way. But as exemplary public performances of punishment, trials can be and have been used for a variety of political ends. Indeed, in transitions, courts are not independent institutions immune from political pressures. Rather, they sustain the legitimacy of the successor regime, indicating in powerful terms how new leaders distance themselves from the past. It is not uncommon for trials to be employed to generate social solidarity through the persecution of identifiable enemies, or "teach" a civic solidarity lesson about atrocity by scapegoating the accused. In such scenarios, the rule of law, such as it is, risks being undermined through the instrumental use of tribunals.

Ultimately, trials and the retributive framework are based on the assumption that mass atrocities are "ordinary": that is, atrocities are not outside the realm of understanding or morality but rather are open to analysis using pre-existing legal norms and rules to assess criminal behavior and responsibility. Some of these norms and rules will have to be adjusted, but the general applicability of criminal analytical frames is kept intact. Thus, such examples as the Nazi extermination camps, *Einsatzgruppen* killing teams, and popular participation in mass bloodletting in Rwanda can all, in principle, be approached as legal crimes committed by identifiable perpetrators. Such an analytical perspective raises deep ontological and epistemological questions for those genocide studies scholars who have long debated whether genocide constitutes a qualitatively different kind of evil, one that represents a rupture in our ability to make moral sense of human affairs.[22] These discussions about the nature of evil have a long and sophisticated philosophical pedigree, and I cannot do them justice here. Rather, I suggest that alternative ethical frameworks have surfaced in response, though they are fraught with their own challenges.

RESTORATIVE JUSTICE

Given the limitations of retributive justice, a number of analysts and practitioners have sought other ways of achieving morally acceptable responses to the past. The main alternative is captured in the concept of "restorative justice," which refers to policies and measures that seek the comprehensive restoration of social relations. The restorative approach focuses on the needs of victims and broader society rather than the more narrow demand of punishing violators. It frames political violence not only as the violation of the law or an individual's legal rights, but as a social phenomenon that undermines community well-being. The aim, then, is to restore broken social relations by reconciling former enemies through public and sustained efforts of truth-telling. This includes acknowledging the wrongs committed against victims and – in the stronger formulations of restorative justice – encouraging forgiveness and the psychological and moral transformation of all those affected by the violence. Punishment is not eschewed, but rather subordinated to these goals. As a social–transformative model of justice, then, its remit is broader than the state or individual wrongdoers.[23]

The restorative paradigm has been adopted in a variety of postconflict scenarios, most tellingly through the use of truth commissions (TCs).[24] Originally employed in limited fashion during the Latin American transitions of the 1980s and 1990s, truth commissions have become central tools of transitional justice across the globe. There have been about thirty TCs used since the 1980s as well as a variety of more limited "commissions of inquiry."[25] Truth commissions are normally sanctioned by the state but differ from trials since they focus on investigating broad-based patterns of abuse rather than individual violations, normally operate for a limited period of time, and publish a final report of their findings upon completion of their work. Unlike trials, TCs cannot hold individuals criminally liable for their actions and rarely have subpoena powers, though in some cases they name perpetrators in their reports as a form of social shaming and thus limited accountability. Most TCs are mandated with providing recommendations on institutional and security sector reform and reparations, though they do not administer reparations programs. Furthermore, truth commissions may occasionally hold public sessions where victims and others can tell their stories in non-adversarial settings. These have proven to be the most dramatic elements of commissions, and since their original use in South Africa's Truth and Reconciliation Commission have become increasingly common.

The early generation of truth commissions was seen as the best available option where legal amnesties prevented the prosecution of major violators. Given that (retributive) "justice" was impossible, successor elites and civil society groups opted for public "truth," as it was often put at the time. This old debate between justice and truth has been superseded, however, and now it is more common to see commissions and trials operating together in a variety of ways. In Peru, for instance, the truth commission completed its work and forwarded a number of its files to the national prosecutor's office for further investigation and criminal indictments. In Sierra Leone, the commission worked in limited fashion with that country's hybrid court but only after a great deal of debate and tension over how to share information. Nevertheless, the increasing collaboration between trials and truth commissions does not erase their fundamentally different understandings of justice. For TCs, the guiding principle of restorative justice is manifested in the assumption that the public dissemination of the truth focused on victims' stories is the path to reconciliation. Individual stories give greater meaning to understandings of violations and establish counter-narratives that highlight the dignity of victims and survivors. Although forgiveness is not a constitutive part of TCs, confession and forgiveness are often encouraged in public hearings as a form of social catharsis and healing.

Limitations

The restorative approach has gained wide support from human rights practitioners and advocates for its holistic approach to social reconstruction. At the center of restoration is truth – an accurate understanding of past events, patterns of violence, actors and responsibility. Without an account of the past and "who" was responsible for "what," reconciliation is impossible, for people will not know whom to reconcile with and for what. Thus, the first step of any restorative project is to report and publicize past crimes. Commissions have been at the center of these efforts, and the most successful commissions have employed a variety of investigative techniques including archival research, interviews, and field investigations (such as unearthing mass graves) to provide detailed histories of violence. By combining multiple investigative methods, TCs can often provide comprehensive macro perspectives that are lacking in transitional contexts. Peru's truth commission report documents a 20-year conflict between guerrillas and the state that resulted in the deaths of approximately 70,000 people, nearly three times the previously estimated number. Argentina's commission documented the disappearances of nearly 9,000 people, providing the foundation for future investigations into the military's atrocities against its population. And South Africa's Truth and

Reconciliation Commission detailed thousands of cases of disappearances, torture, and executions that had remained hidden during the apartheid period.[26]

Nevertheless, restorative efforts face some serious challenges. The first concerns the conception of truth at work in restorative justice. In a post-violence setting, any attempt at making sense of the past is fraught with difficulties because of the political and ethical issues involved. Such attempts do not merely catalogue past crimes, but create new historical narratives that place events in culturally intelligible and persuasive interpretive frames. The narratives are established through the selection – and implicit non-selection – of particular facts and people in efforts to create a broader coherent story about political responsibility. Not all politically motivated tortures, murders, and other violations can receive equal attention in these accounts. Some become paradigmatic examples of political atrocities, presenting perpetrators and victims in vivid ways that reinforce general accounts of violence and responsibility. The Nyarubuye Church massacre in Rwanda, in which about 20,000 people were killed, is a case in point. The mass killings carried out by Hutu government forces against unarmed Tutsi and Hutu civilians symbolize the terrible ferocity of the Rwanda genocide and politicide in stark terms; but other atrocities may be downplayed for lack of political salience, questions about perpetrator motivation, or other reasons that do not support the general narrative.[27]

The problem of selection – and thus the problem of constructing historical truths and collective memory – becomes significantly more acute in the context of official truth efforts. Official truth commissions, for instance, are tasked with synthesizing enormously complex historical events into coherent stories while still maintaining "objectivity." In fact, they are closer to morality plays, "a grand meta-narrative of redemption ... recounting of an epic of collective destruction and rebirth."[28] Commission reports often sketch a narrative arc that reinforces a three-stage history: an antediluvian period of increasing prejudice, hate and fear, followed by a cataclysmic orgy of violence, and ending in the present, a struggle for reconstructing the basic norms necessary for re-establishing (or in some case, establishing for the first time) a functioning liberal democratic order and reconciling a traumatized people. In practice, the goal of constructing this narrative account may come into tension with the messy reality on the ground, where violence may be multidirectional, victims may also be perpetrators, and local atrocities are not always motivated by the ideological claims of elites and their core supporters.[29] Indeed, recent ethnographic work sharply questions whether official truth-telling adequately captures local realities and notes how problematic or subaltern histories and experiences are written out of the master narrative.[30] Official histories smooth over the complexity of violence, and in the process they function both to delegitimize past actors and legitimize present ones. They are thus irreducibly political tools. Michel Foucault noted, correctly, that all official truths seek to repress aporias and internal inconsistencies, and "if one controls people's memory, one controls their dynamism. It is vital to have possession of this memory, to control it, to administer it, tell it what it must contain."[31]

It is also the case that official truth efforts may have little impact on the population, especially those groups associated with the perpetrators. The perceived imposition of a master narrative may generate a host of counter-narratives that deny past abuses, justify them, or seek to create historical equivalencies – we may have slaughtered your people, but you did the same to us. For instance, the current Rwandan government's refusal to acknowledge atrocities committed by its own forces during and after the genocide has eroded its moral and political capital and strengthened the hand of Hutu genocide deniers and those who argue there was a "double genocide."[32]

In rejecting the retributive impulse behind prosecutions, which are seen as reinforcing social divisions, restorativists instead emphasize the importance of political forgiveness. Part of this emphasis is practical – most truth commissions lack prosecutorial or even subpoena powers and instead rely on other strategies to do their work. Nevertheless, restorativists defend forgiveness on more than practical grounds. Supporters contend that truth-telling, followed by repentance on the part of violators and forgiveness from victims, marks a sharp break with the past and represents a first step along the road to societal reconciliation.[33]

The meaning of forgiveness in post-violence contexts is not fixed.[34] In its most general sense, forgiveness emphasizes overcoming resentment, bitterness and anger, forswearing vengeance, and laying the foundations for a new future without violence. Christian formulations have been particularly influential in transitional justice debates, with their focus on the ontological transformation of perpetrators and victims and the presumed ability of the forgiveness process to promote compassion and generosity.[35] A number of critics have argued that post-conflict forgiveness discourse often masks a form of Western religious expectation on the proper ways to engage with the past (the same criticism of Western imposition, incidentally, is made of international courts and retributive justice). These criticisms miss an important point, however: forgiveness practices are found in a wide variety of cultural contexts and transitional settings, even if their normative foundations differ from one another.[36]

A more central question than whether forgiveness is a foreign imposition concerns whether forgiveness, normally practiced between individuals, can serve as an adequate social response to mass atrocity. Here, the evidence is mixed. The South African truth commission did not formally institutionalize forgiveness, but commission chairman Archbishop Desmond Tutu's endorsement of repentance and forgiveness, as well as his equally strong criticisms of retributive justice, ensured that forgiveness became a dominant norm during the transition and was seen by South Africans as the government's preferred policy. Indeed, several analysts and practitioners have sought to make forgiveness a viable *political* practice that emphasizes transformed relations and social harmony.[37] Nevertheless, a number of critics have noted that top-down political forgiveness programs are potentially coercive. They create a social expectation that victims ought to abandon moral outrage and legitimate anger in favor of political needs for stability and "moving on." In essence, expecting forgiveness – especially in the absence of accountability measures – effectively instrumentalizes victims and robs them of moral agency.[38] One South African survivor of apartheid complained bitterly about the truth commission, stating that it was "trying to dictate my forgiveness."[39] This is not a problem unique to South Africa – similar responses have come from Cambodia, Rwanda, and Argentina, among other places.

The upshot of political forgiveness efforts is that they may limit legitimate political dissent and reinforce the interests of the new regime, a particular problem in contexts with successor rulers who are already skeptical of democratic pluralism. Calls for widespread forgiveness, similar to calls for deep social reconciliation, often rely on a substantive conception of social solidarity that tends to smooth over pronounced and legitimate differences that are a part of any political order. Political forgiveness theories face a challenge in defining the difference between significant political conflict that may degenerate into renewed violence versus forceful political dissent that is a basic element of democratic discourse. This may be because these theories rarely detail what legitimate post-atrocity politics should look like, and the antagonistic element of politics is lost in favor of consensus.[40]

REPARATIONS AND DISTRIBUTIVE JUSTICE

Reparations for large-scale violence have a long history, though prior to World War II they were normally understood as payments made by defeated nations to the victors. Those reparations had little normative force – they were not ethical claims, but rather an expected cost of losing a war. After 1945, however, reparations as an ethical acknowledgement of responsibility for abuses gained greater resonance. In particular, West Germany's payment to Israel of about DM3 billion for crimes associated with the Holocaust, including slave labor, persecution and stolen or destroyed property, helped establish the moral underpinnings of reparations. Beginning in the 1960s indigenous groups around the world also mobilized to demand reparations for the legacies of violent colonialism, and African American activists revived calls for reparations from the United States government.[41] Over the past three decades reparations claims have become a fixture of political debates in Eastern and Central Europe, Africa, Latin America, and Asia, and have now become entrenched in transitional justice discourse, though reparations are still relatively rare in practice.[42]

The restorative justice paradigm has long noted the importance of reparations for victims of political violence. In many respects, this is in keeping with its victim-centric focus and general shift away from prosecutions and perpetrator punishment. Nevertheless, recent reparations scholarship and practice has sought to reframe them as part of long-term efforts at economic development and democratization, and thus serve as a means of assisting the consolidation of democracy. Pablo De Greiff argues that reparations can build civic trust and promote the rule of law by recasting victims as citizens with legal rights that must be recognized by the state,[43] with the eventual goal of "normalizing" post-conflict social and political life. With this goal in mind, a substantial literature on material reparations has developed that treats it as a subset of economic development programs.[44] However, reparations retain some distinctions from development programs.

Broadly speaking, reparations are those policies and initiatives that attempt to restore to victims their sense of dignity and moral worth and eliminate the social disparagement and economic marginalization that accompanied their targeting, with the goal of returning their status as citizens.[45] Reparations programs vary significantly, but can be understood according to how recipients are categorized (collectively or individually) and what type of victim acknowledgment they provide (symbolic or material).

In most cases of large-scale atrocity including genocide and crimes against humanity, violence is directed at some type of group, such as ethnic, religious, national, ideological, political, racial, or economic groups. Frequently, targeted groups span different categories and may contain other transversal categories – such as gender – whose members were the targets of specific types of violation. This broadly collective dimension of violence requires *collective symbolic* reparations for victim groups. Recognizing targeted groups means bringing public attention to the fact that violations were not simply discrete "excesses" but the result of planned strategies of repression (and occasionally extermination) against designated "enemies." Symbolic recognition of groups, then, means recognizing (a) the way strategies of repression targeted them *as* groups, and (b) the society's obligation to meet the demands of groups to recognize their experiences and treat them as equal citizens. Commitment to the latter means opposing discourses arguing that groups somehow "deserved" what happened to them because of their group identity or history. Symbolic benefits can be accorded in a number of different ways, including public acts of atonement and official apologies, creating public spaces to pay homage to victims, and establishing museums, monuments, and days of remembrance to preserve collective memory.

Individual symbolic acknowledgment consists of the need to recognize victims as individuals and not simply reduce them to an amorphous group of passive, voiceless survivors. This type of acknowledgment includes developing ways of underscoring how oppression and terror affected individuals *as such*; how the term *victims' experiences* is not simply the aggregate of mostly similar stories but reflects actual, distinct individuals whose lives were changed in personal and profound ways. In other words, it must include sensitivity to the multiplicity of distinct experiences that victims recount. While in practice it is impossible to recognize *all* victims individually in any meaningful sense, individual symbolic recognition emphasizes the importance of remembering that victims are not merely a statistic but actual people who often suffered intolerable cruelties. The suffering of an individual – whoever it may be – will always be more than a symbol of systematic crimes; suffering is always deeply personal, and proper recognition requires attention to this fact. Sensitivity to victims as individuals is an important step to reaffirming their status as human beings and citizens. Without recognition of victims as individuals *and* as equals who deserve respect, it is unlikely that they will secure their status as citizens.

Symbolic recognition – both individual and collective – may be important for helping victims recapture their sense of dignity and self-worth, but symbolic acknowledgment is not enough. In many cases, the devastation wrought by systematic violence and oppression also leaves victims in a position of economic vulnerability, something that cannot be remedied only through symbolic means. Thus, victim recognition also requires a concern with distributive justice.

The *collective material* element of reparatory justice focuses on distributive justice issues. It seeks to provide resources to victimized groups with the aim of creating the material basis and security necessary for them to become full participants in social, political, and economic life. This provision of resources may take several forms, such as developing programs for housing and employment for groups whose economic condition was directly affected by the violence, as well as health initiatives (psychological and physical) to address the traumas that victims experience. Where victims belong to historically devalued communities whose positions worsened during political violence, provision of resources may require broader infrastructural investments, including better roads, rural education programs, and credit initiatives for economic development. While the specifics of such programs must be tailored to particular contexts, the programs are collective in that they help groups that were targets of violence. All these programs entail the redistribution of economic resources with the goal of enhancing the livelihood of victims. For example, truth commissions in Peru, Guatemala, and El Salvador called for significant investments in public education, housing, employment, and economic development in indigenous areas most affected by the violence.

Finally, there is an *individual material* component to reparations. This too is a form of distributive justice, insofar as it addresses the importance of redistributing resources to victims. However, it places greater emphasis on the autonomy of individuals than the collective dimension discussed above. Certainly, no compensation can substitute for death or torture, and in this sense money – or any reparatory measure – is always insufficient. But compensation can have an impact for economically destitute victims and shows that the state's recognition of victims is not merely an empty symbolic gesture but also a commitment backed by material support. Individualized reparation schemes are varied, but they normally include familial rehabilitation through access to medical, psychological, and legal services, compensation for financially assessable losses, economic redress for harms that are not easily quantifiable, and restitution of lost, stolen, or destroyed property. Guatemala's truth commission strongly recommended that the state create a National Reparations Program to include compensation for serious injuries and losses, psychological rehabilitation initiatives, the restitution of or compensation for stolen or destroyed property, and other measures to be developed in tandem with affected communities. In particular, the commission emphasized the importance of individual reparations, with consideration given to the type of violation, the economic and social status of the victim, and special attention to certain categories of people, such as minors, widows, and the elderly.

Material reparations do face certain challenges. For many survivors, material reparations of any sort do not provide an adequate moral response to their suffering. They may see it as a kind of "blood money" or attempt by the state to wash its hands of future responsibility. But even where reparations are accepted as moral, it is not apparent how we should connect, conceptually, reparatory justice initiatives with general economic development and distributive programs (normally referred to as "development"). While most of society would benefit from an increase in development, there is a question of whether the specifically normative dimension of reparations risks being subsumed under these general distributive programs, clouding the normative distinction between reparative justice aimed at victims *per se* and more general state policies to combat poverty. For many victims, reparations are not simply about financial compensation but also about the moral force of state acknowledgment, and therefore collapsing reparations into development is normatively problematic. Indeed, what the state may call reparations for victims may be viewed as part of the state's duties to all citizens, allowing the government to build moral and political capital while actually satisfying (or claiming to satisfy) basic obligations.

Part of the difficulty stems from a lack of clarity regarding what, exactly, is meant by development. For some scholars, policy makers and activists, development includes not only narrowly tailored strategies to promote economic growth (the traditional focus), but also a wider host of policies related to institutional, political and social factors that together affect material and psychological well-being. The United Nations Development Programme evaluates development needs according to a broad range of practical opportunities individuals ought to have in order to exercise meaningful rational agency.[46] Peter Uvin, however, argues that development is about strengthening basic human rights: it concerns "the realization that the process by which development aims are pursued should itself respect and fulfill human rights."[47] These somewhat competing theoretical frames result in different policy recommendations.[48] However, there are compelling reasons to tie reparations to development. Rethinking reparations as not only backward-looking devices of commemoration and compensation, but as part of a future-oriented enterprise of economic justice may contribute to working toward the non-repetition of crimes. Often, the structural causes of mass violence persist after formal peace has returned and significant enclaves of economic marginalization and resentment still exist that may ignite future violence. South Africa, Rwanda, Sierra Leone, and Mozambique have all sought, in various ways, to promote development not only for strictly economic reasons but also as a way to curtail the possible return of violence (albeit with mixed success).

In any case, the relation between reparations and development is still undertheorized precisely because so much research and practice conceptualizes "transitional justice" (the period when reparations are supposed to be applied) as a liminal period between the termination of violence and the consolidation of a functioning liberal democratic order.[49] Thus, development questions are seen as better suited to the domain of "ordinary" liberal democratic politics. This conceptual division, neat in theory but problematic in practice, has its roots in liberal assumptions about the sources of mass violence: a breakdown of liberal codes of tolerance, the erosion of the rule of law, and a rise of violent, politicized "ethnic" or other collective identity claims. In this reading, it follows that what is needed is the establishment of constitutional order with a protection for basic liberal rights (the core of the retributive model presented earlier).[50] The move to incorporate development strategies into transitional justice debates forcefully contests some of these basic liberal assumptions about the causes of violence and peace.[51] These efforts to open the transitional justice field are ongoing, but signal a fundamental and welcome rethinking of what societal goals should be. Genocide studies can contribute directly to these debates by highlighting how structural conditions of marginalization can lead to political instability and mass violence. The structuralist theories of Mark Levene, Adam Jones and other genocide scholars, for instance, are well positioned to enrich transitional justice thinking on reparations and development.[52]

EMPIRICAL CHALLENGES

The previous sections outlined the main parameters of transitional justice scholarship and presented the strengths and limitations of various theoretical paradigms.

However, the options available to transition architects are often limited by specific political, social, and economic constraints.[53] This section presents several factors that affect the viability of transitional justice mechanisms across cases.

The first factor concerns the degree of *institutionalization and legitimacy of the previous regime*. The relative degree of institutionalization and legitimacy of the perpetrating regime affects the likely success of efforts to seek legal recourse for political crimes. Institutionalization means that the regime: ruled through the use of formal and bureaucratic mechanisms, so that different aspects of governance were managed and coordinated by various departments; penetrated civil and political society systematically and deeply; and was generally stable and durable. Institutionalized perpetrator regimes are two-faced, for they assemble complex legal justifications for their actions, bureaucratize violence, and generally rationalize all forms of repression, yet also engage in extra-legal terror against political opponents and the broader population, particularly through the use of secret police, death squads, disappearances, and massacres. Institutionalization often includes extensive legal justifications for crimes through the emergence of a large body of state-security law that justifies state practices, giving legal respectability to a violent state. The upshot may be a large body of law and archival evidence identifying the organization and systematization of state-sponsored violence. The more institutionalized and centralized the terror, the more likely it is that a significant body of documentation delineating the coordination of bureaucracies and security forces will exist. Of course, accessing this information may be difficult, as it was in Argentina, Chile and Guatemala following the removal of their military regimes. However, systematized state terror complemented by a robust body of documentation can facilitate the truth seeking and prosecutorial goals of tribunals, and thus institutionalized regimes are good for trials. Strong and well-documented links between superiors and subordinates illuminate hierarchies of legal (and moral) responsibility, making it more likely that prosecutions will be successful.

Nevertheless, institutionalization can also complicate prosecutions: complex, multilayered systems of repression complicate the criminal–legal understanding of responsibility, especially where there was a wide web of repression implicating numerous bureaucracies and agencies (e.g., as in South Africa and Eastern Europe, in different ways) and enjoying widespread support or at least acquiescence – and thus arguably legitimacy.

An important factor in assessing the viability of accountability measures is the *mode of political transition* between regimes. Transitions that are achieved through a complete victory in war or other radical break with the past give successor elites sufficient political capital to impose trials. The Tokyo and Nuremberg tribunals, as well as successor trials in Rwanda, underscore the wide latitude that victors have in pursuing retribution. Transitions that are negotiated, or "pacted," make trials less politically viable.[54] Previous elites may still retain enough power to prohibit or limit prosecutions through the threat of renewed violence. Other transitional justice mechanisms that are less retributive, such as truth commissions and broad reparations packages, may provide an acceptable alternative to prosecutions.

The *independence of the judiciary* strongly affects the likelihood of post-atrocity justice. In pacted transitions the judiciary remains an enclave of prior regime support (such as in El Salvador) and trials are unlikely to secure meaningful justice. Truth commissions may be a preferred alternative. The rise of regional and international judicial fora such as the Inter-American Court of Human Rights and the International Criminal Court, as well as case-specific tribunals, have provided important alternatives to domestic prosecutions. Regardless, the reconstruction of the national judiciary remains the best hope for domestic accountability and a crucial instrument against future impunity.

Benjamin Valentino has shown that genocide and mass killings require a relatively small group of well-organized killers and wider popular support, or at least indifference.[55] In some cases there are comparatively few overt perpetrators and many "beneficiaries," or persons who benefit from violence without necessarily participating in violations. In South Africa, all white South Africans were beneficiaries of the apartheid regime regardless of their political views. In other cases the proportion of perpetrators to beneficiaries is higher. For example, the Rwandan genocide seems to have included the active participation of many Hutu civilians. In Cambodia, the Khmer Rouge did not enjoy wide-ranging support outside their own ranks, and thus there were relatively few beneficiaries of the regime who were not implicated in gross human rights violations.

In all of these cases, tribunals can offer an important, though limited, contribution to accountability. Where there are relatively few overt perpetrators and many beneficiaries, the latter cannot be held legally accountable. A truth commission can serve as an important complement to trials by highlighting that complicity and responsibility go well beyond the narrowly understood notions of criminal liability that are characteristic of criminal prosecutions. In South Africa, the commission investigated the role that business, legal, medical, religious, and other professional communities played in supporting the apartheid regime. Investigations of this sort illuminate the wide support that some repressive states enjoy by morally implicating beneficiaries and countering claims that the latter were ignorant of the state's violence. Nevertheless, even this is insufficient; a robust public sphere open to critical reflection is an important resource for ensuring that state institutions like the judiciary or commissions do not wholly determine complex normative issues of historical memory, responsibility and perpetrator definition. Civil society actors can raise many of the difficult questions of responsibility, such as the moral status of bystanders and beneficiaries, in ways that are not possible through trials and even truth commission investigations.

Transitional justice programs are expensive, and poor countries emerging from a conflict with a devastated infrastructure and weak economy may be unable to pursue these expensive institutional responses, at least not without significant foreign support. *Material, financial, and personnel resources* affect the scope of prioritization and scope of strategies a country can pursue. A trial of a high-level perpetrator can cost millions of dollars and draw resources away from other pressing needs, including reparations, victim support programs and economic development initiatives. It may be a mistake to reject prosecutions solely on budgetary grounds, but budgetary constraints are real. Cambodia's hybrid tribunal has cost over $30 million a year since it began operations, and the ICTY and ICTR have cost about $150 million a year each.[56] Domestic efforts are cheaper, but still expensive: South Africa spent approximately $18 million a year on its commission, a sum unmatched by any other similar body, and commissioners nevertheless felt their work was underfunded.

Political will is related to these resource issues. Human rights advocates have often found a great deal of rhetorical governmental support for their ambitious projects, only to realize later that the regime has little interest pursuing politically delicate policies. The lack of interest is, unsurprisingly, reflected in the lack of money and resources available for trials, commissions or reparations. Uganda assembled two commissions – in 1974 and 1986 – that were duly ignored by the state, and Ecuador's 1996 commission ended inconclusively after 5 months without producing a report of its findings. Zimbabwe's 1985 state-sanctioned commission, investigating massacres in the Matabeleland, never released its report; the government quashed its publication, claiming the findings would unleash "ethnic conflict."[57] For many years, Cambodia resisted efforts at prosecutions of Khmer Rouge cadres for fear they would reveal extensive connections to the government. And yet political will and sufficient resources are crucial if institutional responses to the past are to succeed. Otherwise, they will amount to nothing more than empty promises.

A final cluster of factors concerns the *salience of specific cultural discourses for furthering justice and reconciliation*. International human rights organizations have developed an enormous literature on "lessons learned" about transitional justice – programmatic reports on justice packages, sequencing and implementation – which together constitute a systematized and highly rationalized body of knowledge whose primary findings are meant to be applied in a variety of contexts. This is partly a result of the general professionalization of the field over the past 20 years, which has received significant financial infusion from the UN, Western countries and various foundations.[58] This process of internationalization and standardization has marginalized local experiences and practices and created a deep disconnect between "expert" and local knowledge, often to the detriment of the latter. Nevertheless, justice and reconciliation are unlikely to have much of an impact if they do not draw from cultural discourses for legitimacy. In South Africa, local leaders frequently called for a collective spirit of *ubuntu*, roughly meaning "humaneness," to emphasize the importance of re-establishing just and meaningful social relations. Northern Ugandans have drawn on *mato oput*, a local reconciliation practice, to solidify community relations and permit former combatants to re-enter society through public expressions of repentance. These practices and others offer deep discursive sources that may feed broader efforts at encouraging reconciliation, understood in culturally relevant terms. Drawing on local discourses may help ensure that reconciliatory efforts will have greater resonance in the population.

CONCLUSION

This chapter has outlined some of the key developments and theoretical frameworks in the transitional justice literature as a first step toward encouraging genocide scholars to move beyond a handful of cases when examining post-genocide developments. While genocide scholars have often discussed the role of trials after genocide, the general normative and empirical findings of transitional justice – and their applicability to genocide – are rarely explored in any systematic fashion.

There are also contributions that genocide studies can make to transitional justice. Genocide scholars are well positioned to provide historically informed accounts of the past that resist reification of group and actor categories typical of the transitional justice literature. As discussed earlier, transitional justice studies often treat ethnic groups in rather static ways, seeking to end violence through "justice and reconciliation" programs between easily identifiable and stable groups. In the process these studies reproduce the same assumptions of ethnic homogeneity used by perpetrators to justify the conflict in the first place. Genocide researchers can bring further nuance to analyses of how collective identities develop and show how extremist claims of group identity often do not reflect realties on the ground. Researchers can also advance more sophisticated understandings of perpetrator, victim and bystander categories, which are often treated rather reductively in trials. Naturally, these efforts complicate transitional justice programs that employ uniform "lessons learned" approaches across many cases, but they are more empirically accurate and open context-sensitive opportunities for more substantive reconciliation and justice efforts.

Genocide research can also problematize dominant accounts of violence at the heart of mainstream transitional justice literature, which occasionally assumes that mass violence is the product of the erosion (or absence) of standard liberal universalist principles like tolerance, reasoned debate, and the rule of law. Sophisticated studies of the causes and dynamics of violence, including structural and contingent factors in explaining policy radicalization, require of trials and truth commissions more complex understandings of perpetrator intentionality and motives. This has direct consequences for the kinds of histories written in courtrooms and truth commission reports.

The points of interest between genocide and transitional justice research are many, and each field has much to offer the other. Greater knowledge and interaction between the two will enrich our understandings of mass violence and aid in efforts to reckon with terrible pasts.

NOTES

1 International Center for Transitional Justice ICTJ, 2008, "What is Transitional Justice?" Available HTTP: www.ictj.org/en/tj. Also see N. Kritz, ed., *Transitional Justice: How Emerging Democracies Reckon With Former Regimes*, 3 vols, Washington, DC: United Institute of Peace, 1997; R. Teitel, *Transitional Justice*, Oxford: Oxford University Press, 2000.

2   See *The Transitional Justice Database* at http://sites.google.com/site/transitionaljusticedatabase/

3   K. Theidon, "Whose Justice? Global and Local Approaches to Justice," *International Journal of Transitional Justice* 3/3, 2009, 1.

4   This is especially evident in articles published in the two main genocide studies journals, *Genocide Studies and Prevention* and *Journal of Genocide Research*. K. P. Apuuli, "Procedural Due Process and the Prosecution of Genocide Suspects in Rwanda," *Journal of Genocide Research* 11/1, 2009, 11–30; R. Wolf, "Judgment in the Grey Zone: The Third Auschwitz (Kapo) Trial in Frankfurt 1968," *Journal of Genocide Research* 9/4, 2007, 617–35; J. Burnet, "The Injustice of Local Justice: Truth, Reconciliation and Revenge in Rwanda," *Genocide Studies and Prevention* 3/2, 2008, 173–94; M. Bergsmo and E. Novic, "Justice After Decades in Bangladesh: National Trials for International Crimes," *Journal of Genocide Research* 13/4, 2011, 503–11; J. N. Clark, "The Crime of Crimes: Genocide, Criminal Trials and Reconciliation," *Journal of Genocide Research* 14/1, 2012, 55–77. Also see V. Dadrian and T. Akçam, *Judgment at Istanbul: The Armenian Genocide Trials*, New York: Berghahn Books, 2012. H. Earl, *The Nuremberg SS-Einsatzgruppen Trial, 1945–1958*, Cambridge: Cambridge University Press, 2009; M. Drumbl, *Atrocity, Punishment and International Law*, New York: Cambridge University Press, 2007; V. Peskin, *International Justice in Rwanda and the Balkans*, New York: Cambridge University Press, 2008. An exception is J. M. Kamatali, "Accountability for Genocide and Other Gross Human Rights Violations: The Need for an Integrated and Victim-based Transitional Justice," *Journal of Genocide Research* 9/2, 2007, 275–95.

5   D. Bloxham and A. D. Moses, eds., *The Oxford Handbook of Genocide Studies*, Oxford: Oxford University Press, 2010.

6   A. Jones, ed., *New Directions in Genocide Research*, New York: Routledge, 2012. The same point holds for other critical reviews of genocide studies, including: S. Totten and W. Parsons, eds., *Century of Genocide: Critical Essays and Eyewitness Testimony*, New York: Routledge, 2009; D. Stone, ed., *The Historiography of Genocide*, New York: Palgrave Macmillan, 2008; and two issues devoted to "Critical Reflections on the State and Future of Genocide Studies" in *Genocide Studies and Prevention* 6/3, 2011 and 7/1, 2012. Many works in the field that discuss genocide's aftermath are normally limited to analyzing prosecutions in select cases, and rarely examine systematically the broader normative questions raised in post-conflict settings.

7   L. Huyse and M. Salter, eds., *Traditional Justice and Reconciliation After Violent Conflict: Learning from African Experiences*, Stockholm: IDEA, 2008.

8   A. L. Hinton, ed., *Transitional Justice: Global Mechanisms and Local Realities After Genocide and Mass Violence*, New Brunswick, NJ: Rutgers University Press, 2010; A. L. Hinton and K. L. O'Neill, eds., *Genocide: Truth, Memory and Representation*, Durham, NC: Duke University Press, 2009. Adam Jones' genocide textbook also devotes a chapter to "Justice, Truth and Redress": see *Genocide: A Comprehensive Introduction*, 2nd edition, London: Routledge, 2010.

9   E. Higonnet, "Restructuring Hybrid Courts," *Arizona Journal of International and Comparative Law* 23/2, 2006, 347–435.

10 M. Minow, *Between Vengeance and Forgiveness: Facing History After Genocide and Mass Violence*, Boston: Beacon Press, 1998.

11 L. Huyse, "Tradition-Based Approaches in Peacemaking, Transitional Justice and Reconciliation Policies," in Luc Huyse and Mark Salter, eds., *Traditional Justice and Reconciliation after Violent Conflict: Learning from African Experiences*, Stockholm: Institute for Democracy and Electoral Assistance, 2008, pp. 1–21; E. Baines, "The Haunting of Alice: Local Approaches to Justice in Northern Uganda," *International Journal of*

Transitional Justice 1/1, 2007, 91–114; T. Longman, "Justice at the Grassroots? Gacaca Trials in Rwanda," in Naomi Roht-Arriaza and Javier Mariezcurrena, eds., *Transitional Justice in the Twenty-First Century: Beyond Truth* v. *Justice*, Cambridge: Cambridge University Press, 2006, pp. 206–28.

12 S. Straus and L. Waldorf, eds., *Remaking Rwanda: State Building and Human Rights after Mass Violence*, Madison: University of Wisconsin Press, 2011.

13 P. Clark, *The Gacaca Courts, Post-Genocide Justice and Reconciliation in Rwanda: Justice Without Lawyers*, Cambridge: Cambridge University Press, 2010. Rwanda has also used work and re-education programs, known as the TIG/RCS, to aid the return of released genocidaires into society.

14 E. Verdeja, *Unchopping a Tree: Reconciliation in the Aftermath of Political Violence*, Philadelphia, PA: Temple University Press, 2009, pp. 97–8.

15 J. Elster, *Closing the Books: Transitional Justice in Historical Perspective*, Cambridge: Cambridge University Press, 2004.

16 G. Bass, *Stay the Hand of Vengeance: The Politics of War Crimes Tribunals*, Princeton, NJ: Princeton University Press, 2001, p. 1.

17 H. Kim and K. Sikkink, "Explaining the Deterrence Effect of Human Rights Prosecutions for Transitional Countries," *International Studies Quarterly* 54/4, 2010, 939–63; D. Bloxham, *Genocide on Trial: War Crimes Trials and the Formation of Holocaust History and Memory*, Oxford: Oxford University Press, 2001.

18 This is especially evident in the work of Human Rights Watch, Amnesty International, and the International Center for Transitional Justice.

19 See H. Cobban, (2003) "Healing Rwanda: Can an International Court Deliver Justice?" *Boston Review*. Online. Available HTTP: http://bostonreview.net/BR28.6/cobban.html (accessed October 5, 2011).

20 A. M. Danner and J. S. Martinez, "Guilty Associations: Joint Criminal Enterprise, Command Responsibility, and the Development of International Criminal Law," *California Law Review* 93, 2005, 74–170.

21 M. B. Dembour and E. Haslam, "Silencing Hearings? Victim Witnesses at War Crimes Trials," *European Journal of International Law* 15/1, 2004, 156.

22 For instance, Z. Bauman, *Modernity and the Holocaust*, Ithaca, NY: Cornell University Press, 1989.

23 J. Braithwaite, *Crime, Shame and Reintegration*, Cambridge: Cambridge University Press, 1989., E. Kissi, "Moral Ambition within and Beyond Political Constraints," in Robert Rotberg and Dennis Thompson, eds., *Truth* v. *Justice: The Morality of Truth Commissions*, Princeton, NJ: Princeton University Press, 2001.

24 Occasionally also called TRCs, or truth and reconciliation commissions. M. Freeman, *Truth Commissions and Procedural Fairness*, Cambridge: Cambridge University Press, 2006.

25 The United States Institute of Peace keeps a useful list here: www.usip.org/publications/truth-commission-digital-collection (accessed December 9, 2011).

26 Peru *Informe Final de la Comisión de la Verdad y Reconciliación*, Lima, Peru: 2003, Available HTTP: www.cverdad.org.pe (accessed October 9, 2011); Argentina National Commission on the Disappeared *Nunca Más: Report of the Argentine National Commission on the Disappeared*, New York: Farrar, Straus and Giroux, 1986; South African Truth and Reconciliation Commission, *South African Truth and Reconciliation Final Report*, 5 vols, New York: Grove's Dictionaries, 1995.

27 J. Meierhenrich, "Topographies of Remembering and Forgetting: The Transformation of Lieux de Mémoire in Rwanda," in Scott Straus and Lars Waldorf, eds., *Remaking Rwanda: State Building and Human Rights after Mass Violence*, Madison: University of Wisconsin Press, 2011, pp. 283–96.

28 M. Osiel, "Ever Again: Legal Remembrance of Administrative Massacres," *University of Pennsylvania Law Review* 1/144, 1995, 275.

29 L. A. Fujii, *Killing Neighbors: Webs of Violence in Rwanda*, Ithaca, NY: Cornell University Press, 2009; C. Nordstrom, *A Different Kind of War Story*, Philadelphia: University of Pennsylvania Press, 1997.

30 A. L. Hinton, ed., *Transitional Justice*; J. DeShaw Rae, *Peacebuilding and Transitional Justice in East Timor*, Boulder, CO: Lynne Rienner, 2009.

31 M. Foucault, "Film and Popular Memory," *Radical Philosophy* 11, 1969, 25; P. Nora, ed., *Realms of Memory: Rethinking the French Past*, New York: Columbia University Press, 1996; D. Stone, "Genocide and Memory," in Donald Bloxham and A. Dirk Moses, eds., *The Oxford Handbook of Genocide Studies*, Oxford: Oxford University Press, 2010, pp. 102–19.

32 L. Waldorf, "Instrumentalizing Genocide: The RPF's Campaign Against Genocide Ideology," in Scott Straus and Lars Waldorf, eds., *Remaking Rwanda: State Building and Human Rights after Mass Violence*, Madison: University of Wisconsin Press, 2011, pp. 48–66; J. Pottier, *Re-imagining Rwanda: Conflict, Survival and Disinformation in the Late Twentieth Century*, Cambridge: Cambridge University Press, 2002.

33 D. Tutu, *No Future Without Forgiveness*, New York: Doubleday, 1999.

34 M. U. Walker, *Moral Repair: Reconstructing Moral Relations After Wrongdoing*, Cambridge: Cambridge University Press, 2006.

35 M. Volf, *Exclusion and Embrace: A Theological Exploration of Identity, Otherness, and Reconciliation*, Nashville, TN: Abingdon Press, 1996; M. Marty, "The Ethos of Christian Forgiveness," in Everett L. Worthington, ed., *Dimensions of Forgiveness: Psychological Research and Theological Forgiveness*, Philadelphia, PA: Templeton Foundation Press, 1998, pp. 9–28; L. W. Hinson, director, *As We Forgive*, film, Washington, DC: Image Bearer Pictures, 2007.

36 D. Philpott, *Just and Unjust Peace: An Ethic of Political Reconciliation*, Oxford: Oxford University Press, 2012.

37 P. Digeser, *Political Forgiveness,* Ithaca, NY: Cornell University Press, 2001; T. Govier, *Forgiveness and Revenge*, London: Routledge, 2002; T. Govier, *Taking Wrongs Seriously: Acknowledgment, Reconciliation, and the Politics of Sustainable Peace*, New York: Humanity Books, 2006.

38 T. Brudholm, "On the Advocacy of Forgiveness after Mass Atrocities," in Thomas Brudholm and Thomas Cushman, eds., *The Religious in Responses to Mass Atrocity*, Cambridge: Cambridge University Press, 2009.

39 W. Verwoerd, "Toward an Answer to Criticism of the South African TRC," in Trudy Govier, ed., *Dilemmas of Reconciliation: Cases and Concepts*, Waterloo, Ontario: Wilfrid Laurier University Press, 2003, p. 246.

40 D. Shriver, *An Ethic for Enemies: Forgiveness in Politics*, Oxford: Oxford University Press, 1998. For a sustained critique, see A. K. Hirsch, ed., *Theorizing Post-Conflict Reconciliation: Agonism, Restitution and Repair*, New York: Routledge, 2012.

41 A useful general treatment of twentieth-century reparations movements is found in E. Barkan, *The Guilt of Nations: Restitution and Negotiating Historical Injustices*, Baltimore, MD: Johns Hopkins University Press, 2000.

42 J. C. Torpey, *Making Whole What Has Been Smashed: On Reparations Politics*, Cambridge, MA: Harvard University Press, 2006. The UN has also endorsed the importance of reparations. See T. Van Boven, *United Nations Commission on Human Rights: Study Concerning the Right to Restitution, Compensation, and Rehabilitation for Victims of Gross Human Rights Violations and Fundamental Freedoms: Final Report.* UN doc. E/CN.4/1990/10, 1990. New York: United Nations, July 8, 1993.

43 P. De Greiff, "Repairing the Past: Reparations for Victims of Human Rights Violations," in Pablo De Greiff, ed., *The Oxford Handbook on Reparations*, Oxford: Oxford University Press, 2006, pp. 1–20.

44 N. Roht-Arriaza and K. Orlovzky, "A Complementary Relation: Reparations and Development," in Pablo De Greiff and Roger Duthie, eds., *Transitional Justice and Development: Making Connections*, New York: International Center for Transitional Justice, 2009, pp. 170–212.

45 E. Verdeja, "A Normative Theory of Reparations in Transitional Democracies," *Metaphilosophy* 37/3–4, 2006, 449–68; also see M. U. Walker, *What Is Reparative Justice?* Aquinas Lecture, Milwaukee, WI: Marquette University Press, 2010.

46 United Nations Development Programme, www.undp.org (accessed February 23, 2012). The key theoretical justification is found in "capabilities theory." See A. Sen, *The Idea of Justice*, Cambridge, MA: Harvard University Press, 2009.

47 P. Uvin, *Human Rights and Development*, Bloomfield, CT: Kumarian Press, 2004, pp. 175–6.

48 P. De Greiff and R. Duthie, eds., *Transitional Justice and Development*, New York: International Center for Transitional Justice, 2009.

49 T. Carothers, "The End of the Transition Paradigm," *Journal of Democracy* 13/1, 2002, 5–21; P. McAuliffe, "Transitional Justice's Expanding Empire: Reasserting the Value of the Paradigmatic Transition," *Journal of Conflictology* 2/2, 2011, 32–44.

50 J. Charvet and E. Kaczynska-Nay, *The Liberal Project and Human Rights: The Theory and Practice of a New World Order*, Cambridge: Cambridge University Press, 2008.

51 D. Philpott and G. Powers, eds., *Strategies of Peace: Transforming Conflict in a Violent World*, Oxford: Oxford University Press, 2010; R. Mani, *Beyond Retribution: Seeking Justice in the Shadows of War*, London: Polity Press, 2002; J. Smith and E. Verdeja, eds., *Globalization, Social Movements and Peacebuilding*, Syracuse, NY: Syracuse University Press, 2013.

52 M. Levene, *Genocide in the Age of the Nation-State*, 2 vols, London: I. B. Tauris Books, 2005; A. Jones, "Genocide and Structural Violence: Charting the Terrain," in Adam Jones, ed., *New Directions in Genocide Research*, pp. 132–52.

53 The empirical literature on transitional justice has grown significantly over the past three years. See B. Gordsky, "Re-ordering Justice: Towards A New Methodological Approach to Studying Transitional Justice," *Journal of Peace Research* 46/6, 2009, 819–37; T. Olsen, L. Payne and A. Reiter, "Transitional Justice in the World: 1970–2007: Insights from A New Dataset," *Journal of Peace Research* 47/6, 2010, 803–9.

54 G. O'Donnell, P. Schmitter, and L. Whitehead, eds., *Transitions from Authoritarian Rule*, 4 vols, Baltimore, MD: Johns Hopkins University Press, 1986.

55 B. Valentino, *Final Solutions: Mass Killing and Genocide in the Twentieth Century*, Ithaca, NY: Cornell University Press, 2004.

56 Extraordinary Chambers in the Courts of Cambodia "How Much Will the Trials Cost?" Available HTTP: www.eccc.gov.kh/en/faq/how-much-will-trials-cost; International Criminal Tribunal for the Former Yugoslavia, "The Cost of Justice," available HTTP: www.icty.org/sid/325; International Criminal Tribunal for Rwanda "Budget and Expenses," available HTTP: www.unictr.org/BSD/132/Default.aspx (all accessed January 3, 2012).

57 P. Hayner, *Unspeakable Truths: Transitional Justice and the Challenge of Truth Commissions*, New York: Routledge, 2010, p. 55.

58 C. Bell, "Transitional Justice, Interdisciplinarity and the State of the 'Field' or 'Non-Field,'" *International Journal of Transitional Justice* 3/1, 2009, 5–27.

REFERENCES

ACLED (2012) *Armed Conflict Location and Event Dataset*. Online. Available HTTP: www.acleddata.com/

R. Adalian, "The Armenian Genocide," in Samuel Totten, William S. Parsons and Israel W. Charny, eds., *Century of Genocide: Eyewitness Accounts and Critical Views*, New York: Garland Publishing, 1997.

T. Adorno, E. Frenkel and D. Levinson, *The Authoritarian Personality: Studies in Prejudice*, New York: W. W. Norton & Co. Inc., 1993.

D. Aikman, "The Situation in Cambodia," in Jack Nusan Porter, ed., *Genocide and Human Rights: A Global Anthology*, Lanham, MD: University Press of America, 1982.

T. Akçam, *The Young Turks' Crime Against Humanity: The Armenian Genocide and Ethnic Cleansing in the Ottoman Empire*, Princeton, NJ: Princeton University Press, 2012.

A. Alvarez, *Governments, Citizens, and Genocide: A Comparative and Interdisciplinary Approach*, Bloomington, IN: Indiana University Press, 2001.

M. Apple and L. K. Christian-Smith, eds., *The Politics of the Textbook*, London: Taylor & Francis, 1991.

J. Apsel, "Educating a New Generation: The Model of the Genocide and Human Rights University Program," *Human Rights Review* 12/4, 2011, 465–86.

J. Apsel, ed., *Darfur: Genocide Before Our Eyes,* 3rd edition, New York: Institute for Study of Genocide, 2007.

——, *Teaching About Human Rights*, Washington, DC: American Sociological Association, 2005.

J. Apsel and H. Fein, *Teaching about Genocide: A Guidebook for College and University Teachers: Critical Essays, Syllabi and Assignments*, 3rd edition, Washington, DC: American Sociological Association, 2002.

Argentina National Commission on the Disappeared *Nunca Más: Report of the Argentine National Commission on the Disappeared*, New York: Farrar, Straus, Giroux, 1986.

H. Arendt, *The Origins of Totalitarianism*, New York: Harcourt Brace & Company, 1973.

—— *Eichmann in Jerusalem: A Report on the Banality of Evil*, Harmondsworth, England: Penguin, 1994.

K. D. Askin, "Sexual Violence in Decisions and Indictments of the Yugoslav and Rwanda Tribunals: Current Status," *American Journal of International Law* 93/1, 1999, 97–123.

E. Baines, "The Haunting of Alice: Local Approaches to Justice in Northern Uganda," *International Journal of Transitional Justice* 1/1, 2007, 91–114.

Ban Ki-moon, "On Responsible Sovereignty: International Cooperation for a Changed World," Berlin, SG/SM11701, July 15, 2008.

T. Barta, "Mr. Darwin's Shooters: On Natural Selection and the Naturalization of Genocide," in A. Dirk Moses and Dan Stone, eds., *Colonialism and Genocide*, New York: Routledge, 2007, pp. 20–41.

G. Bass, *Stay the Hand of Vengeance: The Politics of War Crimes Tribunals*, Princeton, NJ: Princeton University Press, 2001.

O. Bartov, "Locating the Holocaust," *Journal of Genocide Research* 13/1, 2011, 121–9.

Y. Bauer, *Holocaust in Historical Perspective*, Seattle: Washington University Press, 1978.

—— "Genocide Prevention in Historical Perspective," *Dapim* 25, 2011, 319.

Z. Bauman, *Modernity and the Holocaust*, Ithaca, NY: Cornell University Press, 1989.

BBC, "Commentary Calls for Joint Efforts to Fight Against War Criminals in Sudan," *BBC Monitoring Middle East*, April 7, 2009.

G. Beckerman, "Top Genocide Scholars Battle over How to Characterize Israel's Actions," *Forward: The Jewish Daily*, February 16, 2011, online. Available HTTP: www.forward.com/articles/135484/ (accessed February 21).

C. Bell, "Transitional Justice, Interdisciplinarity and the State of the 'Field' or 'Non-Field,'" *International Journal of Transitional Justice* 3/1, 2009, 5–27.

A. Bellamy and Paul D. Williams, "On the Limits of Moral Hazard: The 'Responsibility to Protect,' Armed Conflict and Mass Atrocities," *European Journal of International Relations* 18/3, 2012, 539–71.

D. Bergen, "Challenging Uniqueness: Decentering and Recentering the Holocaust," *Journal of Genocide Research* 13/1-2, 2011, 129–34.

D. Bergoffen, *Contesting the Politics of Genocidal Rape: Affirming the Dignity of the Vulnerable Body*, London: Routledge, 2011.

Y. Bilinsky, "Was the Ukrainian Famine of 1932–1933 Genocide?" *Journal of Genocide Research* 1/2, 1999, 147–56.

D. Bloxham, *Genocide on Trial: War Crimes Trials and the Formation of Holocaust History and Memory*, New York: Oxford University Press, 2001.

—— *The Great Game of Genocide: Imperialism, Nationalism and the Destruction of the Ottoman Armenians*, Oxford: Oxford University Press, 2005.

—— *The Final Solution: A Genocide*, Oxford: Oxford University Press, 2009.

D. Bloxham and T. Kushner, *The Holocaust: Critical Historical Approaches*, Manchester: Manchester University Press, 2005.

D. Bloxham and A. D. Moses, eds., *The Oxford Handbook of Genocide Studies*, Oxford: Oxford University Press, 2010.

J. H. Bodley, *Victims of Progress*, 3rd Edition, Mountain View, CA: Mayfield, 1990.

Book of Numbers, *The Bible: Authorized King James Version*, Oxford: Oxford University Press, 1997.

J. Braithwaite, *Crime, Shame and Reintegration*, Cambridge: Cambridge University Press, 1989.

C. Browning, *Ordinary Men: Reserve Police Battalion 101 and the Final Solution in Poland*, New York: Harper Perennial, 1992.

—— *The Origins of the Final Solution: The Evolution of Nazi Jewish Policy, September 1939–March 1942*, Lincoln, NE: University of Nebraska Press and Jerusalem: Yad Vashem, 2004.

S. Brownmiller, *Against Our Will: Men, Women, and Rape*, New York: Fawcett Columbine, 1993.

T. Brudholm, "On the Advocacy of Forgiveness after Mass Atrocities," in Thomas Brudholm and Thomas Cushman, eds., *The Religious in Responses to Mass Atrocity*, Cambridge: Cambridge University Press, 2009.

Bryce, Viscount, *The Treatment of the Armenians in the Ottoman Empire, 1915–16: Documents Presented to Viscount Grey of Fallodon, Secretary of State for Foreign Affairs by Viscount Bryce*, Compiled by Arnold Toynbee, London: HMSO, 1916.

A. Bullock, *Hitler: A Study in Tyranny*, New York: Harper Perennial, 1991.

M. Byers and S. Chesterman, "Changing the Rules about Rules? Unilateral Humanitarian Intervention and the Future of International Law," in J. L. Holzgrefe and Robert Keohane, eds., *Humanitarian Intervention*, Cambridge: Cambridge University Press.

Cambodia: Extraordinary Chambers in the Courts of Cambodia, Transcript of Proceedings – "Duch" Trial, Phnom Penh, Cambodia: Extraordinary Chambers in the Courts of Cambodia, August 31, 2009.

G. Cameron and J. Goldstein, "The Ontology of Modern Terrorism: Hegel, Terrorism Studies, and Dynamics of Violence," *Cosmos and History: The Journal of Natural and Social Philosophy* 6/1, 2010, 60–90.

T. Carothers, "The End of the Transition Paradigm," *Journal of Democracy* 13/1, 2002, 5–21.

L. Cederman, A. Wimmer and B. Min, "Why Do Ethnic Groups Rebel? New Data and Analysis," *World Politics* 62/1, 2010, 87–119.

D. Cesarani, "Does the Singularity of the Holocaust Make It Incomparable and Inoperative in Commemorating, Studying and Preventing Genocide? Britain's Holocaust Memorial Day as a Case Study," *Journal of Holocaust Education* 10/2, 2001, 40–56.

G. Chaliand and Y. Ternon, *The Armenians: From Genocide to Resistance*, Tony Berrett, trans., London: Zed Press, 1983.

F. Chalk and K. Jonassohn, *The History and Sociology of Genocide*, New Haven, CT: Yale University Press, 1990.

D. Chandler, *Brother Number One: A Political Biography of Pol Pot*, revised edition, Boulder, CO: Westview Press, 1999.

I. Charny, *How Can We Commit the Unthinkable? Genocide: The Human Cancer*, Boulder, CO: Westview Press, 1982.

J. Charvet and E. Kaczynska-Nay, *The Liberal Project and Human Rights: The Theory and Practice of a New World Order*, Cambridge: Cambridge University Press, 2008.

A. Chua, *World on Fire: How Exporting Free Market Democracy Breeds Ethnic Hatred and Global Instability*, New York: Anchor Books, 2004.

W. Churchill, *A Little Matter of Genocide: Holocaust and Denial in the Americas, 1492 to the Present*, San Francisco, CA: City Lights Books, 1997.

P. Clark, *The Gacaca Courts, Post-Genocide Justice and Reconciliation in Rwanda: Justice Without Lawyers*, Cambridge: Cambridge University Press, 2010.

V. Clark, "Rape Thy Neighbour", in Human Rights Watch, *Bosnia and Hercegovina: "A Closed, Dark Place" – Past and Present Human Rights Abuses in Foca*, 6 (Section D) ed., vol. 10, 1998.

H. Cobban, "Healing Rwanda: Can an International Court Deliver Justice?," *Boston Review* (2003). Online. Available HTTP: http://bostonreview.net/BR28.6/cobban.html. Accessed October 5, 2011.

B. Cohen, "Jewish Studies," in Jean-Marc Dreyfus and Daniel Langton, eds., *Writing the Holocaust*, London: Bloomsbury Academic, 2011, pp. 108–24.

D. Cohen, "Comparative History: Buyer Beware," in Deborah Cohen and Maura O'Connor, eds., *Comparison and History*, New York: Routledge, 2004.

R. Conquest, *The Harvest of Sorrow: Soviet Collectivization and the Terror-famine*, New York: Oxford University Press, 1987.

—— *Stalin: Breaker of Nations*, New York: Penguin Books, 1991.

S. Craig, "The Interdependence and Permeability of Human Rights Norms: Toward a Partial Fusion of the International Covenants on Human Rights," *Osgoode Hall Law Journal* 27/53, 1989, 769–878.

I. Cotler, "Genocide Starts With Incitement to Hate," *Africa News Service*, April 8, 2009.

V. Dadrian, *Warrant for Genocide: Key Elements of the Turko-Armenian Conflict*, New Brunswick, NJ and London: Transaction Publishers, 1999.

W. A. Dando, "Man-made Famines: Some Geographical Insights from an Exploratory Study of a Millennium of Russian Famines," *Ecology of Food and Nutrition* 4/4, 1976.

A. M. Danner and J. S. Martinez, "Guilty Associations: Joint Criminal Enterprise, Command Responsibility, and the Development of International Criminal Law," *California Law Review* 93, 2005, 74–170.

"Darfur: Women Raped Even After Seeking Refuge," Human Rights Watch, online. Available HTTP: http://hrw.org/english/docs/2005/04/11/sudan10467.htm. (accessed July 14, 2012).

C. Davenport, "State Repression and Political Order," *Annual Review of Political Science* 10, 2007, 1–23.

D. Davies, *The Last of the Tasmanians*, New York: Barnes & Noble, 1974.

J. Davies and T. Gurr, *Preventive Measures: Building Risk Assessment and Crisis Early Warning Systems*, Lanham, MD: Rowman & Littlefield, 1998.

L. Dawidowicz, *The War Against The Jews, 1933–1945,* New York: Holt, Rinehart and Winston, 1975.

P. De Greiff, "Repairing the Past: Reparations for Victims of Human Rights Violations," in Pablo De Greiff, ed., *The Oxford Handbook on Reparations*, Oxford: Oxford University Press, 2006.

P. De Greiff and R. Duthie, eds., *Transitional Justice and Development*, New York: International Center for Transitional Justice, 2009.

M. B. Dembour and E. Haslam, "Silencing Hearings? Victim Witnesses at War Crimes Trials," *European Journal of International Law* 15/1, 2004, 151–77.

M. Derdarian, *Vergeen: A Survivor of the Armenian Genocide*, Los Angeles, CA: Atmus Press, 1996.

J. DeShaw Rae *Peacebuilding and Transitional Justice in East Timor*, Boulder, CO: Lynne Rienner, 2009.

A. de Waal and B. Conley-Zilkic, "Reflections on How Genocidal Killings Are Brought to an End," *Social Science Research Council*, December 22, 2006. Available HTTP: http://howgenocidesend.ssrc.org/de_Waal/geq.

P. Digeser, *Political Forgiveness*, Ithaca, NY: Cornell University Press, 2001.

F. Dikötter, *Mao's Great Famine: The History of China's Most Devastating Catastrophe, 958–1962*, London: Bloomsbury Publishing, 2010.

J. Donnelly, *International Human Rights*, Boulder, CO: Westview Press, 2006.

M. W. Doyle, "International Ethics and the Responsibility to Protect," *International Studies Review* 13/1, 2011, 72–84.

M. Drumbl, *Atrocity, Punishment, and International Law*, Cambridge: Cambridge University Press, 2007.

H. Earl, *The Nurenberg Einsatzgugpen Trial, 1945-1958: Atrocity, Law, and History*, Cambridge: Cambridge University Press, 2010.

W. Easterly, R. Gatti and S. Kurbat, "Development, Democracy, and Mass Killing," *Journal of Economic Growth* 11, 2006, 129–56.

L. Einstein, "The Armenian Massacres," *Contemporary Review* 111, 1917, 494. 83.

K. Ellinghaus, "Biological Absorption and Genocide: A Comparison of Indigenous Assimilation in the United States and Australia," *Genocide Studies and Prevention* 4/1, 2009, 59–79.

J. Elster, *Closing the Books: Transitional Justice in Historical Perspective*, Cambridge: Cambridge University Press, 2004.

M. Esparza, H. Huttenbach and D. Feierstein, *State Violence and Genocide in Latin America: The Cold War Years*, New York: Routledge, 2011.

R. Evans, "'Crime Without a Name': Colonialism and the Case for 'Indigenocide,'" in A. Dirk Moses, ed., *Empire, Colony, Genocide: Conquest, Occupation, and Subaltern Resistance in World History*, New York: Berghahn Books, 2008, pp. 133–47.

Extraordinary Chambers in the Courts of Cambodia, "How Much Will the Trials Cost?" Available HTTP: www.eccc.gov.kh/en/faq/how-much-will-trials-cost (accessed January 3, 2012).

D. Feierstein, *El genocidio como práctica social: Entre el nazismo y la experiencia argentina: Hacia un análisis del aniquilamiento como re organizador de las relaciones sociales*, Buenos Aires, Argentina: Fondo de CulturaEconómica, 2008.

H. Fein, *Accounting for Genocide: National Responses and Jewish Victimization During the Holocaust*, Chicago: University of Chicago Press, 1984.

—— "Accounting for Genocide After 1945: Theories and Some Findings," *International Journal on Group Rights* I, 1993, 88–92.

—— *Genocide: A Sociological Perspective*, London: Sage, 1993.

—— *The ISG Newsletter*, 9, Fall 1992. New York.

—— *The ISG Newsletter,*10, Spring 1993. New York.

—— "Genocide by Attrition 1939–1993: The Warsaw Ghetto, Cambodia, and Sudan: Links between Human Rights, Health, and Mass Death," *Health and Human Rights* 2/2, 1997, 10–45.

—— *Human Rights and Wrongs: Slavery, Terror and Genocide*, Herndon, VA: Paradigm Publishers, 2007.

J. Fearon and D. Laitin, "Ethnicity, Insurgency and Civil War," *American Political Science Review* 97/1, 2003, 75–90.

M. Finnemore, "Paradoxes in Humanitarian Intervention," in Richard Price, ed., *Moral Limit and Possibility in World Politics*, Cambridge: Cambridge University Press, 2008, pp. 197–224.

J. Fitzpatrick, ed., *Human Rights Protection for Refugees, Asylum-seekers, and Internally Displaced Persons: A Guide to International Mechanisms and Procedures*, Ardsley, NY: Transnational Publishers, 2002.

S. Fitzpatrick, *The Russian Revolution*, New York: Oxford University Press, 1994.

G. Fleming, *Hitler and the Final Solution*, Berkeley: University of California Press, 1982.

J. Flint and A. De Waal, *Darfur: A Short History of a Long War*, London: Zed Books, 2005.

M. Foucault, "Film and Popular Memory," *Radical Philosophy* 11, 1969, 24–9.

A. Frank, *Diary of a Young Girl*, New York: Doubleday Books, 1967.

Frankfurter Rundschau, March 3, 1993, quoted in R. Seifert, "War and Rape: A Preliminary Analysis," in Alexandra Stiglmayer, ed., *Mass Rape: The War against Women in Bosnia-Herzegovina*, Lincoln, NE: University of Nebraska Press, 1994, p. 55.

V. Frankl, *Man's Search for Meaning*, New York: Pocket Books, 1997.

M. Freeman, *Truth Commissions and Procedural Fairness*, Cambridge: Cambridge University Press, 2006.

S. Friedländer, *Reflections of Nazism: An Essay on Kitsch and death*, New York: Harper and Row, 1984.

—— *The Years of Persecution: Nazi Germany and the Jews: 1933–1939*, New York: HarperCollins, 1997.

—— *The Years of Extermination: Nazi Germany and the Jews: 1939–1945*, New York: HarperCollins, 2007.

L. A. Fujii, *Killing Neighbors: Webs of Violence in Rwanda*, Ithaca, NY: Cornell University Press, 2009.

A. Garbarini, "Reflections on the Holocaust and Jewish History," *Jewish Quarterly Review* 102/1, 2012, 81–90.

Z. Garber, *Shoah, the Paradigmatic Genocide: Essays in Exegesis and Eisegesis*, Lanham, MD: University Press of America, 1994.

R. Gellately and B. Kiernan, eds., *The Specter of Genocide: Mass Murder in Historical Perspective*, Cambridge: Cambridge University Press, 2003.

Genocide Prevention Task Force, *Preventing Genocide: A Blueprint for US Policymakers*, Washington, DC: US Institute for Peace, 2008.

C. Gerlach, *Extremely Violent Societies: Mass Violence in the Twentieth Century World*, Cambridge: Cambridge University Press, 2010.

T. Gingerich and J. Leaning, *The Use of Rape as a Weapon of War in Darfur, Sudan*, report prepared for the US Agency for International Development/OTI, October 2004.

Global Center for the Responsibility to Protect, *The 2009 General Assembly Debate: An Assessment*, New York: Global Center for the Responsibility to Protect Report, August 2009, Available HTTP: http://globalr2p.org/media/pdf/GCR2P_General_Assembly_Debate_Assessment.pdf.

Global Database, "Guiding Principles on Internal Displacement," *Global Database*, online. Available HTTP: www.idpguidingprinciples.org (accessed July 15, 2012).

D. Goldhagen, *Hitler's Willing Executioners: Ordinary Germans and the Holocaust*, New York: Vintage Books, 1997.

B. Goldsmith, C. Butcher, D. Semenovich and A. Sowmya, "Forecasting the Onset of Genocide and Politicide: Annual Out-of-Sample Forecasts on a Global Dataset, 1988–2003." Online. Available HTTP: http://ssrn.com/abstract=2027396 or http://dx.doi.org/10.2139/ssrn.2027396 (accessed March 20, 2012).

P. Gordon and K. Crehan, *Dying of Sadness: Gender, Sexual Violence and the HIV Epidemic*, New York: HIV and Development Programme, United Nations Development Programme, 1999.

B. Gordsky, "Re-ordering Justice: Towards a New Methodological Approach to Studying Transitional Justice," *Journal of Peace Research* 46/6, 2009, 819–37.

P. Gourevitch, *We wish to inform you that tomorrow we will be killed with our families*, New York: Picador Books, 1999.

T. Govier, *Forgiveness and Revenge*, London: Routledge, 2002.

J. Gross, *Neighbors: The Destruction of the Jewish Community in Jedwabne Poland*, Princeton, NJ: Princeton University Press, 2001.

F. Grünfeld and A. Huijboom, *The Failure to Prevent Genocide in Rwanda: The Role of Bystanders*, Leiden, Netherlands: Martinus Nijhoff, 2007.

J. Hagan, *Justice in the Balkans: Prosecuting War Crimes at the Hague Tribunal*, Chicago: University of Chicago Press, 2003.

R. Hamilton, *Fighting for Darfur*, New York: Palgrave, 2011.

B. Harff, "No Lessons Learned From the Holocaust? Assessing Risks of Genocide and Political Mass Murder Since 1955," *American Political Science Review* 97, 2003, 57–73.

H. G. Haupt and J. Kocka, eds., *Comparative and Transnational History: Central European Approaches and New Perspectives*, New York: Berghahn Books, 2009.

P. Hayner, *Unspeakable Truths: Transitional Justice and the Challenge of Truth Commissions*, New York: Routledge, 2010.

Helsinki Watch, *War Crimes in Bosnia-Hercegovina*, New York: Human Rights Watch, 1993.

M. Hiebert, "The Three 'Switches' of Identity Construction in Genocide: The Nazi Final Solution and the Cambodian Killing Fields," *Genocide Studies and Prevention* 3/1, 2008, 5–29.

E. Higonnet, "Restructuring Hybrid Courts," *Arizona Journal of International and Comparative Law* 23/2, 2006, 347–435.

R. Hilberg, *The Destruction of the European Jews*, London: W. H. Allen, 1961, 3 vols.

C. Him, *When Broken Glass Floats: Growing Up Under the Khmer Rouge*, New York: W. W. Norton, 2001.

L. W. Hinson, director, *As We Forgive*, Film, Washington, DC: Image Bearer Pictures, 2007.

A. Hinton, *Why Did They Kill? Cambodia in the Shadow of Genocide*, Los Angeles, CA: University of California Press, 2005.

A. Hinton, ed., *Annihilating Difference: The Anthropology of Genocide*, Los Angeles, CA: University of California Press, 2002.

—— *Transitional Justice: Global Mechanisms and Local Realities after Genocide and Mass Violence*, New Brunswick, NJ: Rutgers University Press, 2010.

A. Hinton and K. O'Neill, eds., *Genocide: Truth, Memory and Representation*, Durham, NC: Duke University Press, 2010.

H. Hirsch and R. Smith, "The Language of Extermination in Genocide," in Israel W. Charny, ed., *Genocide: A Critical Bibliographic Review, Volume Two*, London: Mansell Publishing Limited, 1991.

R. K. Hitchcock and S. Totten, eds., *Genocide of Indigenous Peoples*, New Brunswick, NJ: Transaction, 2011.

S. L. Hoffman, ed., *Human Rights in the Twentieth Century*, Cambridge: Cambridge University Press, 2011.

O. Holter, "A Theory of Gendercide," *Journal of Genocide Research* 4/1, 2010, 11–38.

I. Horowitz, *Taking Lives: Genocide and State Power*, 4th edition, New Brunswick, NJ: Transaction Publishers, 1997.

R. Hovannisian, "Etiology and Sequelae of the Armenian Genocide," in George J. Andreopoulos, ed., *Genocide: Conceptual and Historical Dimensions*, Philadelphia, PA: University of Pennsylvania Press, 1994.

R. Hukanovic, *The Tenth Circle of Hell: A Memoir of Life in the Death Camps of Bosnia*, London: Little, Brown, 1997.

Human Rights Watch, *"We'll Kill You if You Cry." Sexual Violence in the Sierra Leone Conflict*, New York: Human Rights Watch, 2003.

L. Huyse, "Tradition-Based Approaches in Peacemaking, Transitional Justice and Reconciliation Policies," in Luc Huyse and Mark Salter, eds., *Traditional Justice and Reconciliation after Violent Conflict: Learning from African Experiences*, Stockholm: Institute for Democracy and Electoral Assistance, 2008, pp. 1–21.

L. Huyse and M. Salter, eds., *Traditional Justice and Reconciliation After Violent Conflict: Learning from African Experiences*, Stockholm: Institute for Democracy and Electoral Assistance (IDEA), 2008.

International Center for Transitional Justice (ICTJ) (2008) *What Is Transitional Justice?* Available HTTP: www.ictj.org/en/tj.

International Commission of Inquiry on Darfur, *Report of the International Commission of Inquiry on Darfur to the United Nations Secretary-General*, January 25, 2005.

International Criminal Tribunal for the Former Yugoslavia (ICTY), "The Cost of Justice." Available HTTP: www.icty.org/sid/325 (accessed January 3, 2012).

—— *The Prosecutor v. Gojko Janković, Janko Janjić, Zoran Vuković, Dragan Zelenović, Radovan Stanković*, IT-99-33-A, October 1999.

—— *Prosecutor v. Goran Jelisić* (Appeal Judgment), IT-95-10-A, July 2001.

—— *Prosecutor v. Radislav Krstić* (Appeal Judgment), IT-98-33-A, April 2004.

International Criminal Tribunal for Rwanda (ICTR), "Budget and Expenses." Available HTTP: www.unictr.org/BSD/132/Default.aspx (accessed January 3, 2012).

—— *The Prosecutor v. Jean-Paul Akayesu*, case no. ICTR-96-4-T, September 1998.

—— *The Prosecutor v. Clément Kayishema and Obed Ruzindana* (Trial Judgment), ICTR-95-1-T, May 1999.

—— *The Prosecutor* v. *Georges Anderson Nderubumwe Rutaganda* (Judgment and Sentence), ICTR-96-3-T, December 1999.

—— *The Prosecutor* v. *Alfred Musema* (Judgment and Sentence), ICTR-96-13-T, January 2000.

R. Jackson, *The Global Covenant*, Oxford: Oxford University Press, 2000.

K. Jenkins, *Re-thinking History*, New York: Routledge, 1991.

E. von Joeden-Forgey, "Gender and Genocide," in *The Oxford Handbook of Genocide Studies*, ed. D. Bloxham and A. D. Moses, Oxford: Oxford University Press, 2010.

A. Jones, *Gendercide and Genocide*, Nashville, TN: Vanderbilt University Press, 2004.

—— *Genocide: A Comprehensive Introduction*, 2nd edition, New York: Routledge, 2010.

—— *New Directions in Genocide Research*, London: Routledge, 2012.

D. Kahneman and A. Tversky, "Prospect Theory: An Analysis of Decision Under Risk," *Econometrica* 47/2, 1979, 263–92.

S. Kalyvas, *The Logic of Violence in Civil War*, Cambridge: Cambridge University Press, 2006.

H. Kelman, "Violence Without Moral Restraint: Reflection on the Dehumanization of Victims by Victimizers," *Journal of Social Issues* 29/4, 1973, 25–61.

H. Kelman and V. Hamilton, *Crimes of Obedience*, New Haven, CT: Yale University Press, 1990.

I. Kershaw, *Hitler 1936–1945: Nemesis*, London: Allen Lane, the Penguin Press, 2000.

B. Kiernan, *Blood and Soil: A World History of Genocide and Extermination from Sparta to Darfur*, New Haven, CT: Yale University Press, 2007.

H. Kim and K. Sikkink, "Explaining the Deterrence Effect of Human Rights Prosecutions for Transitional Countries," *International Studies Quarterly* 54/4, 2010, 939–63.

R. King and D. Stone, eds., *Hannah Arendt and the Uses of History: Imperialism, Nation, Race, and Genocide*, Oxford: Berghahn Books, 2007.

E. Kissi, "Moral Ambition Within and Beyond Political Constraints," in Robert Rotberg and Dennis Thompson, eds., *Truth* v. *Justice: The Morality of Truth Commissions*, Princeton, NJ: Princeton University Press, 2001.

—— *Revolution and Genocide in Ethiopia and Cambodia*, Lanham, MD: Lexington Books, 2006.

J. Knowlton and T. Cates, eds., *Forever in the Shadow of Hitler? Original Documents of the Historikerstreit, The Controversy Concerning the Singularity of the Holocaust*, Atlantic Highlands, NJ: Humanities Press International, 1993.

L. Kolakowski, *Modernity on Endless Trial*, Chicago: University of Chicago Press, 1990.

M. Krain, "State Sponsored Mass Murder: The Onset and Severity of Genocides and Politicides," *Journal of Conflict Resolution* 41/3, 1997, 331–60.

N. Kristof, "Genocide in Slow Motion," *The New York Review of Books* 53/2, February 9, 2006.

N. Kritz, ed., *Transitional Justice: How Emerging Democracies Reckon With Former Regimes*, 3 vols., Washington, DC: United Institute of Peace, 1997.

L. Kuper, *Genocide: Its Political Uses in the Twentieth Century*, New Haven, CT: Yale University Press, 1983.

J. Laber, "Bosnia: Questions About Rape," *New York Review of Books* XL/6, 1993.

G. Lakoff, *Women, Fire, and Dangerous Things: What Categories Reveal about the Mind*, Chicago: Chicago University Press, 2007.

P. Landesman, "The Minister of Rape," *New York Times Magazine*, September 15, 2002.

B. Lang, *Post-Holocaust: Interpretation, Misinterpretation, and the Claims of History*, Bloomington: Indiana University Press, 2004.

T. Lawson, *Debates on the Holocaust*, Manchester: Manchester University Press, 2010.

R. Lemarchand, ed., *Forgotten Genocides: Oblivion Denial and Memory*, Philadelphia: University of Pennsylvania Press, 2010.

R. Lemkin, *Axis Rule in Occupied Europe: Laws of Occupation, Analysis of Government – Proposals for Redress*, Washington, DC: Carnegie Endowment for International Peace, 1944.

M. Levene, *Genocide in the Age of the Nation State*, London: I. B. Tauris, 2005, 2 vols.

P. Levi, *Survival in Auschwitz*, New York: Classic House Books, 2009.

G. Lewy, *The Nazi Persecution of the Gypsies*, Oxford: Oxford University Press, 2000.

—— *The Armenian Massacres in Ottoman Turkey: A Disputed Genocide*, Salt Lake City: University of Utah Press, 2005.

—— "Can There be Genocide Without the Intent to Commit Genocide?" *Journal of Genocide Research* 9/4, 2007, 661–74.

R. Lifton, *Nazi Doctors: Medical Killing and the Psychology of Genocide*, New York: Basic Books, 2000.

P. Longerich, *Holocaust: The Nazi Persecution and Murder of the Jews*, Oxford: Oxford University Press, 2010.

T. Longman, "Justice at the Grassroots? Gacaca Trials in Rwanda," in Naomi Roht-Arriaza and Javier Mariezcurrena, eds., *Transitional Justice in the Twenty-First Century: Beyond Truth* v. *Justice*, Cambridge: Cambridge University Press, 2006, pp. 206–28.

Y. Lozowick, *Hitler's Bureaucrats: The Nazi Security Police and the Banality of Evil*, New York: Continuum, 2002.

E. Luck, "A Response," *Global Responsibility to Protect* 2/1-2, 2010, 161–6.

K. Maas Weigert, "Structural Violence," in Lester Kurtz, ed., *Encyclopedia of Violence, Peace and Conflict*, Oxford: Elsevier Press, 2008.

J. Mace, "Soviet Man-Made Famine in Ukraine," in Samuel Totten and William S. Parsons, eds., *Century of Genocide: Critical Essays and Eyewitness Accounts*, 3rd Ed., New York: Routledge, 2009.

P. McAuliffe, "Transitional Justice's Expanding Empire: Reasserting the Value of the Paradigmatic Transition," *Journal of Conflictology* 2/2, 2011, 32–44.

C. McCauley and D. Chirot, *Why Not Kill Them All? The Logic and Prevention of Mass Political Murder*, Princeton, NJ: Princeton University Press, 2006.

C. Mackinnon, "Turning Rape into Pornography: Postmodern Genocide," *Ms.*, July/August 1993, 24–30.

R. Mani, *Beyond Retribution: Seeking Justice in the Shadows of War*, London: Polity Press, 2002.

M. Mann, *The Darkside of Democracy: Explaining Ethnic Cleansing*, New York: Cambridge University Press, 2007.

MAR: Minorities at Risk Project (2010). Online. Available HTTP: www.cidcm.umd.edu/mar/.

D. Marcus, "Famine Crimes in International Law," *American Journal of International Law* 97/2, 2003, 245–81.

E. Markusen, "Genocide and Total War: A Preliminary Comparison," in Isidor Wallimann and Michael N. Dobkowski, eds., *Genocide and the Modern Age: Etiology and Case Studies of Mass Death*, Syracuse, NY: Syracuse University Press, 1987, pp. 97–123.

E. Markusen and D. Kopf, *The Holocaust and Strategic Bombing: Genocide and Total War in the Twentieth Century*, Boulder, CO: Westview Press, 1995.

M. Marrus, *The Holocaust in History*, New York: Plume Books, 1989.

M. Marty, "The Ethos of Christian Forgiveness," in Everett L. Worthington, ed., *Dimensions of Forgiveness: Psychological Research and Theological Forgiveness*, Philadelphia, PA: Templeton Foundation Press, 1998, pp. 9–28.

F. Mazian, *Why Genocide: The Armenian and Jewish Experiences in Perspective*, Ames, IO: Iowa University Press, 1990.

M. Mazower, "After Lemkin: Genocide, the Holocaust and History," *Jewish Quarterly* 5, 1994, 5–8.

—— "Strange Triumph of Human Rights 1922–1950," *Historical Journal* 47, 2004, 379–98.

Médecins Sans Frontières, *The Crushing Burden of Rape: Sexual Violence in Darfur*, March 8, 2005.

J. Meierhenrich, "Topographies of Remembering and Forgetting: The Transformation of Lieux Mémoire in Rwanda," in Scott Straus and Lars Waldorf, eds., *Remaking Rwanda: State Building and Human Rights after Mass Violence*, Madison: University of Wisconsin Press, 2011, pp. 283–96.

R. Melson, *Revolution and Genocide: On the Origins of the Armenian Genocide and the Holocaust*, Chicago: University of Chicago Press, 1992.

A. Menen, "The Rapes of Bangladesh," *New York Times Magazine*, July 23, 1972.

M. Midlarsky, *The Killing Trap: Genocide in the Twentieth Century*, Cambridge: Cambridge University Press, 2005.

D. Miller and L. Miller, *Survivors: An Oral History of the Armenian Genocide*, Berkeley: University of California Press, 1993.

M. Minow, *Between Vengeance and Forgiveness: Facing History After Genocide and Mass Violence*, Boston: Beacon Press, 1998.

M. Morris, K. Leung, D. Ames and B. Lickel, "Views from Outside and Inside: Integrating Emic and Etic Insights about Culture and Justice Judgment," *Academy of Management Review* 24/4, 1999, 781–96.

A. D. Moses, "Conceptual Blockages and Definitional Dilemmas in the 'Racial Century': Genocides of Indigenous Peoples and the Holocaust," *Patterns of Prejudice* 36/4, 2002, 7–36.

—— (2008) "Toward a Theory of Critical Genocide Studies," *Online Encyclopedia of Mass Violence*. Available HTTP: www.massviolence.org/Toward-a-Theory-of-Critical-Genocide-Studies. Accessed March 20, 2012.

—— "Redemptive anti-Semitism and the Imperialist Imaginary," in Paul Betts and Christian Wiese, eds., *Years of Persecution, Years of Extermination: Saul Friedländer and the Future of Holocaust Studies*, London: Continuum Books, 2010, pp. 233–54.

—— Canadian Museum for Human Rights: "The 'Uniqueness of the Holocaust' and the Question of Genocide," *Journal of Genocide Research* 14/2, 2012, 215–38.

A. D. Moses, ed., *Genocide and Settler Society: Frontier Violence and Stolen Indigenous Children in Australian History*, New York: Berghahn, 2004.

—— *Empire, Colony, Genocide: Conquest, Occupation, and Subaltern Resistance in World History*, New York: Berghahn Books, 2008.

—— *Genocide: Critical Concepts in Historical Studies*, London: Routledge, 2010.

A. D. Moses and D. Stone, eds., *Colonialism and Genocide*, London: Routledge, 2007.

D. Moshman, "Conceptual Constraints on Thinking About Genocide," *Journal of Genocide Research* 3/3, 2001, 431–50.

P. Nora, ed., *Realms of Memory: Rethinking the French Past*, New York: Columbia University Press, 1996.

C. Nordstrom, *A Different Kind of War Story*, Philadelphia: University of Pennsylvania Press, 1997.

P. Novick, *The Holocaust in American Life*, New York: Houghton-Mifflin, 1999.

G. O'Donnell, P. Schmitter and L. Whitehead, eds., *Transitions from Authoritarian Rule*, 4 vols., Baltimore, MD: Johns Hopkins University Press, 1986.

D. Ofer, "Israel," in David S. Wyman and Charles H. Rosenzveig, eds., *The World Reacts to the Holocaust*, Baltimore, MD: Johns Hopkins University Press, 1996, pp. 836–924.

Office of the United Nations High Commissioner for Human Rights, "Questions and Answers about IDPs," United Nations online. Available HTTP: www.ohchr.org/EN/Issues/IDPersons/Pages/Issues.aspx (accessed July 18, 2012).

T. Olsen, L. Payne and A. Reiter, "Transitional Justice in the World: 1970–2007: Insights from a New Dataset," *Journal of Peace Research* 47/6, 2010, 803–9.

M. Osiel, "Ever Again: Legal Remembrance of Administrative Massacres," *University of Pennsylvania Law Review* 1/144, 1995, 463–680.

H. Patomäki, *The Political Economy of Global Security: War, Future Crises and Changes in Global Governance*, London: Routledge, 2008.

W. L. Patterson and P. Robeson, eds., *We Charge Genocide: The Historic Petition to the United Nations for Relief from a Crime of the United States Government Against the Negro People*, New York: International Publishers, 1970.

G. Perl, *I Was a Doctor in Auschwitz*, New York: Arno, 1979.

Peru, *Informe Final de la Comisión de la Verdad y Reconciliación*, Lima, Peru: 2003. Available HTTP: www.cverdad.org.pe (accessed October 9, 2011).

D. Philpott, *Just and Unjust Peace: An Ethic of Political Reconciliation*, Oxford: Oxford University Press, 2012.

D. Philpott and G. Powers, eds., *Strategies of Peace: Transforming Conflict in a Violent World*, Oxford: Oxford University Press, 2010.

PITF: Political Instability Task Force (2011) *Internal Wars and Failures of Governance: 1955–2008*. Online. Available HTTP: http://globalpolicy.gmu.edu/pitf/pitfdata.htm.

L. Poliakov, *Harvest of Hate: The Nazi Program for the Destruction of Jews in Europe*, New York: History Library, 1956.

J. N. Porter, *Genocide and Human Rights: A Global Anthology*, Washington, DC: University Press of America, 1982.

J. Pottier, *Re-imagining Rwanda: Conflict, Survival and Disinformation in the Late Twentieth Century*, Cambridge: Cambridge University Press, 2002.

S. Powers, *A Problem from Hell: America and the Age of Genocide*, New York: Basic Books, 2003.

P. du Preez, *Genocide: The Psychology of Mass Murder*, London: Boyars/Bowerdean, 1994.

G. Prunier, *Darfur: A 21st Century Genocide*, Ithaca, NY: Cornell University Press, 2008.

S. Ratner and J. Abrams, *Accountability for Human Rights Atrocities in International Law: Beyond the Nuremberg Legacy*, Oxford: Oxford University Press, 2001.

E. Reeves, "The 'Two Darfurs': Redefining a Crisis for Political Purposes," *Sudan Tribune*, 20 May 2005.

—— "Genocide by Attrition: Agony in Darfur," *Dissent* 52/1, 2005, 21–5.

—— "Children Within Darfur's Holocaust," Sudanreeves.org, December 23, 2005, online. Available HTTP: www.sudanreeves.org/2006/03/13/children-within-darfurs-holocaust-december-23-2005/.

—— "Whitewashing Darfur," *Guardian*, June 14, 2009.

Report of the UN secretary-general, *Implementing the Responsibility to Protect* (UN doc. A/63/677, January 12, 2009).

—— *Early Warning, Assessment and the Responsibility to Protect* (UN doc. A/64/864, July 14, 2010).

The Responsibility to Protect (UN doc. A/RES/63/308, October 7, 2009).

M. Richarz, "Luftaufnahme—Die Schwierigkeiten der Heimatforschermit der jüdischen Geschichte," *Babylon* 8, 1991, 27–33.

W. Riker, "The Political Psychology of Rational Choice Theory," *Political Psychology* 16/1, 1995, 23–44.

N. Roht-Arriaza and K. Orlovzky, "A Complementary Relation: Reparations and Development," in Pablo De Greiff and Roger Duthie, eds., *Transitional Justice and Development:*

Making Connections, New York: International Center for Transitional Justice, 2009, pp. 170–212.

S. Rosefelde, *Red Holocausts*, New York: Routledge, 2009.

A. Rosenbaum, *Is the Holocaust Unique? Perspectives on Comparative Genocide*, Boulder, CO: Westview Press, 1988.

S. P. Rosenberg, "Genocide Is a Process, Not an Event," *Genocide Studies and Prevention* 7/1, 2012, 16–23.

M. Rothberg, *Multidirectional Memory: Remembering the Holocaust in the Age of Decolonization*, Stanford, CA: Stanford University Press, 2009.

K. Roy, "Feelings and Attitudes of Raped Women of Bangladesh Towards Military Personnel of Pakistan," in Israel Drapkin and Emilio Viano, eds., *Victimology: A New Focus, Vol. V: Exploiters and Exploited: The Dynamics of Victimization*, Lexington, MA: Lexington Books (D. C. Heath and Company), 1975.

R. Rozett, "Diminishing the Holocaust: Scholarly Fodder for a Discourse of Distortion," *Israel Journal of Foreign Affairs* 6/1, 2012, 53–64.

R. Rubenstein, *The Cunning of History: The Holocaust and the American Future*, New York: Harper Torchbooks, 1975.

R. Rummel, *Death By Government*, New Brunswick, NJ: Transaction Publications, 1994.

V. Sanford, *Buried Secrets: Truth and Human Rights in Guatemala*, New York: Palgrave Macmillan, 2003.

W. Schabas, *An Introduction to the International Criminal Court*, Cambridge: Cambridge University Press, 2001.

—— *Preventing Genocide and Mass Killing: The Challenge for the United Nations*, London: Minority Rights Group International, 2006.

D. Schaller and J. Zimmerer, "Late Ottoman Genocides: The Dissolution of the Ottoman Empire and Young Turk Population and Extermination Policies – Introduction," *Journal of Genocide Research* 10/1, 2008, 7–14.

D. Scheffer, "Genocide and Atrocity Crimes," *Genocide Studies and Prevention* 1/3, 2006, 229–50.

J. Sémelin, *Purify and Destroy: The Political Uses of Massacre and Genocide*, New York: Columbia University Press, 2007.

A. Sen, *The Idea of Justice*, Cambridge, MA: Harvard University Press, 2009.

S. Sewell, D. Raymond, and S. Chin, *Mass Atrocity Response Operations: A Military Planning Handbook*, Cambridge, MA: Carr Center for Human Rights Policy/US Army Peacekeeping and Stability Operations Institute, 2010.

A. Shapira, "The Eichmann Trial: Changing Perspectives," in David Cesarani, ed., *After Eichmann: Collective Memory and the Holocaust since 1961*, London: Routledge, 2005, pp. 18–39.

M. Shaw, "From Comparative to International Genocide Studies: The International Production of Genocide in 20th-century Europe," *European Journal of International Relations* 7, 2001, 1–24.

M. Shaw, *War and Genocide: Organized Killing in Modern Society*, Cambridge: Polity Press, 2003.

—— *What Is Genocide?* Cambridge: Polity Press, 2007.

D. Shriver, *An Ethic for Enemies: Forgiveness in Politics*, Oxford: Oxford University Press, 1998.

J. Singer, *A General System Taxonomy for Political Science*, New York: General Learning Press, 1971.

A. Smeulers and L. Hoex, "Studying the Microdynamics of the Rwandan Genocide," *British Journal of Criminology* 50, 2010, 435–54.

J. Smith and E. Verdeja, eds., *Globalization, Social Movements and Peacebuilding*, Syracuse, NY: Syracuse University Press, 2013.

R. Smith, "Women and Genocide: Notes on an Unwritten History," *Holocaust and Genocide Studies* 8/3, 1984, 315–34.

—— "State, Power, and Genocidal Intent: On the Uses of Genocide in the Twentieth Century," in Levon Chorbajian and George Shirinian, eds., *Studies in Comparative Genocide*, New York: St. Martin's Press, 1999, pp. 3–14.

T. Snyder, *Bloodlands: Europe Between Hitler and Stalin*, New York: Basic Books, 2010.

South African Truth and Reconciliation Commission, *South African Truth and Reconciliation Final Report*, 5 vols, New York: Grove's Dictionaries, 1995.

G. Stanton, "Blue Scarves and Yellow Stars: Classification and Symbolization in the Cambodian Genocide," *The Faulds Lecture*, Warren Wilson College, Swannanoa, North Carolina, March 1987.

—— "The 8 Stages of Genocide." Online. Available at: www.genocidewatch.org/aboutgenocide/8stages.htm. Accessed February 20, 2012.

—— "How We Can Prevent Genocide: Building an International Campaign to End Genocide," *Genocide Watch*, online. Available HTTP: www.genocidewatch.org/howpreventgenocideic.html. Accessed July 18, 2012.

E. Staub, *The Roots of Evil: The Psychological and Cultural Origins of Genocide and Other Forms of Group Violence*, Cambridge: Cambridge University Press, 1989.

—— "The Psychology and Culture of Torture and Torturers," in Peter Suedfeld, ed., *Psychology and Torture*, New York: Hemisphere Publishing Corporation, 1990, pp. 64–6.

J. Steiner, "The SS Yesterday and Today: A Sociopsychological View," in Joel E. Dimsdale, ed., *Survivors, Victims, and Perpetrators; Essays on the Nazi Holocaust*, New York: Hemisphere Publishing Corporation, 1980.

A. Stiglmayer, ed., *Mass Rape: The War against Women in Bosnia-Herzegovina*, Lincoln: University of Nebraska Press, 1994.

Stockholm International Forum on the Holocaust, Conference on Education, Remembrance and Research, Stockholm, Sweden, January 26–8, 2000, proceedings. Stockholm: Regeringskansliet, 2000.

D. Stone, *The Historiography of Genocide*, London: Palgrave Macmillan, 2010.

—— *Histories of the Holocaust*, Oxford: Oxford University Press, 2010.

—— "Genocide and Memory," in Donald Bloxham and A. Dirk Moses, eds., *The Oxford Handbook of Genocide Studies*, Oxford: Oxford University Press, 2010, pp. 102–19.

S. Straus, *The Order of Genocide: Race, Power and War in Rwanda*, Ithaca, NY: Cornell University Press, 2006.

—— "Second Generation Research on Comparative Genocide," *World Politics* 59/3, 2007, 476–501.

S. Straus and L. Waldorf, eds., *Remaking Rwanda: State Building and Human Rights after Mass Violence*, Madison: University of Wisconsin Press, 2011.

P. Suedfeld, "Torture: A Brief Overview," in Peter Suedfeld, ed., *Psychology and Torture*, London: Taylor and Francis, 1990.

S. Tarrow, *Power in Movement: Social Movements, Collective Action, and Politics*, Cambridge: Cambridge University Press, 1994.

—— "Bridging the Quantitative–Qualitative Divide in Political Science," in Henry E. Brady and David Collier, eds., *Rethinking Social Inquiry: Diverse Tools, Shared Standards*, Lanham, MD: Rowman & Littlefield, 2004, pp. 171–9.

Task Force for International Cooperation on Holocaust Education, Remembrance, and Research, ed., "Holocaust, Genocide, and Crimes Against Humanity," online.

Available at: www.hedp.org.uk/_files/Documents/holocaust_genocide_and_crimes_against_humanity.pdf. Accessed May 12, 2012.

C. Tatz, "Genocide and the Holocaust: The Need for a Richter-Scale," keynote lecture at the conference "The Holocaust and Legacies of Race in the Postcolonial World, 1945 to the Present," University of Sydney, April 10–12, 2012.

C. C. Taylor, *Sacrifice as Terror: The Rwandan Genocide of 1994*, London: Berg Publishers, 1999.

R. Teitel, *Transitional Justice*, Oxford: Oxford University Press, 2000.

K. Theidon, "Whose Justice? Global and Local Approaches to Justice," editorial note in special issue of *International Journal of Transitional Justice* 3/3, 2009, 295–300.

T. Todorov, *The Conquest of America: The Question of the Other*, New York: Harper & Row, 1984.

J. C. Torpey, *Making Whole What Has Been Smashed: On Reparations Politics*, Cambridge, MA: Harvard University Press, 2006.

S. Totten and S. L. Jacobs, eds., *Pioneers of Genocide Studies*, New Brunswick, NJ: Transaction Publishers, 2002.

S. Totten, P. Bartrop and S. Jacobs, eds., *Teaching About the Holocaust: Essays by College and University Teachers*, New York: Praeger Books, 2004.

S. Totten and R. Ubaldo, eds., *We Cannot Forget: Interviews with Survivors of the 1994 Genocide in Rwanda*, Piscataway, NJ: Rutgers University Press, 2011.

B. Tovias, "Navigating the Cultural Encounter: Blackfoot Religious Resistance in Canada (c. 1870–1930)," in A. D. Moses, ed., *Empire, Colony, Genocide: Conquest, Occupation, and Subaltern Resistance in World History*, New York: Berghahn Books, 2008, pp. 271–95.

H. Travis, *Genocide in the Middle East: The Ottoman Empire, Iraq and Sudan*, Durham, NC: Carolina Academic Press, 2010.

D. Tutu, *No Future Without Forgiveness*, New York: Doubleday, 1999.

UCDP/PRIO, *Uppsala Data Conflict Armed Conflict Dataset v.4–2011: 1946–2010*. 2011. Online. Available HTTP: www.pcr.uu.se/research/ucdp/datasets/ ucdp_prio_armed_conflict_dataset/.

L. Ung, *First They Killed My Father: A Daughter of Cambodia Remembers*, New York: Harper Perennial, 2001.

U. Üngör, "Fresh Understandings of the Armenian Genocide: Mapping New Terrain with Old Questions," in Adam Jones, ed., *New Directions in Genocide Research*, New York: Routledge, 2012, pp. 198–214.

United Nations Commission on Human Rights, *Report of the Representative of the Secretary-General, Mr. Francis M. Deng, Submitted Pursuant to Commission Resolution 1997/39 – Addendum: Guiding Principles on Internal Displacement*, Principle 10(1), February 11, 1998, E/CN.4/1998/53/Add.2.

United Nations Economic and Social Council, *Ad Hoc Committee on Genocide: Summary Record of the Fourth Meeting*, UN doc. E/AC.25/SR.4, 14, April 15, 1948.

United Nations General Assembly, *United Nations Convention on the Prevention and Punishment of Genocide*, UN General Assembly resolution 260 (III) (December 9, 1948). Full text available at: www.un.org/ga/search/view_doc.asp?symbol=a/res/260(III). Accessed June 23, 2012.

—— *2005 World Summit Outcome*, UN doc. A/60/L.1, October 24, 2005).

United Nations Security Council, *Final Report of the Commission of Experts Established Pursuant to Security Council Resolution 780 (1992)*, May 27, 1994 S/1994/674.

United States Department of State, *Dispatch*, 3/46, Washington, DC: United States Department of State, November 16, 1992.

P. Uvin, *Human Rights and Development*, Bloomfield, CT: Kumarian Press, 2004.

B. Valentino, *Final Solutions: Mass Killing and Genocide in the Twentieth Century*, Ithaca, NY: Cornell University Press, 2004.

B. Valentino, P. Huth and D. Balch-Lindsay, "'Draining the Sea': Mass Killing and Guerrilla Warfare," *International Organization* 58, 2004, 375–407.

P. van den Berghe, *State Violence, and Ethnicity*, Niwot: University of Colorado Press, 1990, p. 1.

A. Varshney, *Ethnic Conflict and Civic Life: Hindus and Muslims in India*, New Haven, CT: Yale University Press, 2003.

E. Vedeja, "A Normative Theory of Reparations in Transitional Democracies," *Metaphilosophy* 37/3–4, 2006, 449–68.

—— *Unchopping a Tree: Reconciliation in the Aftermath of Political Violence*, Philadelphia, PA: Temple University Press, 2009.

—— "Genocide: Clarifying Concepts and Causes of Cruelty," *Review of Politics* 72, 2010, 513–26.

—— "The Political Science of Genocide: Outlines of An Emerging Research Agenda," *Perspectives on Politics* 10/2, 2012, 307–21.

W. Verwoerd, "Toward an Answer to Criticism of the South African TRC," in Trudy Govier, ed., *Dilemmas of Reconciliation: Cases and Concepts*, Waterloo, Ontario: Wilfrid Laurier University Press, 2003, p. 246.

M. Volf, *Exclusion and Embrace: A Theological Exploration of Identity, Otherness, and Reconciliation*, Nashville, TN: Abingdon Press, 1996.

M. U. Walker, *Moral Repair: Reconstructing Moral Relations After Wrongdoing*, Cambridge: Cambridge University Press, 2006.

J. Waller, *Becoming Evil: How Ordinary People Commit Genocide and Mass Killing*, Oxford: Oxford University Press, 2007.

M. Walzer, *Just and Unjust Wars: A Moral Argument with Historical Illustrations*, New York: Basic Books, 2003.

Washington Post, "U.N. Genocide Action Sought on Red Bloc," January 18, 1953. M3.

M. Weiner-Hanks, *Historical Comparisons*, Washington, DC: American Historical Association, 2007.

A. Weiss-Wendt, "Problems in Comparative Genocide Scholarship," in Dan Stone, ed., *The Historiography of Genocide*, New York: Palgrave Macmillan, 2010, pp. 42–70.

E. Weitz, *A Century of Genocide: Utopias of Race and Nation*, Princeton, NJ: Princeton University Press, 2005.

A. Wendt, "Anarchy is What States Make of It: The Social Construction of Power Politics," *International Organization* 46/2, 1992, 391–425.

The White House, *National Security Strategy of the United States*, Washington, DC: The White House, May 2010.

E. Wiesel, *Night*, New York: Ballantine Books, 1960.

P. D. Williams, "Briefing: The Road to Humanitarian War in Libya," *Global Responsibility to Protect* 3/2, 2011, 248–59.

P. D. Williams and A. J. Bellamy, "Principles, Politics and Prudence: Libya, the Responsibility to Protect and the Use of Force," *Global Governance* 18/3, 2012, 273–97.

S. Wills, *Protecting Civilians: The Obligations of Peacekeepers*, Oxford: Oxford University Press, 2009.

P. Wolfe, "Structure and Event: Settler Colonialism: Time and the Question of Genocide," in A. Dirk Moses, ed., *Empire, Colony, Genocide: Conquest, Occupation, and Subaltern Resistance in World History*, New York: Berghahn Books, 2008.

L. Woocher, "The Responsibility to Prevent: Towards a Strategy," in Frazer Egerton and Andy Knight, eds., *The Routledge Handbook of the Responsibility to Protect*, Abingdon, UK: Routledge, 2012.

A. Woolford, "Ontological Destruction: Genocide and Aboriginal People," *Genocide Studies and Prevention* 4/1, 2009, 81–97.

J. Zimmerer, *Deutsche Herrschaftüber Afrikaner: StaatlicherMachtanspruch und Wirklichkeit-imkolonialen Namibia*, Münster/Hamburg: LIT Verlag, 2002.

—— "Colonialism and the Holocaust: Towards an Archaeology of Genocide," in A. Dirk Moses, ed., *Genocide and Settler Society*, New York: Berghahn Books, 2004, pp. 49–76.

—— "The Birth of the Ostland Out Of the Spirit of Colonialism: A Postcolonial Perspective on the Nazi Policy of Conquest and Extermination," *Patterns of Prejudice* 2/39, 2005 202–24.

J. Zimmerer and D. Schaller, eds., *The Origins of Genocide: Raphael Lemkin as a Historian of Mass Violence*, London: Routledge, 2009.

INDEX

Note: Page numbers in **bold** type refer to **figures**
Page numbers in *italic* type refer to *tables*
Page numbers followed by 'n' refer to notes